THE
TRAVELER'S
WEB

To Marcia

[signature]

6/3/07

THE
TRAVELER'S
WEB

An EXTREME Searcher Guide
to Travel Resources on the Internet

Randolph Hock

CyberAge Books
Medford, New Jersey

First Printing, 2007

The Traveler's Web: An Extreme Searcher Guide to Travel Resources on the Internet

Library of Congress Cataloging-in-Publication Data

Hock, Randolph, 1944-
    The traveler's web : an extreme searcher guide to travel resources on the Internet /
Randolph Hock.
        p. cm.
    Includes index.
        ISBN: 978-0-910965-75-0
1. Travel--Computer network resources   I. Title
    G149.7.H63 2007
    025.06'9104--dc22

                                                                    2007000610

Printed and bound in the United States of America.

President and CEO: Thomas H. Hogan, Sr.
Editor-in-Chief and Publisher: John B. Bryans
Managing Editor: Amy M. Reeve
VP Graphics and Production: M. Heide Dengler
Book Designer: Kara Mia Jalkowski
Cover Designer: Shelley Szajner
Copyeditor: Barbara Brynko
Proofreader: Bonnie Freeman
Indexer: Sharon Hughes

To Pamela, Matthew, Stephen, and Elizabeth

Contents

Figures
and Tables

Foreword

According to a recent survey by the Travel Industry Association of America, nearly 80 million Americans turned to the Internet for help with travel planning in 2005. The same survey reports that the Internet is now used for some aspect of travel planning in more than 75 percent of all trips. You can count on these numbers rising in the years ahead.

Why is the Internet revolutionizing the way we research, plan, and book travel? Because it saves time, and because online information is often more current and timely than what's available in printed guidebooks and brochures. This can make a big difference in the quality of our travel experiences.

Most of what you'll find on the Web is both free and accessible around the clock, but sifting through the sea of available travel information can present a tremendous challenge. There are so many available travel sites that most travelers stick with the few they know best, missing a great deal of valuable information as a result. This is what makes *The Traveler's Web* such a useful tool. Ran Hock covers scores of sites readers might otherwise miss, helping travelers sort through all the noise on the Internet to hone in on the information they need.

With this new book, Hock has created a compendium of travel-related Web sites relevant to a wide range of travelers. He covers virtually every mode of transportation and a variety of trip styles, from adventure to luxury travel. He goes beyond the basics, tackling such practical topics as where to find weather reports, subway maps, and cyber cafes, and recommending specialized travel sites for seniors, families, gays and lesbians, and other groups.

The Traveler's Web provides insight into the content and utility of each profiled site, but that's only the beginning: The book also teaches readers how to search to get the most out of each resource.

Throughout his long and distinguished career, Ran Hock has taught librarians, researchers, and many others how to search online databases. For these highly educated practitioners, unlocking the information in online databases is a function of their everyday jobs. In this book, Hock shares many of the searching techniques he teaches information professionals, including concepts like "precision" and "Boolean Logic" that are not readily known to the general public.

The Traveler's Web is the fourth title in Hock's "Extreme Searcher" series, but it is more than just another reference book: Readers are invited to visit Hock's own Web site, where new information is posted regularly and readers can communicate directly with the author regarding their specific information needs.

With this timely book, the travel research and planning process just got much easier. Readers will find themselves marking pages in the book that describe Web sites they have never used. I found myself constantly returning to the Internet to check out one or another site described by Hock that I had never tried before.

If you enjoy traveling and want to get the most out of every trip, *The Traveler's Web* is a must. Once you've read it, you'll never want to plan a trip without it.

David Grossman
USA TODAY

David Grossman is a librarian and journalist covering travel for *USA TODAY*, as well as libraries for *Searcher* magazine. He developed Internet booking tools for airlines and databases for publishers such as Rand McNally. Mr. Grossman holds an MBA from Northwestern University and library science and journalism degrees from the University of Michigan.

Acknowledgments

The most overwhelming acknowledgement I owe is to the creators of the hundreds of Web sites covered in this book. Some of those sites of course are commercial, and though "altruism" is not their goal, the services those sites provide have changed in a very positive way the ways in which we plan our travel. Other sites in this book were created as "a labor of love" and deserve another level of acknowledgement for the hundreds or thousands of hours that their creators have put into creating sites that provide travelers with extraordinarily useful information. Just as we all do when we travel, in creating this book, I have very much relied "on the kindness of strangers." I am very grateful for the exceptionally fine Web sites provided by organizations and individuals I don't personally know.

There are also many people that I do know who deserve credit for getting and keeping this book on its journey, particularly the many wonderful people at Information Today. Foremost, I thank Amy Reeve, Managing Editor, for her skills, insights, knowledge, understanding, and flexibility. Not far behind is John Bryans, Editor-in-Chief and Publisher, to whom I owe thanks for his support, enthusiasm, and numerous other attributes that I am sure he would be happy for me to mention but for which there is just not enough space here. I am also grateful to Heide Dengler (VP of Graphics and Production), Kara Mia Jalkowski (Book Designer), Sharon Hughes (Indexer), Shelley Szajner (Cover Designer), and Rob Colding (Marketing Coordinator) for all of the hard work and creativity they have applied to getting the book on its way. I also extend my thanks to Tom Hogan, Sr., President and CEO xx The Traveler's Web

of Information Today, for having had the wisdom to identify and hire all these talented people.

I am also very grateful to David Grossman who wrote the Foreword. It has been a pleasure getting to know him again after a hiatus of more than 20 years.

Finally, I thank my wife, Pamela Pope Hock, for her continued support, patience, and love, and generally for continuing to put up with me.

About The Extreme Searcher's Web Page

www.extremesearcher.com

As a supplement to this book (and his other books), the author maintains The Extreme Searcher's Web Page at www.extreme searcher.com. There you will find information about and links to sites included in *The Traveler's Web* and his other books. The collection of links for all of the Web sites included in this book can be found at that site or by going directly to extremesearcher.com/travel. URLs for sites in this book occasionally change, and once in a while (hopefully not very often), a Web site covered may just disappear. The Web site is updated on a continuous basis to account for such changes, and you sometimes also find new sites added there. (If you should find a "dead link" on the site before the author does, you are encouraged to report it to the e-mail address below.)

Since links to all Web sites in the book are on the Extreme Searcher's site, if you make use of that site (and bookmark it), you will not have to type in any of the URLs included in the book. You should find the site particularly helpful for browsing through the sites covered here.

Enjoy your visit to The Extreme Searcher's Web Page and please send any feedback to ran@extremesearcher.com.

Disclaimer:

Introduction

New horizons, the urge to know what is over that next hill, to feel what it is like to stand in a 13th-century cathedral, to walk an Irish lane—these are among the broad range of reasons we travel. Whatever the motivation, one thing that ardent travelers have in common is an enhanced "awareness" of what the world beyond their hometowns feels like and has to offer. While one of my goals with *The Traveler's Web* is to show how the Internet can help you get somewhere and make the most of your time there, the book itself has an underlying theme of "awareness." Most travelers have come to know what the Internet has to offer by being told about a site, doing a quick search, or stumbling across a useful resource. Relatively few have taken the time to sit down and become fully aware of the breadth and depth of travel information that is available online. This book aims to provide such an awareness and, in a somewhat systematic way, to give you a feel for what is out there on the Internet to help the traveler.

This Introduction is a guide to using *The Traveler's Web*, and taking a few minutes to read it will help you get the most out of the book. In the following pages, I describe for whom this book is written, what sites are included, and what you can expect to learn about each site. I also provide advice on signing up for sites, discuss the roles of resource guides and search engines in finding travel information, offer some comments about travel agencies, and explain the Web page that supports the book.

The Intended Audience

The audiences I kept in mind while writing *The Traveler's Web* were both the leisure and the business traveler. Just by glancing at the names of Web sites covered, it may appear that the book is heavily weighted toward the leisure traveler, and in a sense, it is. For one thing, there are far more leisure-oriented travel sites on the Web than there are sites for business travelers. However, a large number of sites covered—reservation sites, for instance—are equally useful for both audiences. In any event, I believe business travelers owe it to themselves to consider working in a little leisure when circumstances permit.

The Traveler's Web is for travelers, and while I hope it may prove of use to travel agents and other travel professionals, I have not covered sites designed primarily for the travel industry.

What Web Sites Are Included

Choosing which Web sites to include was by far my greatest challenge in writing the book. My overall aim is to provide manageable (not exhaustive) coverage of sites. Thus, in general, for each chapter I have identified a few key sites plus additional sites that serve as examples of the broader variety available. Among the considerations when deciding whether to include a site were the following:

- Is the site well known?

- Is the site exemplary of unique types of travel *information* available on the Internet?

- Does the site offer unique, useful *features*?

- Has the site received good reviews or positive mention on other reputable sites, in travel magazines, etc.?

- Does the site have broad geographic coverage? (Those that do were preferred over those with narrower coverage. However, a site with narrower coverage was often included as an example of sites at the country, state, or provincial level.)

- For sites that provide directories and search capabilities, if two or more Web sites are similar, which has the greater searchability (search criteria), the larger database, and the most comprehensive information?

- Does the site seem to have longevity, as indicated by having been around for a time, being owned by a well-established organization, etc.?

- What is the site's reputation among consumers, as indicated in online discussion groups? (This applies particularly to travel agency sites.)

Of these criteria, typically no single one either qualified or disqualified a site for inclusion (the notable exception being the "reputation" criterion, which knocked out a couple of fairly well-known travel agency sites). The length of the book was an important consideration in choosing sites, as producing a 1,000-page book would have defeated the "manageability" aim. As a result, for most categories of sites discussed, many good ones were not included. If, for example, a hotel reservations site does nothing significantly different or better than other hotel sites, it was not included. Particularly challenging was deciding which travel agency sites to include. For just the U.S. and the U.K., there are thousands of such sites. For a travel agency to be included, its site had to do something unique and/or provide supplemental information (guides, forums, etc.) so that a stop there was more valuable than a stop at other sites. (A bit more will be said later about assessing travel agency sites.) Travel agency sites that serve only U.S. customers, only U.K. customers, etc., were typically not included. Likewise, the book does not list individual airline, car rental company, or hotel chain Web sites, except where they provide something unique or extraordinary. The book does, however, tell you how you can very quickly get to such sites.

With few exceptions, the sites I've included here are "free," or at least offer some useful free resources. There are many fine travel sites (such as Travel News Today) that provide excellent information, but for a significant subscription price. Generally speaking, I think there is enough free information out there to satisfy the needs of most travelers.

The book references substantially more U.S. Web sites than sites from other countries largely because so many more English language travel Web sites come from U.S. sources than from other countries. I have tried, however, to provide an ample number of non-U.S. Web sites to make the book valuable for English-speaking travelers who are not Americans. (Actually, proportionally to population, U.K. Web sites are probably overrepresented here. I will confess up front to latent Anglophilic tendencies.) U.K. readers will need to do a little "translation," as American English is used. (For instance, car rental vs. car hire, vacation vs. holiday, etc.—an awareness of which is important, , particularly when searching on keywords. Search a U.K. site for *car rental* and you may miss major sites.)

What Is Included About Each Site

What you will find here about each site will vary considerably depending upon the nature and size of the site. For each, you will get an overview of what the site is about, along with a description of the main types of content offered and information about any particularly useful or unique content. If the site has a search capability, you will be told what you need to know to take best advantage of it (except where it is so obvious that no explanation is necessary). I have tried to avoid overwhelming the reader with too much detail. For some resources, such as the major reservation sites (Orbitz, Expedia, and Travelocity), you will find many pages and encounter references in several chapters. However, for most sites you will find one or two short paragraphs of description. When a section of a site—for example, the car rental section at Travelocity—is discussed, the URL for that specific section will usually be shown. In some cases, the URL for a specific page or part of a site is extremely long and ugly. In such instances the URL for the main site will be given; from there you will have to click on a link or tab in order to get to the appropriate page.

I have taken care to ensure that the descriptions of the various Web sites are correct. Undoubtedly, if you look closely enough you will find some things that have changed since we went to press. Hopefully any such "errors" are minor and limited to such things as a link having moved on the page or wording on a page having changed slightly. Quite often, sections of Web sites are renamed. A section that was called "Articles" yesterday may be referred to as "Topics" today, but the overall content of a site is less likely to change. The Extreme Searcher's Web Page that supports the book (www.extreme searcher.com/travel) is updated on a continuing basis—if a URL listed in the book has changed, you should find it corrected on this site. If it isn't, please let me know.

Increasingly, travel sites provide a version compatible with mobile devices. In some cases this is mentioned when it seems particularly relevant and useful, but no attempt is made to identify every site that has such a feature (partly because this is changing so rapidly). You'll find a resource guide for the mobile versions of travel sites in Chapter 10, "Bits and Pieces and Practicalities."

Owners or admirers of Web sites that I have neglected to mention are welcome to contact me. Where they can make a strong case for a site (meeting the criteria I described earlier), I will consider adding a link at The Extreme Searcher's Web Page.

"Signing Up" for Web Sites

Many sites offer an option to sign up and/or sign in. For the vast majority of sites covered here, signing up is free. If a portion of a site is not free, you will typically be told that very clearly. (If you are asked for a credit card number, that's a pretty good clue that you are moving beyond the free zone.) Signing up is necessary for sites where you are at the point of making a purchase and for sites where you request additional information, such as newsletters. I am signed up for most of the sites covered in this book, and, contrary to what many people expect, as far as I can tell it has not caused me to receive significantly more spam than I would otherwise have received. In my view, the additional information and services you can get from a site are usually worth the minute or two it typically takes to sign up.

What you see on a Web page will occasionally differ depending on whether or not you have signed in. Throughout the book, it is safe to assume that what I have described as appearing on the page is what you will see when signed in.

The Role of Resource Guides

Merely because the number of sites included in *The Traveler's Web* is limited to several hundred does not mean that these are all the sites to which the book provides access. In many sections, you will find at least one site that serves as an Internet resource guide, offering links to other sites on the topic. For instance, Chapter 8, "Sites for Special Groups and Special Needs," features 48 sites. Several of these sites, however, are resource guides that point you to hundreds of other relevant sites. Thus, the resource guides you'll read about here will put you a mere click or two away from thousands of travel sites.

The Role of Search Engines

In addition to descriptions of specific sites, in many sections you will encounter the suggestion, "Try a search engine search." Search engines can be extremely helpful—especially when you are researching a very precise travel topic, such as salmon fishing on the Golsovia River in Alaska or August cooking classes in Tuscany. In general, though, keep in mind that search engines do not bring together collections of travel information in as useful a manner as do the specialized sites. In fact, search engines do not necessarily even index the detailed content of many of the sites I cover—particularly those that include searchable databases.

When a search engine is suggested, if there is a type of search phrase that works particularly well (even a very simple, perhaps obvious search phrase), you will often see such a recommendation. When an example of a search is given—for example, *cuisines Latvia*—what you would type in is indicated in italics to distinguish it from other words in the sentence. By the way, capitalization is not necessary as most search engines are case insensitive. In most examples, I have capitalized names of countries and cities simply because it is the natural way to write them.

Assessing the Quality of Travel Agency Web Sites for Yourself

As I have already mentioned, there are thousands of travel agency sites on the Internet that are not included in this book, though many if not most of them are reputable and reliable. You will frequently bump into their ads (and links to their sites), and they may be able to provide you with some great deals (or not). Before you either too quickly ignore or buy from one of these sites, you should do an assessment of your own.

The following questions will help you assess a site's legitimacy and reliability. This is not a foolproof evaluation method: If some (or even most) of the questions do not draw an affirmative answer for a given site, that should not automatically disqualify it. There are no doubt a number of good travel agency sites that haven't had time to establish a reputation, and as we know, smaller and newer companies sometimes "try harder." That said, these questions will provide a good starting point for assessing any agency site.

- Has the agency been in business for at least 3 years?

- Is the site owned by an organization you recognize?

- Is the site endorsed by a reputable organization?

- Does the agency belong to professional or trade associations?

- Has the site or agency won any awards or been featured in any magazine? (If so, the site will readily tell you.)

- Has the site been discussed positively in established travel forums?

- Does the site itself reflect quality and care (professional-looking design, up-to-date content, correct grammar and spelling, etc.)?

- Does the site provide an address and phone number?

- Is there an "About Us" or similar link that gives significant information about the company?

- Has the firm gone to the trouble of providing users with additional useful information, such as background information on destinations, travel tips, etc.?

- Does the site offer competitive prices without seeming too good to be true?

- When you do a Web search on the agency, do you find it mentioned elsewhere in a consistently positive way?

What About Real Live Travel Agents and Agencies?

Some people might consider travel agents—the real live kind found in brick-and-mortar travel agencies—an endangered species, and in fact the Bureau of Labor Statistics estimates that the number of travel agents is declining (www.bls.gov/oco/ocos124.htm). Reliance on them has certainly changed with the coming of the Internet, but behind a lot of the travel agency sites on the Internet, there are still people with whom you can talk and get some of the personal touch. For a very good view (yet with a bit of understandable bias) of how the Internet has affected travel agents, see the FAQ page (www.astanet.com/about/faq.asp) on the Web site for the American Society of Travel Agents (wwforw.astanet.com). *The Traveler's Web* is not intended to decrease any reader's reliance on his or her travel agent. Actually, I hope travel agents will be able to make good use of the book.

The Extreme Searcher's Web Page

Links to all the sites referenced in *The Traveler's Web* can be found by going to The Extreme Searcher's Web Page at www.extreme searcher.com (or you can save a click and go directly to www.extreme searcher.com/travel). Make use of this page for easy access to featured sites without having to type in any of the URLs. The Extreme Searcher's Web Page is updated on an ongoing basis to account for any changes in URLs. Occasionally, a new site will be added, but it's likely you will find the site most helpful in letting you easily browse the sites covered in *The Traveler's Web*.

Happy traveling—I look forward to seeing you on the road!

What's Out There?
The Real World and the Cyber World

Whether you're headed to Beijing on business, Cancun on a cruise, or Hawaii to learn the hula, using the Internet can probably make your trip less expensive, more productive, and more fun. The trick is knowing where and how to look, and sometimes, just what to look for. Millions of people have taken advantage of airfare savings they have found by shopping around on travel sites. Fewer, however, have used the Internet to research their destinations, find out what other people are saying about those destinations, plan the details of their routes, check the weather, learn the few words necessary to be "polite" in a foreign country, and generally take advantage of the wealth of travel resources that are available online.

Voyaging around the world and voyaging through the Internet have a lot in common. Both activities are often motivated by curiosity, the urge to explore, the need to relax, a desire to learn, and even profit. On top of that, the techniques, tricks, and general approaches that make these two activities fruitful and fun are actually very similar in several ways. Thus, the marriage between travel and the Internet is a natural one.

This book will explore this marriage by pointing to and describing the Internet resources that are the most useful to travelers. It will also emphasize certain techniques and approaches that work well whether you are at the keyboard or on the road. You will find the following themes reflected throughout the book:

- Click everywhere, go everywhere. Explore around one more corner and try out one more link. Roam!
- So many destinations, so little time.
- Don't take just one person's word as to what is good for you.
- All things in moderation—including moderation itself. There are times to be extreme: Extremism in the pursuit of travel is not a vice. (Extra points for those of you who "get" that one.)

The Web sites covered reflect the breadth of travel-related topics and resources, and I try to demonstrate how to use these types of resources most effectively. Not every possible travel topic and certainly not all of the tens of thousands of travel sites out there will be included. However, for specific topics that are not covered, such as diving safaris, make use of the travel resource guides covered toward the end of this chapter and occasionally throughout the rest of the book. They should help you to easily find additional relevant sites. When somewhat specific topics are addressed, only carefully selected sites are included. The goal is to identify some of the best and most reliable sites, sites that are representative examples in various areas, and sites that provide a particularly useful and/or unique service.

A word about the organization of the book: Throughout, you will find some sites mentioned more than once. Many sites, such as Travelocity, serve many functions, providing online reservation services for flights, cars, cruises, etc., while also offering country and city guides, travel tips, and more. Such sites will be mentioned in more than one chapter, with emphasis on the part of the site that is most relevant to the chapter topic. This should make easy for you to keep track of all major sources for each topic without having to jump back and forth between chapters.

Just What Does the Internet Offer the Traveler?

The Internet offers the traveler much more than just a place to make reservations. Each chapter in this book focuses on particular applications that travelers may use to their advantage. Following is a brief overview of the various applications and resources you will encounter on the Web and in this book.

Travel Guides Online (Chapter 2)

If you are going to spend more than a day in any city or more than a few days in any country, break down and buy a good travel guide—the book kind. These are a traveler's "dream machine," more portable than a computer, and many will fit in your pocket. Even if your travel guide isn't pocketsize, keep it on your nightstand and spend a few minutes with it each night before you doze off. However, no matter how long you plan on staying at any destination, you should take advantage of the free guides that are available on the Internet for virtually any country, for almost any city, and for thousands of specific museums, monuments, and other attractions.

Many of the well-known printed guides, such as the *Rick Steves' Europe Through the Back Door* and *Arthur Frommer's Budget Travel* series, have companion Web sites that provide a surprising amount of information for free. These sites, which provide good overviews and basic details, are a good starting point for planning your adventures. Travel guides are covered in detail in Chapter 2.

Reservation Sites: Flights and More (Chapter 3)

The best-known category of travel sites is reservation sites, where you can go to find rates and schedules and to book reservations. They include online travel agency sites, such as Travelocity, Expedia, and others, as well as sites from airlines, hotel chains, and car rental chains. Although for decades, real live travel agents in general did a great job making travel arrangements, the Internet has drastically changed the picture. Online reservation sites make it easy for an individual to explore an amazingly broad range of options in terms of where and when to go and how much to pay. These sites, which also make it easy to quickly purchase tickets, will be discussed in detail in Chapter 3, with the emphasis there on airline reservations.

Train, Car, and Ferry Travel (Chapter 4)

Most travel agency sites, such as Travelocity, will be more than happy to help you find many modes of transportation in addition to flights. However, when you are driving or traveling by train or ferry, you may need some more specialized information and attention. If you plan on driving, there are numerous sites, such as the various map sites (MapQuest, Yahoo! Local, and Maporama, for example), that will provide you with itineraries, directions, travel times, and other information. If you are taking a train or ferry, you will need timetables, information on accommodations, and other details that can often be found more easily on the Web than anywhere else. How to find this information will be covered in Chapter 4.

Cruises: Ships, Barges, and Boats (Chapter 5)

If you haven't noticed, cruises are "hot" (or "cool," or *de rigueur*, if you please) these days. But take it from someone who was a skeptic: If you haven't been on a cruise yet, chances are extremely good that by the time you return home from your first one, you will be planning another. As with almost any hot topic, there are lots of hot Web sites for cruises. Again, the general online travel agency sites will be helpful, but Chapter 5 will provide considerable detail on using those sites specifically for cruises and also will cover a number of other sites and resources available for planning (and taking) a cruise. "Cruises," of course, can mean a lot more than a vacation aboard a gigantic (but wonderful) 1,000-foot-long floating resort. It can also mean a cruise down the Danube, a week on a barge in France, or a trip aboard a paddle wheeler on the Mississippi.

Finding a Bed and a Meal (Chapter 6)

Travel tastes and pocketbooks lend to a wide range of options for lodging and dining. Here again, the Web offers a lot of resources that are apparent and a lot more that are less apparent but that can help you find just what you are looking for at just the right price. From campsites to hostels to luxury hotels, the Internet can provide not just reservation services, but also background information that will ensure your choice is the best one. For accommodations, you can check out photos of a hotel and find out what previous guests have to say about their stay before you make reservations. For restaurants, you can often read reviews, view the menu ahead of time, and make lunch or dinner reservations online. Lodging and dining options and how to find them are covered in Chapter 6.

Adventure, Outdoor, and Educational Travel (Chapter 7)

You have to define for yourself what qualifies as "adventure travel" since, for many of us, travel of any kind is an adventure. However, if you are looking for those trips that are more extreme in exhilaration, education, exertion, exhaustion, or elevation, Chapter 7 will give you a leg up. The Web not only has information on tours, locations, and activities, but it can help you get ready for just about anything, from how to psychologically prepare to "get in the zone" to how to survive a shark attack.

Sites for Special Groups and Special Needs (Chapter 8)

There are many Web sites and parts of Web sites devoted to the special conditions, preferences, and needs of certain travelers. Families, seniors, gay and lesbian, handicapped, and business travelers can all find Web sites that address their special requirements and offer guides to establishments and activities that are particularly "friendly" to their unique needs and desires. Chapter 8 will lead you to Web sites that cater to special groups.

Exploring Countries and Cultures Online (Chapter 9)

The Internet can really shine in helping you prepare for a trip when you go beyond the kinds of information found on travel-specific sites. You can quickly get detailed information (or less detail, if that's what you want) on cities, states, countries, and regions. You can find out about cultures, traditions, etiquette, religions, politics, economics, the arts, history, cuisines, and much more. Language resources on the Web may even provide the language basics you need to be polite and to be understood when you have simple questions and needs. The Internet also provides ways for you to easily find and read newspapers from thousands of cities around the world, and receive e-mail alerts for events, topics, and locations of specific interest to you. We will take a look at these kinds of resources in Chapter 9.

Bits and Pieces and Practicalities (Chapter 10)

In addition to the types of travel information already discussed, there are lots of bits and pieces of nitty-gritty information on the

Internet that can make your trip easier, more fun, more fulfilling, and safer. These practicalities include such things as passport and visa information; currencies; weather reports; health alerts; country, city, road, airport, and subway maps; and flight tracking. The Web also provides information on communicating effectively and economically while traveling—for example, the locations of cybercafes, and instructions for finding phone numbers in various countries. Almost everyone needs to do some shopping while traveling, and the Web can prepare you for that, too: You'll find information about local shops and products, and related details, such as weights and measures, including clothing sizes.

Resource Guides

You will find links to sites listed in *The Traveler's Web* on The Extreme Searcher's Web Page (www.extremesearcher.com/travel). This resource is not intended to be exhaustive but rather to serve as a gateway to sites offering a wide range of travel services and information. As a starting point for most travel topics, this collection of links should serve you well. The sites I've included are among the most useful, reliable, and popular; some are representative of a certain type of site, while others provide something unique.

There may be times, though, when you want to explore Internet travel resources even more exhaustively and in those situations a travel "resource guide" may be the best place to start. In a manner not unlike this book and its companion Web page, such sites are designed as gateways, providing access to hundreds or even thousands of other significant travel-related sites. As you explore a resource guide to determine if it's right for you, look for categories that meet your specific needs and interests (diving safaris, for instance). The resource guides that follow are among the most popular, having distinguished themselves on the strength of their collections, perspectives, and value-added information.

AardvarkTravel.net

aardvarktravel.net

The AardvarkTravel.net site is large, offering links to more than 20,000 sites. Technically, it is both a travel search engine and a directory; that is, you can use the search box to search for terms or browse Aardvark's directory categories. The directory has 14 main subject headings: one for each continent, Air & Sea Travel, Overland Travel, Specialty Travel, Travel Merchandise, Travel Companions, Travel Resources & Advice, and Tourism (Figure 1.1). The continent categories are further divided by country, making this an excellent choice for identifying selected resources for a given country; U.S. states and Canadian provinces have subcategories for major cities. The section of links for identifying potential travel companions is a somewhat unique feature. In addition, AardvarkTravel.net has a travel forum with more than 30 topic areas (see Chapter 2 for a full discussion of forums).

Yahoo! Travel Directory

dir.yahoo.com/recreation/travel

Yahoo!'s directory of travel sites, a part of Yahoo!'s general Web directory, is gigantic, containing listings for more than 125,000 sites, with cross-links to thousands of other sites found in various Yahoo! Directory sections. The Travel category itself includes more than 86,000 sites listed by region (subdivided by region, country, and U.S. states). There are links to 32,000 Destination Guides and more than 45 other categories, including Air Travel and Travel Agents, as well as specialized categories such as Hitchhiking and Vegetarian. The specialized categories, subcategories, and country sections are what make Yahoo! particularly useful for many travelers.

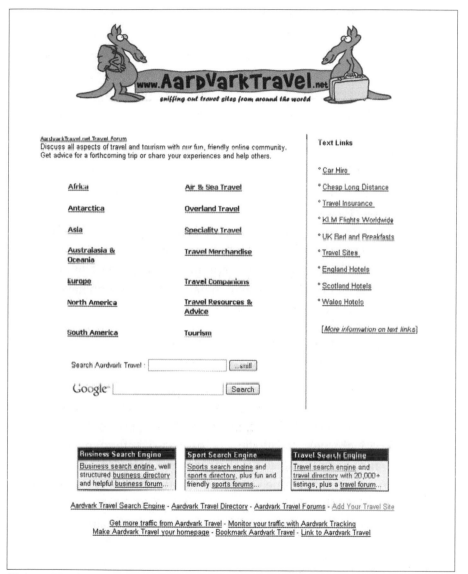

Figure 1.1   Aardvark Travel Directory

Open Directory—Travel

dmoz.org/recreation/travel

The Web's other large general directory is Open Directory, which offers a significant travel collection within its Recreation category. The Specialty Travel subcategory is especially strong, with categories not found in Yahoo!, including Nudism, Volunteering, and Battlefields.

Librarians' Internet Index—Travel

lii.org/pub/topic/travel

Another general yet more selective Web directory is Librarians' Internet Index (LII). Under the Recreation—Travel category are several thousand sites in specific travel-related categories (Camping, Cruising, Cybercafes, etc.) and additional cross-linked sites in categories such as Museums and Transportation (Figure 1.2). In contrast to many other directories, this site contains excellent annotations for each site, adding greatly to its value for browsing.

Forbes.com Best of the Web—Travel

www.forbes.com/bow/b2c/section.jhtml?id=3

On an ongoing basis, *Forbes* magazine provides reviews of sites that it considers to be the Best of the Web. The Travel portion of its selection is divided into 27 categories, each typically listing from seven to 15 choices. In addition to expected categories such as Cruises and Family Vacations, Forbes.com provides some fairly unique or specific categories, such as Expatriate Resources, Scuba Diving, and Wireless Travel. For each site, a one-paragraph review and a description sum up what Forbes considers the site's best and worst aspects.

Travelazer

travelazer.com

LII.org (Home)   About LII   Suggest a Site   Subscribe to New This Week   Contact

LIBRARIANS' INTERNET INDEX
WEBSITES YOU CAN TRUST

Search [Entire Collection ▾] for [_____] in [All Fields ▾] [Search LII.org] Help

Powered by: Siderean's Seamark Navigator

8,740 Sites 🔖 Subscribing to this search

Filters	Remove All ✖
Recreation: Travel	✖

Group results by: ▾   Sort results by: ▾   Results 1-10 of 8740   Next >

Libraries and Hurricane Katrina 🔍 💬 🗃
Collection of resources for libraries and librarians related to the aftermath of Hurricane Katrina. Includes a link to ongoing news coverage, and links to resources for financial donations, book donations, housing, employment, and disaster recovery and preservation. Also includes links to reading resources to help victims cope and to sites with general relief information. From the American Library Association (ALA).
URL: http://www.ala.org/ala/cro/katrina/katrina.htm
Added to LII: 2005-09-12

Recreation: Travel
Geography (2400)
Outdoor Recreation (5800)
Travel Sites by Continent (2312)
More subtopics

Cliff House 🔍 💬 🗃
A brief, illustrated history of this San Francisco landmark and the "various edifices that have carried the name Cliff House." Includes information on Adolph Sutro, the Camera Obscura, and the Musée Mécanique. From the Western Neighborhoods Project.
URL: http://www.outsidelands.org/cliffhouse.html
Added to LII: 2003-04-16

Arts and Humanities
Art (2009)
History (3110)
Literature & Books (2122)
More subtopics

Business
California: Business (255)
Finance (189)
Industries (1156)
More subtopics

The Official Site of the Oakland Athletics 🔍 💬 🗃
The site of this Major League Baseball team from Oakland, Calif., contains a schedule of games, statistics, a player roster, team news, and more.
URL: http://www.oaklandathletics.com
Added to LII: 1998-09-08

Computers
Internet (134)
Technology (1105)
Web Design and Management (21)
More subtopics

Small-Town America: Stereoscopic Views from the Robert N. Dennis Collection 🔍 💬 🗃
This collection of 12,000 stereoscopic photographs of three Mid-Atlantic states (New York, New Jersey, and Connecticut) covers the period from 1850 to 1920. "In addition to showing buildings and street scenes in cities, towns, and villages the photographs show farming, industry, transportation, homes, businesses, local celebrations, natural disasters, people, and costumes." Keyword and phrase searchable; browsable by title, name of photographer or publisher, subject, and format. From the collections of The New York Public Library.
URL: http://digital.nypl.org/stereoviews/
Added to LII: 2001-06-12

Government
International Governments (782)
Law (764)
Politics (809)
More subtopics

Acute Radiation Syndrome: A Fact Sheet for Physicians 🔍 💬 🗃
Fact sheet about "Acute Radiation Syndrome (ARS)... an acute illness caused by irradiation of the entire body (or most of the body) by a high dose of penetrating radiation in a very short period of time (usually a matter of minutes)." Topics include descriptions of types of ARS (such as bone marrow syndrome and gastrointestinal syndrome), symptoms, and patient management. From the Centers for Disease Control and Prevention (CDC).

Health
Diseases & Conditions (211)
Pollutants & Toxic Substances (202)

Figure 1.2   Librarians' Internet Index—Travel

In contrast to other resource guides listed here, Travelazer is not a browsable directory but a travel-specific search engine with a database containing millions of pages. Unlike the general Web search engines (discussed later in this chapter), Travelazer indexes only those pages that have a definite "travel" context. Searching is very simple: If you enter multiple terms, you will receive only those pages that contain all the terms (e.g., *Chicago museums*). Note that there is no automatic "stemming" (a feature available in some search sites that automatically finds variant word endings).

Rick Steves' Europe—Favorite Links

www.ricksteves.com/plan/links_menu.htm

This is the smallest collection of links of any resource guide listed here, but the small size is more than balanced by the fact that the links were chosen by one of the world's best and most famous travel writers, Rick Steves. While these 300+ links emphasize European travel, a number of more general sites on travel tips and planning are also included.

PlanetRider—The Best Travel Sites

www.planetrider.com

PlanetRider is an outstanding collection of travel sites. It is a very large, well-organized collection, with a quarter of a million sites arranged in these categories: Destinations, Activities, Landscapes (outdoor and adventure travel), Maps on the Web, Helpful Resources, 10-Minute Vacations, and Weather. A pull-down Site Shortcuts menu takes you to collections of sites for Skiing Worldwide, Bargain Travel, Road and Travel Maps, and Air Reservations. The site is both searchable and browsable. Another major benefit is that all site listings are rated and include brief reviews. Each site is rated on two criteria: quality of information and ease of navigation.

Johnny Jet

www.johnnyjet.com

This collection of more than 1,000 sites is a labor of love, created because Johnny Jet loves travel and sharing travel information (Figure 1.3). One of the site's most interesting and useful aspects is its variety of specific categories, including Bored in Your Hotel Room?, Flight Attendants, Pilot Info, and Complain. Johnny also has a newsletter and a Weblog.

About.com—Travel
about.com/travel

About.com—Travel is part of the much broader About.com site, which covers a seemingly unimaginable range of topics. Each part of About.com provides a combination of topical articles, links to Web resources, and topic forums. For this reason, it is significantly different from the other resource guides listed here, which are primarily pointers to Web resources. About.com provides its own articles and advice, written by About.com's "guides," each of whom specializes in a particular area. In the Travel section of About.com, you will find articles and links that cover a broad range of travel topics, arranged by destination and by topic. Take advantage of the categories to discover what the site offers.

Searching vs. Browsing for Travel Information

There are many times when it is more effective to simply do a straightforward search in a general Web search engine than to browse collections of sites such as those provided by resource guides (or, for that matter, even this book). The more specific your topic, the greater the chance that a quick search will be your best bet. For example, if you are looking for information on hiking in New Hampshire, trout fishing in Switzerland, or ethnographic museum collections in Canada, you should go to Yahoo!, Google, or another general search engine, enter a few terms, and take a look at the results.

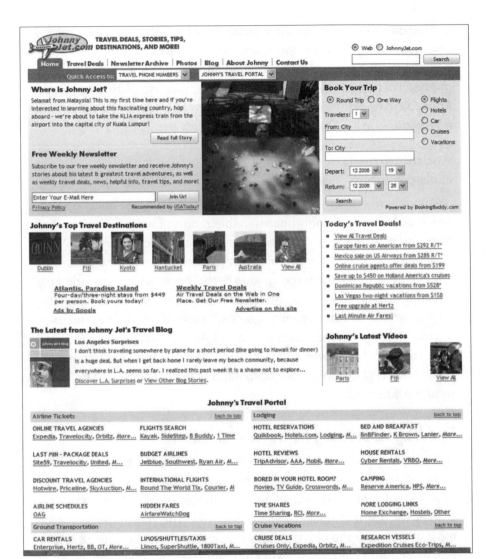

Figure 1.3   Johnny Jet

Throughout this book you will find instances where I suggest doing a simple search, as well as tips designed to make those searches effective. In general, you may find the following advice useful in making the best use of general Web search engines for finding travel information or, for that matter, just about any kind of information. (Throughout this book, when an example of a search is given, the italicized words are those that you would type in the search box.)

Use Multiple Terms

When you enter multiple terms in a major search engine (e.g., *trout fishing Switzerland*), the search will return only Web pages that contain all of the terms. Therefore, the more terms you enter, the more precise your search (for great precision, don't hesitate to use many terms, for example, *tour packages horseback Mayan ruins Tulum*). If the search engine returns too few or no results, just delete one or two of the terms from the search box that is shown on the results page and submit your query again. (By the way, capitalization doesn't matter to the major search engines. If you search for *mexico,* you will get the same results as for *Mexico.*)

Use Quotation Marks When Searching for Phrases

If you want a specific phrase to come up in your search, place quotation marks around the phrase. If you want resorts in New Mexico, for example, search

resorts "new mexico"

instead of

resorts new mexico

The quotation marks around *"new mexico"* guarantee that you will get only results that have the word "new" followed immediately by "mexico." Without the quotation marks (shown in the second example), the search will instead retrieve everything that has the word "new" somewhere and also the word "mexico" somewhere (for example, "New resort hotel opens in Guadalajara, Mexico"). This technique works not only for pairs of words but for longer phrases as well (e.g., "*Royal New South Wales Canine Council*").

Search by Title Words for High Precision

To add greater oomph to your search, insist that your results pages have a particular term (or terms) in the title. In both Yahoo! and Google, this is done by placing "intitle:" in front of the term. For example, a search for

trout fishing intitle:Switzerland

would return all pages that have the terms "trout" and "fishing" any-where on the page, and "Switzerland" in the title. The following search would be even more precise:

trout intitle:fishing intitle:Switzerland

The techniques just discussed are only a few examples of the many that can be used to improve the quality of results from search engines. If you want to take it a step (or many steps) further, click on the Advanced Search link on the search engine's home page and look around on the advanced page for numerous additional options.

One final bit of introductory advice about search engines: Use more than one. Try the same search in both Yahoo! and Google. Because of the ways search engines rank results, you will often see significant differences in the first 10 to 20 results. One search engine may find items that another doesn't. If you don't believe it, try a few searches in both Google and Yahoo! and compare the results.

As I said early on in this chapter, the Internet is much more than just a place to make reservations. The following chapters will introduce you to a broad range of resources that no traveler should be without.

Travel Guides Online

As suggested in Chapter 1, if you plan to spend a substantial amount of time in any particular country or city, shell out a little cash and get a print travel book, or at least, when you get there, stop by the local tourist office and pick up some free brochures. It will be some time before most of us are roaming the streets with full Internet access in our hands. However, in preparation for a trip, or while you are there, take advantage of the amazing amount of useful information online for just about anywhere you might want to visit. If you are spending only part of a day in a city, pulling a few pages off the Internet is a quick and inexpensive way to choose a few prime spots to see. If you are spending more time in a place, the Internet may be able to provide more background and related information on countries, cities, towns, and specific sights such as museums than any single (and perhaps even expensive) guidebook.

In the next few pages we will look at Web sites that offer descriptions of destinations and expert advice on how to get there and what to see and do once you are there. At the end of this chapter, you will find sources for advice and information from fellow travelers: travel forums (discussion groups, boards, etc.). In Chapter 9, "Exploring Countries and Cultures Online," we will look beyond publications written specifically as guides for the traveler and explore resources that go into more detail about countries and cultures.

There are a variety of types of travel guides on the Web. Many of the best known are provided by publishers of print guidebooks. Some guides are general and cover the whole world; others cover particular parts of the world, countries, cities, or specific sites, such as individual museums. Also considered to be "guides" are online versions of periodicals, such as travel magazines and newspaper travel sections and columns. The final category that should be included are sites for radio and TV travel programs, mainly because of the similar travel information they provide. Although every source is different, each provides information and advice to help you select destinations, prepare for your travels, and make the most of your visit.

As is the case whenever you use the Web to find resources, one of the problems with using online travel guides is that there are so many that it is hard to (1) be fully aware of the variety of information they provide, and (2) know which are worth your valuable time. As you explore the differences in these sites, keep in mind that each writer has his or her own style, and as a reader, which guide you go back to most frequently may simply be a matter of whose writing style you prefer. As elsewhere in this book, this chapter is not meant to be exhaustive (for fear of being exhausting to you). Included here you will find the best known guides as well as some lesser-known sites that are particularly interesting or provide good examples of the variety of sites available. Particularly if you are headed to a more out-of-the-way spot, be sure to check more than one guide. There are many other guides on the Web that provide useful information, but those featured on the next few pages could arguably be considered the leaders.

General Travel Guides
Online Versions/Excerpts from Printed Guidebooks

Some of the best-known printed travel books have corresponding Web sites that contain a substantial portion of what you find in the printed book. If you haven't used these sites before, you may be sur- prised how much content you can get for free. You will also find that these sites, when considered together, exemplify a very important characteristic of travel information online: There is a lot of redundancy in the information found on the Web. Often you will find exactly the same information from the same provider in more than one place and on more than one site. Information from Fodor's, for example, can be found at Fodor's own site, as well as in the Destinations section at Expedia (in return, the reservations portion of Fodor's own site is han- dled by Expedia). Another specific example of redundancy is the Rough Guide's description of Morocco: It is used on more than two dozen travel sites and on more than 100 pages on the Web.

Most of these guidebook sites serve multiple functions. They typi- cally include not just destination guides, but also sections for making reservations, booking tour packages, forums, and more. In the descriptions that follow, the destination guides function is empha- sized. Other functions, such as reservations and forums, will be men- tioned briefly and covered in more detail in later chapters that cover those specific topics. Be aware that these guides will typically contain only information for destinations covered in the print version and that you may need to check out more than one guide when looking for information on less-visited locations.

One other general tip: In these travel guides, look for and take advantage of the Print links or buttons so you can print out the content of the pages (usually) without ads, unnecessary graphics, and other peripheral content.

Fodor's
www.fodors.com

Fodor's is an excellent example of what an Internet travel guide can do for you. It contains not just information on destinations and sights but is a guide to hotels, restaurants, and much more. The Travel Wire (short travel articles) section alone would make this site worthwhile.

Fodor's Destinations

The travel guide (Destinations) part of the Fodor's site is accessible either by clicking on the Destinations tab, or link, or by clicking on the map found on Fodor's main page. You will be taken to a clear, straightforward directory of destinations arranged by continent, country, region or state, and city. In all, Fodor's provides these "mini-guides" for nearly 300 cities and regions (Figure 2.1), but the number of destinations is more than 300 if you count the Side Trips links provided for those destinations. For most countries, you will get a mini-guide for several cities. For some smaller countries, such as Slovakia, the information focuses on the country itself. Expect to find mini-guides for major cities, but not for the many smaller cities covered in the corresponding printed guide. Because Fodor's does not publish printed travel guides for all countries, some are notably missing online, particularly some Asian, African, and Middle Eastern countries.

For each city (or region), expect to find an Overview and sections for Sights & Activities, Restaurants, Hotels, Nightlife & the Arts, and Shopping. Click on any of the latter five categories to get a list of places or events with a brief description of basic details. Each of those sections also has an Overview subsection that is particularly useful for getting an overall feel for opportunities for hotels, sights, etc. A Smart Travel Tips section provides information on Arriving & Departing, Getting Around, and Contacts & Resources. You will also find links to suggested itineraries for various lengths of time. Additional Features links take you to information on When to Go, Fodor's Choice, and side trips and special topics relevant to the particular city. For the unique flavor of a city, don't pass up these special topics links—for example, for Sydney, Australia, you may find an article

Figure 2.1   Fodor's Destinations page for Bangkok

on "The Shocking Truth About Australian Wine," and for Chicago, Illinois, one on "Chicago's Gangster Past." Also take advantage of links to Maps, Related Destinations, Weather, and Adventure Travel, provided by Fodor's partner sites, such as Weather.com.

In the Hotels section for any destination, look first at the Lodging Overview link to get a feel for the overall lodging situation for the destination. On a Hotels page, you will find a list of hotels with a price range, a (Fodor's) Guest Rating, and a Book It link. Click on the hotel name to get a more detailed description of the hotel, an address, and phone numbers. The details page may also provide individual ratings and tremendously useful comments from travelers themselves.

In the Restaurants section, check out the Overview subsection first, which is designed just like the Hotels Overview section. From the Overview, use the Go to Restaurants Listings link to get to names and descriptions of restaurants.

Other Sections of Fodor's

Links on Fodor's main page (and at the top of most Fodor's pages) lead to sections for Hotels, Restaurants, Travel Wire, Talk, Booking, and Bookstore. Fodor's does a good job of integrating this variety of content and provides multiple ways to get to a specific bit of information. If you start with the Destinations section for a particular city, you will find subsections for hotels, restaurants, etc. If you start with the Hotels link on the main page, you are then led to a choice of destinations, and so on. Whatever you choose as a starting point, in the end, you get to the same information. Other main sections of Fodor's that deserve attention are:

- Travel Wire – This section alone would make Fodor's a top travel site. Here you will find brief articles (from the last few months) by Fodor's editors, arranged in categories such as, Bargains and Packages, Festivals and Events, Fodor's

Choice, Gear and Gadgets, Just Back From ... , MuseumWatch, New and Fabulous, News, On the Road, Overlooked and Underrated, Tours, Travel Tips, and Worldly Shopper. The search box lets users find articles on a destination or topic of interest. Look for the link on the Travel Wire pages where you can sign up for a free e-mail subscription to the Travel Wire newsletter.

- Talk — Contains forums with comments and questions from travelers. You can read the discussions without registering for Fodor's, but you must be registered to post a message. Look for the Log In/Register section for more information.

- Booking — Takes you to the Expedia site (see Chapter 3, "Reservation Sites: Flights and More").

- Shop — Leads to a catalog of Fodor publications.

Lonely Planet

www.lonelyplanet.com

Although Lonely Planet (both in its free online version and its print books) has much in common with other travel guides, its content is steered by its philosophy that "as part of a worldwide community of travelers, we want to enable everyone to travel with awareness, respect and care." This goal lends a definite and unique perspective to the information you will find at Lonely Planet. With information on far more cities (and countries) than Fodor's site, Lonely Planet is a good starting point if you are interested in a smaller city or out-of-the-way places. On the other hand, the descriptions for each city are likely to be significantly shorter. Some major cities have their own fairly extensive pages, while smaller cities receive coverage only within the Web page for the entire country. Lonely Planet doesn't directly provide lists and reviews of hotels and restaurants, but it does provide links to partner sites for booking flights, lodging, tour packages, and other travel services. A key part of the Lonely Planet site is the input provided by travelers in the Thorn Tree Forum. The Lonely Planet site is easy to navigate, and a search box on the home page allows you to search the Lonely Planet Shop, the overall site, or its forums. The Advanced Search link leads to a sophisticated site search by date and a number of other search criteria. Lonely Planet content is available for mobile devices (wap.lonelyplanet.com and mobile.lonelyplanet.com).

Lonely Planet Destinations (WorldGuide)

Click on the Destinations link and you are taken to Lonely Planet's WorldGuide, where you can pick your destination either by pull-down menus or by clicking on a map. If you want information on a specific city, you will want to use the search box or the pull-down Explore menus instead of the map (which just leads to country-level information). For each country, you will typically find the following categories of information (Figure 2.2), and within each category page, you will find links to city descriptions, a map, the image gallery, travel services, and the Lonely Planet bookshop:

- Introduction – Offers two subsections:
  - At a Glance – A brief traveler's overview of the country and, in some cases, a When to Go section with weather conditions, peak seasons, and more
  - Fast Facts – A brief listing of information about the country, including population of the capital, language, religions, currency, time zone, dial code, electrical voltage and frequency, and electrical outlet used
- See – Provides a brief description of the major sights and locations.

Figure 2.2   Lonely Planet's Destinations page for Norway

- Image Gallery – Displays from three to six pictures; not many, but good.

- Events – Provides a brief overview of what's happening and when, including public holidays for some countries.

- Transport – Tells you how to get there and how to get around once you are there.

- Money – Provides details about the country's economy, but more importantly for the traveler, a Costs list showing the price of typical items, such as movie tickets, a liter of milk, a loaf of bread, a glass of wine, a roll of film, and a daily transport ticket—a tremendously valuable tool in planning a travel budget.

- Background Info – Includes sections on Weather, Time & Place (time, weights and measures, geography), Crossing Borders (customs, visas, passports), Government (names of heads of government, etc.), People & Society (origins and religions), and Culture & History (the origins of the culture, the language, music, literature, and history, so travelers get a sense of the basics).

City information includes similar categories, with much more information about the city's local sights, attractions, events, etc. (However, for individual sights within any city, more information is available on the Fodor's or Frommer's sites than at Lonely Planet.)

Other Sections of Lonely Planet

On Lonely Planet's main page (and other pages), you will find links to the following Lonely Planet features:

- Thorn Tree – One of the most active travel forums on the Web with more than a quarter of a million registered users. For more information about the Thorn Tree forum, see the section on Discussion Groups at the end of this chapter.

- Travel Services – Lonely Planet has teamed up with several well-respected sites to provide the following reservation and travel services: Airline Reservations (from Opodo, Kayak, Zuji); Hostels and Budget Travel (HostelWorld); Hotel Reservations (Opodo, Kayak, Zuji); Travel Insurance (World

Nomads); Global Communication for phones and phone cards (ekit); Adventure Travel (World Expeditions); Personal Trip Web Site (MyTripJournal); Rail and Ferry passes, schedules, and reservations (RailPlus, RailEurope); and Car Rental (Holiday Autos).

- Bluelist – A collection of travel experiences and destinations that are recommended, described, and rated by the Lonely Planet staff, authors, and travelers.

- Travel Ticker – Contains important travel advisories, including new and ongoing warnings, and reminders of other events, such as elections and holidays, that may generate large crowds travelers may wish to avoid.

- Theme Guides – Provides advice on where to go, categorized by a variety of themes, including Art, Beaches, Deserts, Fatal Attractions, Festivals, Food, History, Honeymoons, Islands, Music, Religion, Roadtrips, Safaris, Sport, Twilight Zone, Water, and Sports. Lonely Planet is at its unconventional best with its commentary on places and events: "The sole purpose of the Burning Man Festival is to confirm the widely-held belief that Californians are a loopy lot, in that harmless SoCal magic-crystals-and-inner-child kind of way."

- Digital Guides – Print guides, audio guides, and maps you can purchase

- Travel Features – Browse this mini-travel magazine with articles, podcasts and blogs by Lonely Planet guidebook writers. You can browse by author and by region.

- Postcards – Includes guidebook-type information contributed by Lonely Planet readers and functions somewhat as an update to the printed Lonely Planet guidebooks. Most information falls in the following categories: Visas; Embassies &

Border Crossings; Travel Tips; Moving About; Scams and Warnings; Gems, Highlights & Attractions; Yarns, Fables, and Anecdotes; and others. There's a disclaimer from Lonely Planet warning readers that content here has not been checked by LP editors.

• Travel Links – A useful collection of links that connects to several hundred travel sites arranged by continent and topic.

These sections are found at various places on the site. If you do not find them, use the search box to search for them.

If you have not used Lonely Planet, try it out. You will find it to be a substantially different kind of travel guide with unique perspectives. You can also sign up for the Lonely Planet newsletter, Lonely Planet Comet (www.lonelyplanet.com/comet), or RSS feeds to keep up with Lonely Planet's excellent travel articles.

Frommer's
www.frommers.com

For information on a very large number of destinations, plus excellent articles, travel discussion forums, deals, tips for travelers, and more, the Frommer's site is a great starting place. Frommer's provides information on more than 3,000 destinations, articles that bring together advice, resources, and identification of great travel deals, plus a helpful collection of information in its Tips and Tools section. The site is extensive, with more than 100,000 pages of information, well organized, and easy to use. The Trip Ideas section provides a great place to start if you are looking for ideas. This section lets you browse based on your preference of activities or lifestyles. Frommer's main page has preview sections for major sections of the site: The Destinations section of the main page contains a map and search box for finding information on a particular destination; the Deals & News box provides links to featured articles, along with a Browse All link and search box for accessing all articles and deals; the Trip Ideas box provides links to 16 categories of activities and lifestyles; and the Book a Trip box presents a compact box for making reservations through Frommer's reservation partners. In addition, on the main page you will find links for subscribing to Frommer's newsletters, plus ads for Frommer's publications and services. Take advantage of the search box at the top of the main page to search the entire site, Destinations, Deals & News, the Bookstore, or Message Boards. Tabs near the top of the page take you to each section (which are described in the following paragraphs). The site is very well integrated and conveniently "redundant." For example, although there is a specific section for message boards (Travel Talk), the message boards pertaining to specific destinations are also found in the Destinations section.

Frommer's Destinations

Frommer's is very generous with the amount of information that it provides for free from its extensive catalog of printed guides; it covers more than 3,000 destinations (countries, regions, states, national parks, islands, etc.). From the main Destinations page, you can search using the Destinations search box, or you can browse by clicking on one of the continents on the world map shown there, by clicking on one of the text links to continents, or by choosing a place from a list of Top Destinations. (If you use the Destinations section of Travelocity, you may notice great similarity between what you find there and what you find on Frommer's Destination section, as Travelocity uses Frommer's content for destination descriptions.)

Frommer's search boxes provide more search functionality than search boxes on most travel sites. In addition to just entering one or more words, you can use the Boolean AND, OR, and NOT. (For those not familiar with Boolean, AND narrows your search to only those results that contain all of your words, e.g., *Birmingham AND Alabama*;

OR expands your search to include any term of multiple terms, e.g., *Holland OR Netherlands*; and NOT eliminates a term, e.g., *Birmingham NOT Alabama*.) On search results pages, you will see two lists of results: one for Destinations and the other for From Our Guides. The former takes you to the main page of any guide that matches your search, and the latter displays the title of each individual page (from the Guides) that matches your query.

For most parts of the world, Frommer's provides Guides at several different levels: Countries, Regions, States/Provinces/Territories, and Cities (Figure 2.3). Depending on the level, you will find the following:

- Deals and News – Special deals and articles for the destination.
- Introduction – An overview of the destination.
- Frommer's "Bests" – Best bets in dining, hotels, museums, experiences, outdoor adventures, attractions, etc. These categories will depend on the location. For Thailand, you'll find the Most Fascinating Temples; for Cuba, the Best Beaches; and for London, the Best Pubs.
- Planning a Trip – Contains Fast Facts, Visitor Information, When to Go, Getting There, Regions in Brief, Health & Insurance, Money, Entrance Requirements & Customs, Getting Around, and Trips for Travelers with Special Needs.
- Organized Tours
- Hotels – Provides a fairly extensive listing of hotels with columns for Rating, Price, Name, and Neighborhood. Click on the column heading to sort by that criterion. Click on a hotel name to get a review, facilities, phone numbers, address, price range, Web site, etc.
- Restaurants – Provides a listing of restaurants with columns for Rating, Price, Name, Cuisine Type, and Neighborhood. The details page for each restaurant gives a review, cuisine

Figure 2.3   Frommer's city guide page for Rio de Janeiro

type, hours, location, transportation, address, phone, prices, reservations, credit cards accepted, dress code, and season.

- Attractions – Provides reviews, ratings, hours, locations, transportation, phone numbers, and prices.
- Nightlife – Provides names, reviews, phone numbers, and addresses.
- Shopping – Provides areas, reviews, and locations.
- Side Trips – Provides descriptions, distances, and more.
- Active Pursuits – Talks about sports and fitness facilities at this destination.
- Spectator Sports – Click here if you want to drop some money at the local racetrack or enjoy a soccer or cricket game or other spectator sport.
- Message Boards – Provides excellent active discussion groups.

Other Sections of Frommer's

Frommer's main page provides links to the following features:

- Hotels – Takes you directly to the same hotel information that you will find under individual destinations.
- Trip Ideas – Whether or not you have a pretty good idea of what kind of vacation you want, this section can be a good place to start. Provides articles, deals, selected destinations, carriers, and other information for seven categories of Activities (Beach & Water Sports, Cruise, Cultural Immersion, Outdoor & Adventure, Road Trip, Theme Park, and Winter Sport) and eight categories of Lifestyles (Disabled, Family,

Gay & Lesbian, Honeymoon, Senior, Single, Student, and Women). For each category, a specialized search box is provided to search the articles in that section. The Activities categories provide additional search criteria. In the Outdoor & Adventure category, for example, the search box lets you enter a destination and use a dropdown menu to narrow your search to any of 15 specific sports or other outdoor activities.

- Deals and News – Possibly viewed as Frommer's travel magazine, contains articles by Frommer's staff that are well researched, very informative, yet short enough to read quickly. Each article focuses on one of the following categories: Airfare, Hotels, Car, Bus & Rail, Package, Cruise, Other Discounts, Trip Ideas, or Tips and Tools. These are the same articles listed in the other sections of the site and typically include descriptions, news, and perspectives and links to relevant Web sites and deals. They may cover travel news, specific destinations, activities, travel tips, deals, or other topics, with content ranging from European opera tours to national park passes. While other travel sites may have articles about "deals" that turn out to be ads, Frommer's articles provide links to multiple competitive providers. These articles also make good reading for the armchair traveler. Use the Newsletter link on the Deals & News page to subscribe to an RSS feed or e-mail delivery of new articles (and selected message board postings) three times every week.

- Book a Trip – Make reservations using one of Frommer's partners: Flights (Travelocity), Hotels (Hotels.com), Cars (Thrifty and Travelocity), Packages (iExplore), Cruises (Travelocity and Norwegian Cruiseline), Rail (Rail Europe), and Last-Minute Travel (Travelocity). Since Frommer's is not a travel agency, it does not book its own arrangements. It partners with providers such as these so that you can make reservations through the Frommer's site.

- Tips and Tools – Features recent articles on travel tips and tools, arranged in the following categories: Calendar of Events, Entry Requirements & Customs, Health & Travel Insurance, Money & Currency, Online Updates, Packing Tips, and Photography.

- Travel Talk – Hosts all Frommer's message boards: Destination Boards, Activity Boards, Lifestyle Boards, and Tips, Tools & Deals Boards. For more details, see the Discussion Groups section at the end of this chapter.

- Bookstore – Frommer's catalog of print guidebooks.

- Frommer's Newsletters – Access Frommer's five free e-mail newsletters: Frommers.com Newsletter (three times a week); Ski Newsletter (seasonal); National Parks Newsletter (alerts for new articles in the U.S. National Parks section of Destinations; a Sponsor News and Deals Newsletter (variable frequency); and Cruise Newsletter (twice a month).

Rough Guides—Travel

www.roughguides.com

To quote from Rough Guides' About Us page, for their travel books, the Rough Guides founders "aimed to combine a journalistic approach to description with a thoroughly practical approach to travelers' needs, a guide that would incorporate culture, history and contemporary insights with a critical edge, together with up-to-date, value-for-money listings." They have met this goal.

The site's main page primarily features some of Rough Guides' books, maps, and other products, but by clicking on the Travel tab or by using the pull-down menus, you will be able to find your way to descriptive information for countries and cities and other features, such as Spotlights, Community, Travel Talk, Podcasts, and Newsletter.

Rough Guides' Destinations

To get information on a specific destination from the main Travel page, click on the Destinations link on the main menu. From there, you can use a world map, pull-down menus, a search link, or a geographic directory arranged by continent and country. Whatever you do, don't pass up the country listings; on each country's page, look for links to sections such as "Best of ...", Basics, Language, "Explore ...", etc. (Figure 2.4). Many of these sections go down through multiple levels of information (e.g., Basics > Getting Around > Buses) and provide nitty-gritty facts that you will undoubtedly find useful. Under the Basics section, you will find a variety of subsections, such as Accommodation, Eating, Drinking, Getting Around, Communication, Tour Operators, Hiking and Rough Camping, Costs, Money and Banks, Red Tape and Visas, Phone Numbers, and Security.

The Destination pages for cities contain similar sets of links, but at the city level (you already figured that out, right?). As with the country pages, for whatever topic you choose, you will usually find from one to five paragraphs. Don't forget to look for additional links leading to more in-depth information. Hotel and restaurant recommendations may be found in the Basics section, specifically under the Accomodations and Eating and Drinking subsections.

Other Sections of Rough Guides

Rough Guides' main page provides links to the following features:

- Spotlights – Contains hundreds of articles by Rough Guides authors, typically on a particular country or city. The articles

Figure 2.4   Rough Guides' Destinations page for Chile

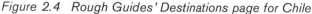

often focus on a specific topic, such as "Spain: Fine Art and Fruit-Throwing Fiestas," "Peru: The Urubamba River by Handmade Raft," or "Florida: Eco-Tourism or Bust," which date back to the start of the Rough Guides site in 1998.

- Community – Provided in conjunction with IgoUgo, a forum where travelers can post their own travel journals (more about IgoUgo at the end of this chapter).

- Travel Talk – An open bulletin board for traveler comments and questions. You don't need to register to read the messages on thousands of topics, but you do need to register (for free) to reply to messages or start a new topic of your own.

- Newsletter and Podcasts – Sign up for the free weekly Rough Guides newsletter for Spotlight articles and other news. Click on the Podcasts link on Rough Guide's menu for regular podcasts that you can listen to online or download to your MP3 player (see the section on podcasts near the end of this chapter).

- Photo Galleries – On the country and city pages, look for the understated See Photos icon, which will take you to a collection of excellent photos that will give you a visual sense of a destination. For some places, you will be treated to dozens of photos.

With its 2006 re-design, the Rough Guides site was both streamlined and enhanced, with the goal of providing detailed information on more than 100 countries. Count on Rough Guides for a really good combination of background and travel details, with bonuses such as discussions and photos.

Rick Steves' Europe Through the Back Door
www.ricksteves.com

Just based on the title, you can see that Rick Steves' Europe Through the Back Door is different from the other sites discussed so far in this chapter. Fodor's, Lonely Planet, Frommer's, and Rough Guides all cover the world at large—most continents, most countries. The Rick Steves' site is primarily about Europe. Besides its narrower coverage, it also differs in its emphasis and purpose. As stated on the site, the mission of Rick's organization is to "inspire, inform and equip Americans to have European trips that are fun, affordable and culturally broadening." The site, which provides unique and detailed guides to destinations, is also a guide to Rick's outstanding television and radio programs. You should not be surprised to find that the site also serves as an online store for Rick's books and videos.

If you have used the site, read his books, watched his videos or TV shows, or listened to him on radio, you will understand the inclination to refer to Rick on a first-name basis. He talks to you as a friend and brings travel to the person-to-person level rather than to the person-to-building level. Use his information to go a step further than the "must-see" places. As well as pointing you to worthwhile spots that others will miss, he doesn't hesitate to tell you what you can skip.

Rick Steves' Plan Your Trip

Most nonadvertising-related content on the site is found under the Plan Your Trip section, and most content related to specific destinations is located under the Best Destinations link. For each of the countries or areas listed, you will find such things as updates to his book on that area, a suggested itinerary, a calendar of festivals, and from 10 to 70 articles about the country, cities, and specific sights, cuisine, and other related topics (Figure 2.5). In the Plan Your Trip section, you will also find:

- Travel Tips – More than 70 topics ranging from "Packing Light and Right" to the "Chunnel User's Guide"
- Favorite Links – Several hundred links on Accommodations, Entertainment, Transportation, Maps, etc., with several categories offering links to specific hotels and tours that Rick recommends
- Graffiti Wall – A travelers' bulletin board with comments, with the majority of messages related to general travel rather than specific destinations

Figure 2.5   Rick Steves' Europe Through the Back Door

Other Sections of Rick Steves' Europe Through the Back Door

Most of the remaining sections of the Rick Steves site focus on his products (books, tours, and Travel Store), but the following deserve particular attention:

- Railpasses – This section provides a lot of good, clear information on how railpasses work, how to plan for using them, and where to buy them (you can also purchase them through the site).

- Rick on TV and Rick on Radio – These sections alert you to when you can catch his shows; the radio section also provides audio from the programs so you can listen to Rick whenever you wish.

If you are heading to Europe, this site is a must. Even if you are not, the Travel Tips section is a worthwhile stop for any traveler.

Michelin Green Guides
(Available through the ViaMichelin maps site at www.viamichelin.com)

The venerable Michelin Green Guides are not available on a site of their own, but information from them is available through the ViaMichelin maps site, discussed in Chapter 4, "Train, Car, and Ferry Travel."

Other General Travel Guides

The preceding general travel guides are all primarily derivatives of print guides. The next three have no print equivalent.

World Travel Guide
www.worldtravelguide.net

World Travel Guide (formerly Columbus Guides) provides a contrast to the preceding guides and a good prelude to the next sections on guides to individual countries and individual cities. Whereas the preceding sites present a combination of commentary and hard facts, World Travel Guide delivers basically "just the facts" (and lots of them), but with little commentary.

For each of the more than 230 countries covered, you will find pages with collections of facts for Contact Addresses, Overview, General Information, Passport/Visa, Money, Duty Free, Public Holidays, Health, Travel—International, Travel—Internal, Accommodation, Sport & Activities, Social Profile, Business Profile, Climate, History and Government, and a map. A very unique and practical feature is the option to create Mini Guides. When on the page for a particular country, click on the Create Mini Guide link and you are given a list of the categories just listed. Click on those of interest and you can print a customized Mini Guide with just that data. For the U.S., Canada, and Australia, you will also find collections of information for individual states and provinces, with the printable Mini Guide option available.

For about 100 cities around the world, similar guides (and Mini Guides) are available on the World Travel Guide site (Figure 2.6), with pages of facts for the following categories: Sport, Shopping, Culture, Nightlife, City Statistics, Special Events, Cost of Living, City Overview, Getting There By Air, Getting There By Water, Getting There By Road, Getting There By Rail, Getting Around, Business, Sightseeing, Key Attractions, Further Distractions, Tours of the City, Excursions, Hotels, and Restaurants. For both countries and cities, an Images link will take you to a photo gallery (unfortunately, many of the photos are unlabeled, so you may have to guess what you are seeing).

Detailed information about airports around the world is available in the Airports section. The Cruises section is fairly minimal, containing just a very brief overview of major cruise destination cities. The Attractions section contains brief descriptions, transportation information, and contact information for several hundred attractions, largely parks, museums, archaeological sites, etc. If you are in the U.K., you can use the Brochures link to order brochures for regions, destinations, and types of holidays. You will also find ads for books, travel insurance, tours, and other travel sites.

The World Travel Guide, which is available in English, German, Spanish, and French, licenses its content to third-party sites, so you may run across this content on other travel sites. The site itself, though, is a great place for getting straightforward facts in a convenient, compact form.

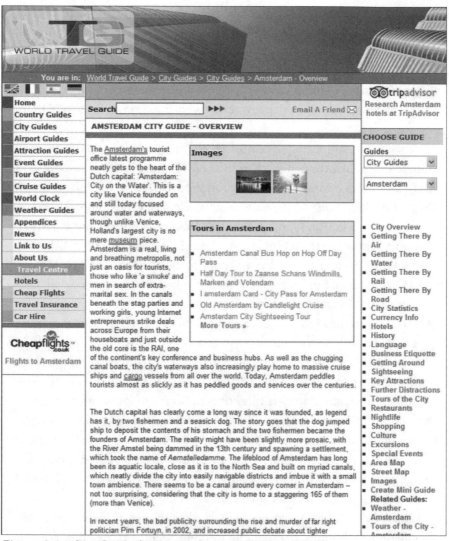

Figure 2.6   City Guide for Amsterdam on World Travel Guide

Wikitravel

wikitravel.org

Wikitravel is an example of a "WikiWiki" site, a type of Web site that is the result of a collaborative project of enthusiasts and allows easy input and online editing of content by any user. Wikitravel has versions in several languages and, among all the versions, contains more than 12,000 articles. Destinations are arranged by continent but can also be located using the search box. As well as articles on countries and cities, Wikitravel contains articles on itineraries and travel topics such as accommodations, transportation, communication, packing, health and safety, special interests, events, and sights.

For each country covered, there are typically sections on individual cities, other destinations, transportation, language, shopping, etiquette, food, hotels, safety and health. The amount of information on each country, city, and topic will vary considerably, depending on the individual contributors. Be aware that for any article, you may be getting unedited information from a single individual.

About.com—Travel

about.com/travel

The About.com site, in general, provides advice, facts, columns, links, and other information on hundreds of topics, ranging from country music to crocheting. The Travel section has numerous sections and subsections on regions and other travel topics, each written by a "Guide" who specializes in that topic. The focused expertise of these Guides is what makes About.com stand out from other travel sites.

The country or region (e.g., Hawaii/South Pacific) sections typically contain the following subsections: Essentials, Offers, Articles & Resources, Buyers Guide, Articles, and Forums. The content of the Essentials section will vary depending on the destination and the Guide. The Essentials section for Canada includes "Do U.S. Citizens

Need a Passport?", Hawaii has a "Beach Guide," Mexico/Central America has "Health Information," Eastern Europe has "Country Profiles," and Southeastern U.S. has articles on "Beaches." To find your way to specific travel destinations in About.com, you may wish to use the search box.

It is in the Articles & Resources subsections (and the rather redundant Articles subsections) that you will find a tremendous variety of valuable advice, information, and links. Since each country, city, etc., has a different Guide, the kinds of articles will vary. This variety of content and perspectives is one of the strengths of the About.com site. Be sure to look around while you're on the Articles & Resources pages for links to more categories, related topics, and headlines.

In addition to About.com's sections for countries and regions, it also has separate sections for Getaways/Vacations, Practical Traveler, Recreation/Outdoors, and Tools. Look in these sections for a useful collection of specialized articles and resources focusing on Adventure Travel, Bed & Breakfasts, Cruises, Honeymoons/Romantic Getaways, Hotels/Resorts/Inns, Spas, Theme Parks, Travel with Kids, Practical Traveler, Air Travel, Budget Travel, Business Travel, Senior Travel, Student Travel, Recreation/Outdoors, Bicycling, Birding/Wild Birds, Camping, Freshwater Fishing, Golf, Hunting/Shooting, Sailing, Saltwater Fishing, Scuba Diving, Skiing, Summer Fun, and U.S./Canadian Parks.

Country-Specific Guides

There are hundreds of sites that provide travel information on a single country. Most countries have an "official" site for travelers, and myriad travel agencies will have country-specific sites. The travel industry within a country may also provide guide sites. You may, of course, prefer to just stick to the general guides discussed (Fodor's, Frommer's, etc.), which may very well have all the information you need (and each of them provides a consistent format from country to country). Guides developed for a single country can, however, provide unique perspectives and content. Keep in mind that the "official" sites are there to market the country, cities, and attractions. You may want to supplement what you find there with information from other guides and from travel forums.

So how do you find these country sites? The easiest way is to go to one of the following sites, which have extensive lists of country sites; you can also do a Web search. From the sites described here, you are just a click or two away from the official tourist site for just about any country. Often, the official link given on these sites will (naturally) be to a version of the site in the country's native language. However, those pages will usually have links to versions of the site in other languages.

Tourism Offices Worldwide Directory
www.towd.com

Tourism Offices Worldwide Directory has links to national tourism sites, office addresses, phone numbers, and e-mail addresses for more than 170 countries, plus offices for U.S. states, Canadian provinces, and Australian territories.

Official Tourist Information Offices Worldwide
www.thebigproject.co.uk/tourist_offices

Official Tourist Information Offices Worldwide links to official tourist information sites for about 100 countries, plus official sites for a number of cities and regions, especially U.K. cities.

Governments on the WWW: Institutions in the Area "Tourism"
www.gksoft.com/govt/en/tourism.html

The overall Governments on the WWW site contains links to all types of official government sites throughout the world and, in the Institutions in the Area "Tourism" section, links to tourism offices in more than 140 countries. The links here may be to sites that are more governmental or business-oriented than to those specifically for tourists. For example, the link for Canada leads to the site for "The Official Business Site of the Canadian Tourism Commission," but that page does contain a link to the site for visitors to Canada.

Travel Industry Sites for Countries

No one has more of a vested interest in encouraging visitors to a particular country than the local travel industry. As a result, organizations of travel agents, hotels, and the like kindly provide great sites to encourage people to visit and offer highlights of what to do while there.

OfficialTravelGuide.com
www.officialtravelguide.com

OfficialTravelGuide.com is a product of the Destination Marketing Association International (DMAI). It contains links to convention and visitor bureau sites, tourism council sites, and sites of similar organizations for more than 1,200 destinations. (It is guilty, unfortunately, of that nasty little trick of placing each link you click on in a window on its own site, making it look as if all 1,200 sites are part of the OfficialTravelGuide.com site.) In addition to the country-level sites, you will find tourism sites for states, provinces, counties, cities, towns, and specific attractions.

Examples of Country Guide Sites

Though space prohibits describing 200 or so country sites here, a small sampling will offer a taste of what to expect on this type of site. Remember that the sites just discussed will give you access to similar sites for about any country.

VisitBritain
www.visitbritain.com

VisitBritain actually has 38 versions to choose from depending on the country *from* which you will be traveling. Each version has sections for Accommodations, Attractions, Events, Flights & Transport, About Britain, Business Tourism, Destinations Guides, Holiday Ideas, and an Online Shop. A Travel Tools section contains a route planner, links to receive brochures and a newsletter, a Web Chat option, a Currency Converter, and more. The Accommodations, Attractions, and Events sections provide databases that are searchable by the type of accommodations, attractions, or events of interest, and by when and where. The Destination Guides provide brief descriptions of cities and regions, plus lists of local accommodations, events, and attractions. The Holiday Ideas section has a selection of featured events, attractions, and topics, as well as the Online Shop that offers travel packages and deals. One additional major section is My Travel Plan. In this section, by registering (for free) you can construct your own itinerary, see it on a map, and book accommodations and tickets.

Canada—Keep Exploring
www.explore.canada.travel

The home page of the Canada—Keep Exploring site, which comes from the Canadian Tourist Commission, offers a selection of featured "Things to Do" and (under "Pure Canada") links to articles on destinations and events. The overall site, though, can be navigated by the tabs for the four main sections of the site: Places to Go, Things to Do, Things to Know, and Maps. Under the Places to Go tab, you will find subsections leading you to guides by Regions, Territories & Provinces, and Cities and Destinations. The Things to Do tab offers events and activities arranged by Festivals & Events, Culture & Heritages, Lifestyle, Attractions, Outdoor, and Touring. The Things to Know section leads to practical information about getting to and around the country. The Maps tab takes you to what at first looks like a rather uninteresting map of the country, but if you make use of the Change Your Map View tool, you can choose from a variety of things to be added to the map (regions, provinces, cities, weather, time zones, roads, rail routes, etc.).

SeeAmerica.org

www.seeamerica.org

SeeAmerica.org links to more than 10,000 travel sites, including airlines, hotels, attractions, convention and visitor bureaus, state tourism offices, and others. The site is arranged by state, and for each state you'll find a list of events and festivals (with details), links to tourism sites for regions and cities within the state, lists of shopping centers, links to restaurant information, basic facts about the state, transportation information, media resources (newspapers, newsletters, etc.), links to travel articles (from Fodor's, *Condé Nast Traveler*, etc.), maps, and more. At a national level, it highlights selected activities, attractions, and travel deals. It also provides a collection of traveler tools for flying, driving, and weather.

Check out these other examples of country-specific sites:

France—Maison de la France

www.franceguide.com

Spain—Welcome to Spain:
The Official Web Site for Tourism in Spain
www.spain.info

Italy—Italia: The Official Web Site
of the Italian State Tourism Board
www.enit.it

China—China National Tourist Office
www.cnto.org

Austria—Welcome to Austria:
The Austrian National Tourist Office
www.austria.info

Visit Mexico
www.visitmexico.com

Germany—Germany Tourism:
The German National Tourist Board
www.germany-tourism.de

Australia—The Official Site of Tourism Australia
www.australia.com

Remember that sites like these are available for almost any country. Use the Tourism Offices Worldwide Directory, Official Tourist Information Offices Worldwide, OfficialTravelGuide.com, or Governments on the WWW sites to find a similar site for whatever country interests you.

Guides for States, Provinces, Etc.

Within any country, most major political units will often have Web sites of their own. The same sites just mentioned (Tourism Offices Worldwide Directory, Official Tourist Information Offices Worldwide, OfficialTravelGuide.com, or Governments on the WWW) can be used to identify these regional sites. A search engine can also get you to these sites quickly if you search for the name and the words "travel" and "guide" (for example, *"New South Wales" travel guide*).

City Guides

Most of the country-specific sites will provide links to information about individual cities, but the information may be fairly brief and in some cases will just cover the larger cities in the country. The general guides (Fodor's, Frommer's, Lonely Planet, and Rough Guides) will have fairly extensive information on many cities, but even some large cities may be missing. But it is easy to quickly find sites with extensive detail on just about any city that interests you.

Using a search engine is one easy way to find a city's Web site. For example, if you search for *Paris* in Yahoo!, among the very first sites that come up are the Paris Tourist Office, The Paris Pages/Les Pages de Paris, and City of Paris, all of which are excellent starting places for a traveler. Above the listing of these search results on Yahoo!, you will also find a link to Yahoo!'s own Paris Visitor Guide. Google (and other search engines) may produce similar results, but without the Visitor Guide link. The search engine approach works well for medium-size cities such as Aberystwyth, and you will often get good results from a search engine if you are looking for a Jindabyne, Kamloops, or Khon Khen. If you don't find what you are looking for, be more specific as to the location or by adding the word "guide" (e.g. *Cleveland Ohio guide*).

There are also some excellent sites that provide guides specifically for cities. Among these are AreaGuides.net and the City Guide portion of Yahoo! In addition, there are sites for particular countries that contain city guides. You will find many additional sites on the Web that contain very similar content, especially a large number of city business directory sites. A number of sites feature similar information, and even similar design, to the ones mentioned here. For example, USA Citylink (www.usacitylink.com) contains information almost identical to Area Gudies.net (and even carries the AreaGuides.net logo).

Wcities
wcities.com

Wcities has many users who will not recognize the Wcities name. The reason is that Wcities content and technology is licensed to and used by a number of other sites, including Yahoo!, Orbitz, and AreaGuides.net (discussed later in this chapter), plus many other sites for reservations, hotels, airlines, etc. These Wcities clients will use various selections of the Wcities data and incorporate it into information and services of their own.

Wcities covers 1,000 cities, the majority of which are in North America and Europe. The main page features a selected city. Use the Change City button to find the city you wish (Figure 2.7). The Guides are among the most extensive and informative collections of city information that you will find on the Web, with information designed for both the leisure and the business traveler. Using the City Guide link from the menu, choose from the following categories: Historical Background, Where to Stay, Dining and Drinking, Entertainment, Recommended Tours, Getting There/Around, and Fun Facts. Within the narrative for each of these are links to the individual establishments and tourist sights. Other menu choices will lead to Events, Hotels, Dining, Nightlife, Attractions, Shopping, Essentials, Business, Etc., and

Figure 2.7   Wcities guide to New Orleans

Movies. Individual sections have further subsections for easy browsing. The Events section enables you to search for events by date range and theme (Family, Concerts, Festivals, etc.).

Be sure to take advantage of the Neighborhood Search that is available under most sections. It gives you a checkbox menu from which you can choose neighborhoods and then make more specific choices regarding price ranges, type of restaurant, etc. The Travel Bag option serves as a way to bookmark information from the site, which can then be viewed or printed for one or more destinations all at once.

Wcities, under its Download links, also provides podcast-type guides to more than 300 cities that can be downloaded to iPods, BlackBerries, and other mobile devices.

AreaGuides.net
www.areaguides.net

This site is in one sense a very sophisticated and extensive "yellow pages" for travelers. It contains 39,000 city guides: 33,000 of them for the U.S. and 6,000 for Canada. Coverage of the rest of the world is skimpier, for example, with only about 30 cities for all of Africa, the Middle East, and Asia. The main menu allows you to select by category of service or type of information, but you will probably want to start by making one of the geographic choices on the left of the page for U.S., Canada, or International. When you work your way down to the page for a particular city, you will find links to a wide variety of local services, local weather and news, etc. For larger cities, the pages will contain a brief description with a More link that takes you to an extensive description. (For city descriptions, AreaGuides.net uses content from Wcities.) Much of the page content for U.S. cities tends to be for people who are "settled in," rather than those there for a short visit. When you get to the International section, you will see a Travel menu on the left of the page that includes links for Travel Services, Attractions, Museums, Religion, and Children. Click on one of these links to find information on that topic (e.g., museums) for the city you choose.

Most of the services under the Concierge and Accommodations sections are provided through Orbitz. A couple of them deserve special note: The Car Service link enables you to find the best way to get any number of people to or from an airport or to special occasions. For golfers, the Golf Tee Times link lets you book a tee time for wherever you are headed.

TimeOut—City Travel Guides

www.timeout.com

The TimeOut Web site, from the publisher of *TimeOut* magazines, provides online guides for 150+ cities, considerably fewer than the guides previously discussed. But for each city, you will find a good general introduction, plus pages for Seasonal (major seasonal events), Restaurants & Bars, Nightlife, Shopping, Hotels, and Nearby (attractions). Also check out the feature articles on the main page and elsewhere. The easiest way to get to the page for a city is probably by using the A–Z Travel tab near the top of the main page

totaltravel.com

www.totaltravel.co.uk

This site covers 10 regions of Great Britain (e.g., West Country, Scotland), 75 areas, and 380 localities.

UKTravel

www.uktravel.com

UKTravel contains brief descriptions for more than 600 towns and cities in England, along with links to accommodations and other traveler services.

Walkabout: The Australian Travel Guide

walkabout.com.au

Walkabout: The Australian Travel Guide provides descriptions, attractions, and the like for 1,500 cities and towns, as well as regional information, tips, Traveller's Tales, and more.

TravelChinaGuide

www.travelchinaguide.com

TravelChinaGuide has descriptions for more than 80 cities on mainland China, plus information on hotels, dining, and attractions for some cities.

For any city, take advantage of the wealth of practical information and insights that can be found in the discussion groups (discussed at the end of this chapter). Discussion groups are excellent places to identify charming out-of-the-way little villages where you may be the only tourist in sight. They may also help identify villages where there is good reason there are no other tourists in sight.

Guides to Particular Attractions

You don't have to wait until you walk into a museum to get a guide. Particularly if your time is very limited, knowing exactly where to go once you enter the building means you can spend more time enjoying the attraction and less time trying to find your way around. The same applies to thousands of other sights and attractions around the world. Once again, a general Web search engine will often be the quickest and easiest way to locate these guides online. For many (maybe most) places, just searching on the name of the place will be enough to find the information you need, and the official Web site for that attraction will often be the first item on the results page. If that doesn't work, add the word "guide" to your search.

Museum sites will be discussed in more detail in Chapter 9, "Exploring Countries and Cultures Online," but in the meantime, if you want to get a sampling of online museum guides, look at the following sites for the Louvre and the Uffizi.

Louvre
www.louvre.fr

Just as the Louvre is a world leader when it comes to museums, its Web site is also a leading example of what a museum site can provide. Not only will you find information about visiting the museum (hours, admission fees, etc.), but you will find virtual tours and previews of what you can see there. Click on the English link for the English version of the site.

Uffizi Gallery
www.uffizi.firenze.it

In case you don't read Italian, you will find a link for the English version at the bottom of the main Uffizi site. On either version, you will find information on when and how to visit the Uffizi, plus information on events and exhibitions.

There are many specialized travel guides on the Web, some of which will be covered in Chapter 8, "Sites for Special Groups and Special Needs," but in the meantime, the following site is a good example of a very "specialized" travel guide.

Roadsideamerica.com: Your Online Guide to Offbeat Tourist Attractions
www.roadsideamerica.com

This site features more than 7,000 Canadian and U.S. tourist attractions, including the Palace of Depression, toilet seat art, cow-chip throwing contests, a 10-foot-tall turkey statue, a cypress knee museum, the death mask of Pretty Boy Floyd, Iowa's largest frying pan, and a coon dog cemetery, as well as classic sights, such as Wall

Drug and South of the Border, that will require a bit more time to fully appreciate. Sure, all of your traveling friends have seen Paris, but this site can help you to earn bragging rights for having seen the world's only double-decker outhouse.

Newspaper Travel Sections

While people who read newspapers frequently may not think of them as "travel guides," it's true that one of the most-used types of travel guides may show up on your doorstep every week: the travel section of your newspaper. Content in travel sections of newspapers is also usually readily available online. Most major newspapers have a travel section and, to a large degree, you will find similar kinds of content among them: travel news and feature articles written by reporters and columnists, local or regional events, destination guides, and travel deals and ads. There are three main reasons to add this category of travel guide to your travel planning toolbox:

1. Get actual news, what events are happening now, airline industry news, etc.

2. For local and regional travel news events and attractions, try the travel section for the large cities in the areas where you are headed. (If you don't know the name or address of the Web site of the newspapers there, you can find it at www.kidon.com/media-link, which will link you to thousands of newspapers around the world.)

3. Find deals from local attractions and travel agents.

The destinations guides found on newspaper Web sites are sometimes written specifically for the particular newspaper, but more often, they will draw upon content from familiar sources such as Lonely Planet or Fodor's. For some papers, information on the site may not appear in the print edition of the paper, for example, traveler comments and reviews. Many sites will require registration, but in most cases, registration is free.

The following five sites are, of course, just a tiny sampling. These particular sites were chosen because they are indeed representative and/or they also have some unique features or content.

New York Times (online)—Travel

www.nytimes.com/pages/travel

Not surprisingly, the *New York Times* Travel section includes lots of information about sights and activities in New York City. The U.S. Guides and World Guides are "powered by Fodor's," though you may find that the content on the *New York Times* site is an abbreviated version of what you will find on the Fodor's site. Drawing on content from other sections of the paper, the Travel section includes an extensive collection of critiques for plays, music, and other events of interest to travelers.

Times Online (London)

travel.timesonline.co.uk

For the traveler either to or from the U.K., the Travel section of the Times Online provides an extensive collection of travel news and feature articles, including more regional coverage such as the article on "A Swinger's Guide: Climbing 60-Foot Trees in Wales." The Destinations section has numerous subsections, including Spas, Gap Travel, and Green Travel, in addition to typical categories. It also offers a free weekly newsletter of travel deals.

Chicago Tribune (online)

www.chicagotribune.com/travel

If you are headed for Chicago, first stop by the online version of the *Chicago Tribune*. In addition to its feature articles, its good coverage of travel news, and lots of information about what Chicago has to offer, it has excellent regional travel information. The Midwest Travel menu leads to articles on each of eight Midwestern states, going back to 1999.

Los Angeles Times (online)
www.latimes.com/travel

Because of its proximity to Mexico, the online version of the *Los Angeles Times* has a good collection of articles on travel to California's southern neighbor, as well as a collection of articles on a variety of travel topics. Notice particularly the Outdoor and the Travel 101 sections, the latter of which provides articles on topics from travel gear and gadgets to health and traveling with kids. To access much of the site, you must register, but registration is free.

USA TODAY (online)
www.usatoday.com/travel/front.htm

The *USA TODAY* online Travel section has a wide selection of articles, guides, and travel tools (such as its Wi-Fi locators). It's an excellent site for travel news at the national level and also has an extensive collection of specialty columns for consumer affairs, airlines, hotels, business, cruising, and other topics. If you are a business traveler, don't miss columns on business travel by David Grossman and Joe Brancatelli.

Travel Magazines

If you have been working too hard, spending your time dealing with boring, mundane daily tasks, focusing too much on spreadsheets or bedsheets, and want a daydreaming fix, you need a travel magazine. Like other literature, for many of us, looking at a computer screen isn't quite the same as leafing through nice, slick, colorful, tactile pages, but some sites can come close—plus do some things

hardcopy magazines can't do. The following are sites for some better-known travel magazines.

Concierge.com (Condé Nast Traveler)

www.concierge.com

Concierge.com combines a number of features such as deals and
destination guides with more than 3,000 travel-inspiring articles and
columns (going back to 1999) from the *Condé Nast Traveler* magazine.
On the main page are tabs that lead to information on Destinations,
Travel Ideas, Lists & Polls, Tools, and Deals. Use these tabs or the
search box on the page to get to the wealth of Condé Nast articles, or
use the pull-down menus to quickly find the Insider Guides for cities
and countries. Pay particular attention to the Tools tab, where you will
find a Destination Finder, a Hotel Finder, Forums, Travel Tips, and more.
The Suitcase option there (powered by Kaboodle) enables you to col-
lect in one place all the information you gather from Concierge.com.

Travel + Leisure online

www.travelandleisure.com

The Travel + Leisure (T+L) site offers articles from the magazine's
monthly issues, going back to 2002. Instead of the usual type of
description provided by travel guides, the site's Destinations section
consists of extensive articles about the places that have appeared in
the magazine, including T+L's recommendations for hotels and dining. Check out the Departments tab for content from the following
magazine sections: Beach, Cities, Cruises, Culture, Driving, Foods,
Hotels, Intersections, News, Obsessions, Outdoors, People,
Preservation, Shopping, Spas, Strategies, Tech News, and Value.
Under the tab for World's Best, you will find T+L's lists for best travel
agents, hotels, design and architecture, and cities. The site is also
home to the online versions of *Travel + Leisure Family* magazine, with

articles and guides for family travel and *Travel + Leisure Golf* for the traveling golfer (or golfing traveler).

National Geographic Traveler
www.nationalgeographic.com/traveler

If you are looking for great photos, *National Geographic* magazines are always a preferred stop. This definitely holds true for the National Geographic Traveler site. Though it contains only a modest selection of magazine articles, the photos here are, as you would expect, exceptional.

Arthur Frommer's Budget Travel Online
www.budgettravelonline.com

Arthur Frommer's Budget Travel magazine and its companion site focus on getting the most for your travel dollar. In addition to the articles on worldwide destinations found in the Destinations section of the main page, take advantage of the Strategies articles. In line with the "budget" theme of the site, these articles provide sound, seasoned advice on making the best choices for Lodging, Airfares, Cruises, and Car Rentals. The link under Spotlight provides strategies for trips with focuses such as genealogy, architecture, arts and crafts, cooking schools, golf, scuba diving, cycling, adventure, skiing, tennis, yoga, spas, singles, seniors, volunteers, women, gay and lesbian, and "chick trips" (for the "chicks" themselves).

TV and Radio Travel Shows and Channels

There are lots of places on TV and radio where you will find travel-related programming, including the Travel Channel, the Discovery Channel, and the History Channel. If you want to find out what travel programs are coming up, check the station's Web site. If you missed a program of interest when it originally aired, the program itself or segments of it may be accessible on those Web sites. The Travel Channel's site is one place on the Web where the primary focus is on travel. Some specific travel shows may have their own sites that give you schedules and other information, such as Rudy Maxa—Traveling in Style for Less (www.rudymaxa.com) and Rick Steves' Europe (www.ricksteves.com). Rick's site even includes full transcripts of shows.

Travel Channel
travel.discovery.com

If you want to find out what shows are coming up and when, the Travel Channel site makes it very easy to do so. In addition to schedules and show descriptions, for some of the shows you will find slide shows and video clips. The site also provides an extensive collection of traveler reviews for destinations, accommodations, restaurants, and attractions. You will find a link on the schedules and elsewhere where you can even elect to have an e-mail reminder sent to you one or two days before a show of your choice is aired.

You *Can* Take It with You: Podcasts

Earlier in this chapter, I said that, for awhile at least, most of us are not likely to be roaming the streets of Rome with full Internet access in our hands. However, you may be roaming those streets with an MP3 player. If so, you can take advantage of the increasing number of travel podcasts. (For those not familiar with podcasts, they are audio files that are "broadcast" on a regular basis, like radio programs, and can be downloaded from the Internet.) More and more travel-related podcasts are becoming available; you can listen to them on your computer or download them to your player (or burn them to a CD). You can then listen to a podcast at (or on the way to) your destination, using it as your virtual travel guide. Sites like Yahoo! Podcasts (podcasts.yahoo.com), audible.

com (www.audible.com), Digital Podcast (www.digitalpodcast. com/browse-travel-31-1.html), and indiepodder.org (www.ipodder.org/ directory/4/podcasts/categories/travel) enable you to identify travel-related digital audio, most of it for free, some for purchase. Expect to see more sites that provide travel-related podcasts. To learn more about podcasts, a good starting point is the Help section of Yahoo! Podcasts (help.yahoo.com/l/us/yahoo/podcasts).

Podcast sites typically also provide a URL for an RSS (Really Simple Syndication) feed that you can use to have links to new episodes sent automatically to your RSS "reader." If you are not familiar with RSS, one of the easiest places to learn about it is MyYahoo!, Yahoo!'s personalized portal. Take a look at my.yahoo.com/s/about/rss/index.html.

The following are a few sites that provide travel-related podcasts.

Rough Guides Podcasts
www.roughguides.com

The Rough Guides Podcasts provide audio guides to cities, and if you wish, you can subscribe to receive a new one each month. You will find a link for the podcasts on the main menu of the Rough Guides Travel page.

Travel with Rick Steves
www.ricksteves.com/radio/podcast.htm

The podcasts from Travel with Rick Steves are broadcasts from his half-hour public radio show. Current shows as well as archived shows are available for download.

The Connected Traveler
www.connectedtraveler.com

On the Connected Traveler site, you can hear—and download— Russell Johnson's programs, which emphasize the cultural and environmental side of travel and tourism.

Lonely Planet Travelcasts
www.lonelyplanet.com/podcasts

Lonely Planet Travelcasts provide reports from Lonely Planet authors at destinations around the world. Current and archived episodes are available.

Amateur Traveler Podcast
amateurtraveler.com

In this weekly half-hour (or longer) podcast, host Chris Christensen covers destinations such as Antelope Canyon, Arizona, and New Orleans, as well as more general travel topics, such as photography and biking. Some episodes include travel news updates.

Wcities Pod CityGuides
ipod.wcities.com

Pod CityGuides provides downloadable guides for more than 300 cities; however, they are not compatible with all MP3 players.

Travel Blogs

Beginning around the year 2000, Weblogs ("blogs") began to take the Web by storm, and within five years, there were literally tens of millions of them out there. (Like much else in life, quality is often inversely proportional to quantity.) Blogs became an easy way for anyone with Internet access to share their thoughts with the world. Of course, you will find blogs on just about any imaginable topic, and some of them are actually valuable. For travel, blogs are indeed somewhat of a natural fit since keeping journals and creating travelogues have a long tradition with travelers. Travel blogs offer another source for getting travelers' opinions and suggestions about destinations and other travel-related topics. Many travel blogs provide an RSS feed so that you can easily get to new entries, and some also provide a podcast version. The first site that follows will introduce you to a number of travel blogs. If you use the second site, you can create your own blog for friends, family, and others to read, and also read similar blogs from other travelers.

About.com—Travel Blogs

weblogs.about.com/od/travelblogs

This part of the About.com Weblogs section lists a number of examples of travel blogs. Try some to see if a trip to the blogosphere is something you may want to pursue.

TravelPod.com

travelpod.com

TravelPod.com, "The Web's Original Travel Blog," is a place where you can create a free travel Weblog of your own, in which you can share your thoughts and photos. You can also read blogs from other travelers. If you use TravelPod.com's Advanced Search page, finding those of interest (by topic or country) is easy.

Travel Discussion Groups and Forums

For many travelers, part of the fun (and usefulness) of planning a trip, and part of the enjoyment after a trip, is talking with others who have visited the same places. Especially on the planning side, getting input from others can make a trip much more enjoyable and help you avoid problems. For most people, though, the chances of bumping into an acquaintance on the street who has been to Zelienople or Zagreb may be pretty slim. But that's not the case on the Internet. By using travel forums and other discussion groups, you can get opinions on just about any destination, any hotel, any sight, and perhaps even restaurants. These types of sites are discussed in this chapter because they are indeed "travel guides"—not official travel guides by professional travel writers, but guidance from fellow travelers. (Near the end of most chapters in this book, you will find discussion groups that are most relevant to the topics covered in that chapter.)

Though you will find substantial differences in the look and content of discussion groups, keep in mind that:

- For most groups, you can read messages without registering for the group, but for many, you will need to sign up if you want to post a message. Registration is usually free for travel discussion groups.

- You should contribute your own advice to whatever degree you feel inclined. That's what makes them work. Also, feel free to simply ask for suggestions and advice about sights, hotels, restaurants, or just about any other topic. For questions of your own, you may want to use a fairly active group. If a group has only a few new messages every month, you are not likely to get a quick answer.

- Don't rule out any hotel, restaurant, or other place on the basis of one or two negative comments about the establishment. Though travelers tend to be open-minded and good-natured, some comments are from the "terminally disgruntled," who are seldom pleased by anything.

The following Web sites are among the best known, most active, and most general. You will find them useful in regard to the topics covered in most of the chapters. We may be stretching the terms "discussion groups" and "forums" a bit with the collection of sites that follow, since some of them do not offer back-and-forth, two-way conversations, but all of these sites are ones where individual travelers have their say.

TripAdvisor

www.tripadvisor.com

TripAdvisor's main thrust is traveler reviews of hotels, restaurants, and other attractions worldwide, and you will find more than 3 million of these on the site. You can search by destination or browse by region. In the forums section, you will find a very broad range of comments beyond just hotels and restaurants. In the Hotels section, you can locate hotels based on member rankings and also compare prices from several online agencies (Orbitz, etc.) The Flights section allows you to similarly compare airfares. The Attractions section (Figure 2.8) takes you to not just comments from the TripAdvisor forums but to guides and reviews from a number of other sites, such as Fodor's, Wcities, PostcardsForYou.com, and IgoUgo. Some travelers check out TripAdvisor before going almost anywhere.

VirtualTourist

www.virtualtourist.com

VirtualTourist contains reviews, articles, and commentary written by its 800,000 members from 220 countries and territories. Membership is free, and members can have their own pages on VirtualTourist, where they can post pictures and commentary on their favorite destinations. Use the Travel Guides tab to search or browse by location to get to commentary on hotels, things to do, restaurants, local customs, nightlife, "Off the Beaten Path," warnings, transportation, parking, shopping, etc. In the Forums section, which is arranged by destination, the discussion goes beyond reviews. You can find or ask for commentary on just about any imaginable travel topic. You can select the content of interest that you find on VirtualTourist to create your own Trip Planner for destinations. The site also provides reservations for hotels, flights, and deals.

Figure 2.8   TripAdvisor's Attractions page

Lonely Planet—The Thorn Tree

thorntree.lonelyplanet.com

Lonely Planet's Thorn Tree forums are among the most popular and active travel forums on the Web. Anyone can read the postings, but you must register with Lonely Planet to post a message. It is also one of the best-organized and most navigable travel forums on the Web. Links at the top of Thorn Tree pages allow you to browse by Branch (directory topics), search by keyword or author, see the featured "Thread of the Day," see who is currently online, get help, and log in.

Frommer's Message Boards

www.frommers.com

Frommer's Message Boards, found under the Travel Talk tab on Frommer's pages, contain thousands of discussions and hundreds of thousands of messages. To find relevant ones, you can either browse the categories or make use of the Search the Boards search box. Anyone can read the messages, but you will need to subscribe to post a message (subscribing is free and easy). Messages can be browsed by destination or by topic, which are arranged in the following categories: Activity Boards (Beach & Water Sports, Cruises, Cultural Immersion, Outdoor & Adventure Travel, Road Trips, Theme Parks, Winter Sport), Lifestyle Boards (Disabled Travelers, Family Travel, Gay & Lesbian Travel, Honeymoons, Senior Travel, Single Travel, Student Travel, Women Travelers), and Tips, Tools & Deals Boards (General, Air Travel, Car Rental, Bus & Rail, Cruises, Frommer's Feedback, Health, Safety & Travel Insurance, Hospitality Exchange, Lodgings, Online Reservations, Packagers & Tour Operators, Photography, Share a Trip).

Rough Guides—Travel Talk

www.roughguides.com

The Travel Talk section of the Rough Guides site is provided in conjunction with IgoUgo (see the next entry).

IgoUgo
www.igougo.com

IgoUgo, as its home page says, is "a community of travelers sharing reviews and photos." Though the content comes from travelers, IgoUgo is arranged very much like the guides covered at the beginning of this chapter. The Destinations portion of the site is browsable by continent, country, and city, or you can find your way to reviews of destinations and attractions by using the main IgoUgo search box. For cities, you will usually find sections of commentary arranged by Journals, Hotels, Things to Do, Restaurants, Nightlife, Experience, Photos, and Deals. For each destination, you can expect to find lots of photos (there are, for example, more than 900 photos of Prague). Reviews and journals can be quite lengthy, even for fairly minor attractions.

World66
www.world66.com

World66, like IgoUgo, is a combination destination guide and traveler review site. It contains more than 100,000 articles on more than 42,000 destinations, all written by travelers themselves. Articles may cover a continent, country, or city, or focus on a more specific aspect, such as Climate, Sights, Accommodations, Dining, Getting Around, Getting There, "A Perfect Day," Museums, Shopping, Nightlife and Entertainment, Internet Cafes, and Bars and Cafes. You will also find collections of photos and maps. For larger cities, the map will identify the location of hotels, restaurants, attractions, etc., with links to corresponding articles.

Independent Traveler Message Boards

boards.independenttraveler.com

In addition to being a travel agency site with an emphasis, obviously perhaps, on "independent" travelers, the Independent Traveler site offers a useful collection of articles, travel news, and links to various other travel resources. It also provides a Boards section with active forums arranged by destination and by topic. The Journals section of Independent Traveler is provided by IgoUgo.

Google Groups (Usenet—Recreation>Travel)

groups.google.com

The content of Google Groups consists of a combination of the well-known Usenet groups going back to 1981 and Google's own much smaller collection of user-created groups, which were initiated by Google in 2004. Since Google Groups cover all topics, you may want to take advantage of the Advanced Groups Search page to search for your topic, entering *rec.travel* in the Group box on that page to retrieve only messages in the rec.travel Usenet group.

Epinions.com—Hotels and Travel

www.epinions.com/trvl

Epinions.com is perhaps the best-known site on the Web for consumer-written reviews for just about any kind of shopping. In its Hotels & Travel section, you will find travelers' opinions of places, services, and products arranged in the following categories: Destinations, Cruises, Ski Resorts, Theatre, Tour Operators, Hotels & Resorts, Transportation & Luggage, Family Travel, and Parks. In addition to reviews, you will see star ratings and can sort the reviews of providers by ratings and average price. Use this site to check out opinions on everything from cruise ships to luggage.

Reservation Sites: Flights and More

Sometimes it seems as if almost every site on the Internet is trying to sell airline tickets as well as something else. Travel reservation sites, probably more than any other category of travel sites, provide a wonderful combination of options for the user. But they also present the problem of "sorting it all out": We still need to figure out where to go for which kinds of information and services.

This chapter will look at the major—and some minor—reservation sites and assess their general natures and the broad range of things they offer. Airline reservations are the central service for most of these sites, and I will explain in detail how to make the best use of what is offered. This chapter will also take a quick glimpse at such things as reservations for cruises, trains, and more, with following chapters focusing more closely on these other types of travel and providing details on reservations and services.

The Different Kinds of Reservation Sites

In "sorting it all out," it's useful to think of Internet reservation sites as falling (for the most part) into the following categories:

- Big, general virtual travel agencies, such as Travelocity, Expedia, and Orbitz, that bring together a lot of reservation services for different kinds of trips and usually do so by partnering with the actual service providers
- Sites for travel agencies that specialize in types of travel (cruises, last-minute, discount, etc.), locality (regional, national, etc.), or audience (seniors, families, gay and lesbian, etc.)
- Sites that are part of a larger site and service, such as American Express Travel and Yahoo! Travel
- Travel providers themselves, such as airlines and car rental companies
- Sites such as Hotwire and American Express Travel that provide reservations primarily through partnering with the big reservation sites
- Price comparison sites such as FareChase and Mobissimo that search many of the sites listed here to provide price comparisons

Some sites may fall into more than one category. Some are true Internet travel sites in that the company was created strictly for the purpose of selling its services over the Internet. Some are an outgrowth of brick-and-mortar travel agencies that existed before the Internet. Though the term "virtual travel agencies" is valid, keep in mind that very few of these are completely virtual in the sense of existing only in a computer. Most reservation sites have real, knowledgeable people at the other end of an 800 number who can assist you in making your reservations online.

The differences are numerous in terms of exactly what each site provides, and it is these differences that will often determine what leads you to use one site instead of another. There are differences in terms of what kinds of reservations you can make (flights, cruises, etc.), what features you can take advantage of when making those reservations, and what other related services—beyond reservations— the site provides. They will also differ in terms of the degree of "human" service provided. Some reservation sites may offer a cheap flight but do not have "live" help, only e-mail contact, and no phone number. You have to balance the savings with the comfort of having a real person with whom you can speak if you wish.

For many people, of all the differences in these sites, the main consideration is price, and you will find significant differences in prices quoted on each for flights, hotels, or cruises. Among the reasons for the price differences is that sites such as Travelocity, Expedia, and Orbitz have deals with airlines, hotels, and other services to purchase blocks of seats and rooms, and can sell them at a price they choose. By doing just a little shopping around on these sites, you can save a significant amount of money. For a flight between the U.S. and Europe or Asia, the savings can add up to literally hundreds of dollars. This chapter will look at each of the big reservation sites and also describe some other sites that can help you make the most of your travel dollar when making reservations online.

The Major Reservation Sites: An Overview

There are a number of characteristics, options, and services that you can expect to find in most or all of the "big" reservation sites, including reservation options for flights, hotels, cars, cruises, vacations, and "deals." All the major sites offer the capability of searching for flights by origin and destination, dates, and number and age of travelers. All provide reservations for hundreds of airlines, tens of thousands of hotels, and dozens of car rental companies. With the exception of colors and layout, even the main pages of the large sites look very similar, with panels for a quick search for flights, tabs for other types of reservations (hotel, car, etc.), and a variety of featured deals. The deals often occupy a good portion of the Web page and provide special pricing and sales for a range of travel options. But it is when we look beyond those standard offerings that we see significant differences—differences that can determine if and how you will use a particular site:

- Search features for flights that allow you to be more precise (or less precise if you wish)
- Additional types of reservations available, including rail, condos, vacation rentals (self-catering), and "last-minute" trips
- Availability and types of destination guides
- Travel news
- Fare alerts (by e-mail)
- Traveler alerts
- Corporate travel services
- A variety of other traveler tools, such as flight tracking, travel tips, driving directions, airport information, and passport information

The descriptions of the reservation sites that follow will emphasize such differences. Extensive detail is given for the three largest sites (Travelocity, Expedia, and Orbitz), and brief descriptions are provided for others. The reason for this approach is that readers are most likely to use the top three and also because the level of detail for them will provide insight into the types of things to look for in *any* reservation site. Among the top three sites, you will find almost all of the variety of content and options that you will find in any of the other reservation sites. If you know those three, you should feel at home navigating and using others. However, there are some tips to keep in mind as you use any (and all) reservation sites.

Tips for Using Reservation Sites Effectively and Efficiently

Most of the things you should consider in making reservations online are probably pretty obvious. Remembering to do them will make these sites easier to use and can save you significant money. Among the things to remember are:

1. Use more than one site to compare prices and options:
    *   Check at least three big sites and at least one comparison site, if price is a priority.
    *   Check the prices for flights (and cruises, etc.) at the providor's (o.g., airlino's) own sitc. Thcrc you may find sales, special "Web fares," and other deals. Sometimes it will be cheaper, but certainly not all of the time. When searching at some airline sites, you will most likely see published prices. Sometimes you will not even find the same flight listed as you found on a travel agency site (the agency may have booked a block of seats or rooms that are now available only from the agency).

2. Bo awaro that "partnoro" may got proforontial troatmont in tho flight listings, which is another reason to use more than one site. Don't look at just the first listings that pop up when you do a search.

3. In deciding between options, keep the risks and benefits in mind. This includes thinking about tho following:
    *   Is it really worth getting up at 3 A.M. instead of 7 A.M. to catch a flight that saves you $20?
    *   For the price comparison sites, is the bargain flight offered from a travel agency you never heard of? The flight may turn out to be a great bargain from a very reputable and trustworthy

company, or maybe not. Check the travel discussion groups to find out what people have said about the agency.

- What are the restrictions and the cancellation and refund policies?

- Keep in mind that after comparing prices on a few different sites, spending another hour trying to save another $10 may not be cost effective.

4. Take advantage of whatever flexibility you have:

- If you can fly on Tuesday, Wednesday, or Thursday, you may save money on a flight. Travelocity, Expedia, Orbitz, and others all offer, on their flight search form, an option for including adjoining days automatically in your search. If you can book a flight on Thursday rather than on Friday, you may save you several hundred dollars.

- Try nearby airports. If I fly out of Baltimore/Washington Airport instead of Washington Dulles, I can often save more than $100. (On the other hand, the drive is 60 minutes instead of 20 minutes and involves traveling on very congested roads. Consider the cost/benefit balance just mentioned). Many times the specific airport (e.g., Gatwick or Heathrow in London) may not matter to you. Travelocity, Orbitz, and CheapTickets all offer an option to automatically search nearby airports. When searching for flights, consider using multi-airport codes for your destination, such as WAS for all three large Washington, D.C., area airports, PAR for both Charles de Gaulle and Orly, and LON for both Gatwick and Heathrow. If you don't know the code, use the city name. For cities served by multiple airports, when you enter a city name, the search reply will typically give you a list of choices, including a choice for all airports. For future reference, make a note of the multi-airport code for the city.

- Consider staying over Saturday night. This can get you big savings, maybe a lot more than the cost of an additional night in a hotel. On a recent trip from Washington to Vienna, Austria, I returned on Sunday instead of Saturday, which meant a savings of more than $1,300, even after figuring in the cost for the extra hotel night and other expenses. Likewise, in some situations, there is a minimum stay of three or four days in order to get a substantially lower fare.

5. Book early. Booking 30, 21, 14, or seven days in advance may incrementally result in a less favorable airfare (i.e., you may pay substantially more if you book six days ahead than if you had booked a month ahead). A lot of "Deals" apply to departures more than six weeks or so in advance. The number of bargain seats available for a specific flight is also very limited and may sell out fast. (By the way, if you received one of those "free" tickets for volunteering to give away your seat on a previous flight, plan to book far, far in advance. When the ticket was given to you, the airline probably gave you no clue as to how early you needed to book if you wanted to use the free ticket. I recently tried to use such a ticket on United and, six weeks out, could not get a Washington-San Francisco seat on any flight within two days of when I wanted to go.)

   On the other hand, "last-minute fares" (flights or cruises) may be greatly discounted. The frustrating thing about all of this is that once you think you understand the "rules," other factors may enter in. You may bump into seasonal changes, you may find a sudden fare war between airlines (if you are really lucky), or an agency may suddenly find itself with unsold seats. How the fare determination really works is one of the great mysteries of the universe.

6. Check prices for "packages." The savings on these combinations of flights and hotels or cars can be significant.

7. Don't forget to enter your frequent flyer number into your account profile, or enter it when you buy the ticket.

8. In some societies, age, rather than youth, is revered. Such is the case on many reservation sites (well, maybe not "revered," but at least acknowledged and courted for your potentially greater supply of leisure time and disposable income). Take advantage of that fact, and if you are at all "long in the tooth," don't forget to look for the appropriate checkbox for such discounts.

9. When looking at fares, note whether they include taxes and fees. Often two prices will be displayed, one with and one without taxes and fees.

The Major Reservation Sites

There is no definition of a major reservation site. The ones discussed here have been identified by the travel industry in recent years as the largest, the ones that are frequently mentioned on the Internet, and ones that, in general, are outstanding for various reasons. There are plenty of other good travel sites out there, too many to go into detail here. Not being listed in this chapter does not mean that a site is not "good." The ones here are those that the most frequent travelers should at least be aware of. In the descriptions, emphasis is placed on what is unique about the site and on the airline reservations portion of the site. Other sections, such as for cruises, are mentioned briefly, with more detail provided in later chapters.

Travelocity
www.travelocity.com

In addition to providing that lovable little gnome in its ads, Travelocity is a reservation site that stands out (Figure 3.1). It is a full-service site, backed by more than 1,000 people, including some at the end of a free phone call. As a matter of fact, if you wish, you can call 888-Travelocity instead of booking online. In addition to flights, Travelocity provides reservation services for hotels, cars, rail, vacations, cruises, and last-minute deals. It has partnered with more than

Figure 3.1   Travelocity main page

700 international airlines, 50,000 hotels (230 hotel chains), nine cruise lines, and more than 50 car rental companies. Throughout the site, you will find a variety of travel deals. As well as its main site, Travelocity has sites in 11 other countries and in nine languages. Travelocity is owned by Sabre, probably the best-known computer reservations system.

Searching for Flights on Travelocity

The search function on Travelocity's main page provides a search for flights, flight-hotel combinations, hotels, and cars. For flight searches, enter the origin and destination, using either city names or airport codes, the dates and times of day you wish to travel, and the number of travelers by age range (2–17, 18–64, 65+). As is typical throughout the Travelocity site, a lot of extra information is available to you. If you click on the question mark next to the age ranges, for example, the site will offer related information, such as details for making reservations for infants.

In addition to the obvious information to fill in for a flight search, the Travelocity search form also provides options to:

- Compare surrounding airports (and automatically include matching flights from those airports in your search results).

- Search either the exact dates you choose, dates within from one to three days of those dates, or "flexible dates." When you choose the "+/- 1 to 3 days" flexible dates option, boxes are provided so you can specify how many days on each side you wish to allow for both departure and arrival dates. With the "flexible dates" option, you are also allowed to choose a range of months.

- Search for one-way flights.

- Search for multiple-destination flights.

- Use "More search options," including specification of class (economy, business, first), fare type (all types or refundable/

changeable only), airline (all or one of about 50 that Travelocity lists), nonstop flights, last-minute deals (flight and hotels), and budget (you can specify cities and a maximum fare, and Travelocity searches for special deals to those cities and provides a calendar showing the dates when those deals are available, usually six or more weeks in advance).

As with most of the major reservation sites, Travelocity shows a summary of least expensive flights by airline on the results pages for a flight search, with one line for nonstops and one for all flights (Figure 3.2). Beneath that on the results pages are details for the first leg of each option. Click on Select for the flight you choose to find the page with options for the second leg of your flight. Note that the prices shown already include taxes and fees. You will also usually notice an option to bundle this flight with a hotel. If you have not already booked a hotel, consider this offer, which can often be very easy as well as economical. While going through the steps of buying a flight on Travelocity, you will find a series of buttons near the top of each page that lets you know how far along you are in the reservation process (Search, Select, Review, Reserve, and Confirm).

At the Review level of the search process, look for the rather inconspicuous link that allows you to "Save this whole itinerary." If you are not ready to purchase your ticket yet, you can use this link to save the information in your list of itineraries and then return to it easily. You can name your itinerary and specify how long you would like Travelocity to save it. When you come back to it, before completing your purchase, you will need to re-price it, because prices may have changed. Saving your itinerary neither reserves the space nor guarantees the price, but it means that you will not have to repeat the entire search process.

Back on Travelocity's main page, if you hold your cursor over the Flights tab near the top of the page, you will see several options that may include Search Flights, Top Deals, Web Fares, Low Fare Alert, and

Your 7 days / 6 nights trip

San Francisco, CA (SFO) to Chicago, IL (CHI)
Departing Wed, Jan 17
Returning Tue, Jan 23
1 Adult

Modify your search | Save to FareWatcher℠ | "Total" for e-tickets incl. taxes & fees. Add'l fees for paper ticket.

	Nearby Airports View Options from $203	Your Search Depart Wed, Jan 17 from $282	Flights + 5 Nights Hotel Save with TotalTrip ℠ from $519					
	Frontier Airlines	Northwest Airlines	United	Alaska Airlines	American Airlines	US Airways	America West Airlines
Nonstops Only 29 flights	0 nonstops	0 nonstops	$448 Total $476	$448 Total $476	$448 Total $476	$858 Total $886	0 nonstops
All 58 Flights displayed below	$238 Total $282	$276 Total $320	$448 Total $476	$448 Total $476	$448 Total $476	$858 Total $886	$2,968 Total $2,996

Featured Package   Flights + 5 Nights Hotel from **$519**

Select Flight for Wed, Jan 17   58 flight options: 1 - 25 | 26 - 50 | 51 - 58

Airline	Departure Time	Arrival Time	Total Travel Time	Roundtrip Price Includes taxes and fees
Frontier Airlines Flight 668 / 531	9:10am San Francisco, CA (SFO)	4:40pm Chicago, IL (MDW)	5hrs 30min - 1 Stop Change planes in Denver, CO (DEN)	$282 per person Select WEB FARE DIRECTV® On-Board more Earn Miles Toward a Free Flight more
View Seats				
Frontier Airlines Flight 668 / 539	9:10am San Francisco, CA (SFO)	6:15pm Chicago, IL (MDW)	7hrs 5min - 1 Stop Change planes in Denver, CO (DEN)	$282 per person Select WEB FARE DIRECTV® On-Board more Earn Miles Toward a Free Flight more
View Seats				
Frontier Airlines Flight 654 / 539	10:50am San Francisco, CA (SFO)	6:15pm Chicago, IL (MDW)	5hrs 25min - 1 Stop Change planes in Denver, CO (DEN)	$282 per person Select WEB FARE DIRECTV® On-Board more Earn Miles Toward a Free Flight more
View Seats				
Frontier Airlines Flight 654 / 541	10:50am San Francisco, CA (SFO)	8:20pm Chicago, IL (MDW)	7hrs 30min - 1 Stop Change planes in Denver, CO (DEN)	$282 per person Select WEB FARE DIRECTV® On-Board more Earn Miles Toward a Free Flight more
View Seats				

Figure 3.2   Travelocity flight search results page

Last-Minute Packages (described later). The Search Flights option takes you to the "More search options" search page, and Top Deals goes to featured airfare deals. Web Fares goes to Internet-only specially priced fares from more than 30 airlines. The Low Fare Alert is an easy way to find cheap flights without even searching: Just enter your origin and destination, and Travelocity replies with fares and dates on which those fares are available. Here and elsewhere on the site you will find links to FareWatcher. With that feature, you can specify up to five city pairs and be notified by e-mail when Travelocity's Low Fares are announced. Flight Status is another option that might appear as one of the Flight tab options or beneath it. With this option, you can check the current status (departure time, etc.) of a flight.

Other Travel Options from Travelocity

Beyond flights, Travelocity provides a wide range of other travel services, including:

- Hotels – Use this option to search and make reservations for 45,000 hotels (230 hotel chains) with Travelocity's "Lowest Prices Over 20,000 Hotels" guarantee.

- Cars/Rail – Rent cars from more than 50 car rental companies and book railway reservations for Europe and Canada.

- Vacations – With this tab, search for vacation deals, hotel-flight combinations, hotels, and escorted and adventure vacations around the world.

- Cruises – In this section, search for cruises from nine cruise lines by destination, date, length, price, departure port, and cruise line.

- Last-Minute Packages – If you have the option of traveling at the last minute (in the next 14 days), like to surprise yourself, or need to get away so badly that you don't really care where you go, look at the deals in this section.

- Travelocity Business – Make reservations through Travelocity's full-service corporate travel agency.

Beyond reservations, there is a varied collection of travel "information" provided by Travelocity. Links to this information are found below the tabs and elsewhere on the site:

- Destination Guides – Travelocity's Destinations Guides are provided by Frommer's (see Chapter 2).
- Travel Info Center – In this section, you can check flight status, check weather conditions anywhere in the world, and get airline timetables, airport codes, traveler reviews, passport information, and more.
- Travel Alerts – This is the place to find reports about storms, strikes, and other events that can affect travel.

Your Travelocity Account

Travelocity puts a lot of emphasis on customer service and on its guarantee of good service. (One very appealing part of the guarantee is that if you book the wrong dates and notify Travelocity within 24 hours of purchasing the ticket, Travelocity will "rebook your airline tickets without charging a change or cancellation fee.") Click on the My Stuff link to get itineraries for trips you have booked, get copies of receipts, set up travel updates to be received on your mobile device or fax (for gate changes and other notifications), edit FareWatcher, change personal information in your account profile, use Travelocity's free photo storage and sharing feature, and find out about Travelocity VIP Rewards. The latter are special deals, coupons, and other rewards that Travelocity provides to its frequent customers.

Travelocity is an extremely rich site. If you get lost navigating the site, use the small Site Map link found at the bottom of the main page.

Expedia
www.expedia.com

As a company, Expedia is very much a travel conglomerate: It owns not just the Expedia.com travel reservation site but also Hotels.com, Hotwire, TripAdvisor, and Custom Classic Vacations, among others. This breadth of natural partnerships allows Expedia to provide a full range of services with very competitive prices. It is less forthcoming than Travelocity about the numbers, but it does cover more than 450 airlines and 65,000 hotel properties. In addition to flight reservations, the site provides reservations for hotels, cars, vacation packages, cruises, and activities (Figure 3.3). Its Activities section offers more than 2,000 activities from more than 250 regions of the world. The site also offers destination guides, maps, driving directions, and other travel tools. In addition to consumer services, Expedia has a corporate travel section and sites for the U.K., Canada, Germany, France, Italy, Australia, and the Netherlands. Expedia has live travel agents available 24/7.

Searching for Flights on Expedia

The search form on Expedia's main page provides a search for flights, hotels, cars, cruises, and combinations for flights and hotel or car, or hotel and car. When searching for flights, you can use additional search capabilities for flexible dates and one-way trips. Clicking on the links for those options takes you to an advanced search page, where you can additionally specify whether you have flexible dates, want to add a hotel or car, or prefer traveling on a certain airline (from about 60 listed) or an airline booking class. You can also request that search results contain only nonstop flights and flights that will avoid

Figure 3.3   Expedia main page

most change penalties. On the left side of the advanced flight search page are links for Fare Compare, Timetable Search, Flight Status, and Coupon Redemption.

The results pages for a flight search on Expedia offer excellent choices that enable you view the results in a way that best suits your needs. As with other sites, a section near the top of the results pages displays the lowest prices by airline, with detailed flight information below that. You also are given options of viewing results by individual flight departure and return segments (the default view) or "top round-trips." As well, results can be sorted by price, shortest flights, departure time, or arrival time. Another handy feature of the results pages is that, for many flights, you are immediately given an option to Review Seat Availability. Not only can you see if you can book a preferred seat location, it also lets you know how many seats remain at that price. If only one or two seats are available, you might want to make up your mind quickly.

The Fare Comparison feature on the results pages enables you to see what prices have actually been paid recently by Expedia customers for popular U.S. city pairs. If you enter the cities and the number of travelers, Expedia returns a calendar that shows the lowest price found for each day (departure) for trips of one to 10 days. You can change the number of days (for example, to a three-to-five night trip) and update the calendar to see the revised figures. This provides a useful benchmark for your own purchase.

Use the Timetable Search to see all scheduled flights for particular cities on particular days, regardless of whether any seats are still available. With Flight Status, you can check the status of current flights. Click on Coupon Redemption to view and redeem your Expedia coupons.

Other Travel Options from Expedia

In addition to airline reservations, with Expedia you can book reservations for hotels, cars, vacation packages, cruises, and activities (events):

- Hotels – Search for accommodations at 65,000 hotel properties. Don't be misled by the predominance of U.S. cities listed on the Hotels page. You can book rooms throughout the world.

- Cars – Search for car rentals worldwide (but the selection of cars is primarily from U.S.-based car rental companies).

- Vacation Packages – With this section, find flight/hotel combinations for one or more destinations, with some spots offering all-inclusive vacations.

- Cruises – Search by destination, departure month, cruise line, departure port, length of cruise, and star rating.

- Activities – Search by destination to find and reserve activities, attractions, tours, excursions, shows, and services around the world, including such esoteric activities as Zero Gravity's weightless flight experience.

- Deals & Destinations – Find deals for flights, hotels, cars, and packages by destination or by type of activity or vacation (skiing, all-inclusive vacations, luxury travel, romantic travel, Disney, golf).

On Expedia's main page and elsewhere throughout the site, you will find a variety of other services, including:

- Maps – Get maps and driving directions for North America and Europe, as well as topographic maps throughout the world. (The amount of topographical detail on these is rather limited.)

- Corporate Travel – Travel services for businesses.

- Destination Guides – These are found primarily as a part of the Deals & Destinations section. When you choose a destination in that section, look for a section labeled "Explore ..." or "Discover ..." (for example, "Explore San Diego"). There you will find maps, as well as information from Fodors.com and CitySearch, with overviews of what the destinations offer and information on Restaurants, Shopping, and Sights & Activities.

- Travel Tools – On the main page and elsewhere, you will find a box of Travel Tools that includes travel alerts (travel warnings and advisories, weather, etc.), flight status (check on current flights), driving directions, a currency converter, airport information (for 65 airports worldwide), a link for deals via e-mail (notification of deals, sales, etc., for routes you choose), and passport information (forms, requirements, etc.).

Your Expedia Account

To view itineraries you have saved or purchased, click on the My Itineraries link. For more information about your account, click on the My Account link to get details about your e-mail settings for Expedia, your password, billing information, coupons, and more.

Orbitz
www.orbitz.com

Orbitz was founded by five major U.S. airlines: American, Continental, Delta, Northwest, and United. However, when using Orbitz, you will find reservations capabilities for more than 455 airlines, plus tens of thousands of hotels, 16 car rental companies, and 17 cruise lines (Figure 3.4). You will also get access to a variety of vacation packages, travel news, city guides, and other travel tools. Throughout the site, you will find special savings and other deals. As the site says, it was "created to address consumers' need for an unbiased, comprehensive display of fares and rates in a single location." The travel news section is part of Orbitz's emphasis on providing customers with constantly updated travel conditions, including weather, automated travel alerts, flight updates, and other information.

Searching for Flights on Orbitz

The Quick Search panel on Orbitz's main page enables you to search for flights, hotels, cars, or packages of a hotel with either a flight or a car. Click on your choice, and the bottom portion of the panel changes to give you the appropriate search options. For flights, you have the usual options of origin, destination, date, time, and number of travelers (by age). If your travel dates are flexible, use of the "Search one day before and after" box.

Two other links in the Quick Search panel may be used to further refine your search: "Find low fares for weekends and flexible trips" and "Expand search options." Click on the "Find low fares ..." link, and you are presented with three ways to save money. With the first option, Weekends, you choose a month and Orbitz will find cheap flights for the weekends in that month. A weekend trip is defined as flights leaving on Thursday, Friday, or Saturday, and returning on Sunday, Monday, or Tuesday. If you are planning a weekend visit and can choose the weekend, this is a great way to find the best fare quickly. The second option, Bonus Days, is an extension of the option on the main page that expands your search one day in either direction from your original travel dates. With Bonus Days, you can expand the flexibility to one, two, or three days before, after, or "before or after" your departure and return dates. The third option, Flexible Stays, allows for flexibility in the length of your stay (two-to-four days, three-to-five days,

Figure 3.4   Orbitz main page

etc.). Enter a beginning and ending date (maximum 30-day span), and Orbitz will find fares for that length of stay within that date range.

The "Expand search options" link on the Quick Search panel supplies a search page where you can search for one-way flights, multicity flights, only nonstop flights, only flights with refundable fares, preferred airlines (up to three from a list of more than 80), and economy, business, or first-class cabin. The Preferred Airlines search also provides a choice of searching for only flights from a particular alliance (oneworld, SkyTeam, or Star Alliance). Consider using this if you are really serious about accumulating the maximum frequent flyer miles.

As with other big reservation sites, the results pages for flight searches on Orbitz show a summary of low fare options by airline, then a detailed flight listing below that. Whereas the first results page on Travelocity shows departing segments and Expedia's gives the option of seeing either segments or round-trips, Orbitz takes a different approach. It shows round-trips, but for each segment of those round-trips, you can choose alternatives for either departure or return. In the end, all three sites basically offer the same options, but Orbitz's approach may allow you to get to the most suitable combination a little more quickly. Orbitz provides additional search flexibility by allowing you to sort results by departure time and shortest flight, as well as the default of lowest price. Orbitz may also provide a substantially larger number of flight combinations than other reservation sites.

On Orbitz results pages, you will see ads for Deeper Discounts from Priceline, which is discussed later.

Other Travel Options from Orbitz

Orbitz also allows you to make reservations for hotels, car rentals, cruises, and vacation packages.

- Hotels – For tens of thousands of hotels throughout the world, search by date and location and, if you wish, hotel name or chain.

- Cars & Rail – Rent from 16 car rental companies, mostly U.S.-based, or purchase train tickets for Amtrak.

- Cruises – Choose cruises from 17 cruise lines (search by destination, cruise line, departure month, ship, and cruise length). If you are 55 or older, check the appropriate box to get a potentially better price for your entire party.

- Vacations – Choose vacations that include flight and hotel, hotel and car, or just hotel. Also, don't miss the Explore by Interest option to find vacations in the following categories: Adventure, All Inclusive, Last Minute, Beach, Family, or Luxury.

- Deals – Check out lots of sales and other special offers that you can browse by location or by type of vacation. With the Orbitz Deal Detector, describe where and when you want to go and set a target price, and you will receive an e-mail when Orbitz finds a new match.

Orbitz also offers helpful travel information through its Vacation Tools/Travel Tips section. It contains travel news from sources such as Reuters and the Associated Press (for example, "U.S. unlikely to suspend airline ticket tax" and "Delta reducing flights at Cincinnati"), weather conditions and alerts, flying forecasts, travel tips, and a collection of travel tools that includes airport guides, airline guides (overview of programs, policies, etc., for more than 70 airlines), city guides (from Wcities), and overseas travel information (passport and other information).

Your Orbitz Account

The My Stuff section at Orbitz contains two subsections: My Trips and My Account. My Trips provides details of current trips booked through Orbitz. The My Account section enables you to change your profile, including password, billing information, e-mail, interests, and alerts settings, and to view your coupons and reward points (if you have an Orbitz credit card).

Some Other General Reservation Sites

Yahoo! Travel

travel.yahoo.com

The strength of Yahoo! Travel, much like the rest of Yahoo!, emerges from its rich meld of services and information that comes from its partners and from information and services that have been created and provided by Yahoo! itself. At Yahoo! Travel, you can book reservations for flights, hotels, cars, vacations, and cruises. The first three (flights, hotels, and cars) are all handled through Travelocity. Vacations are arranged in partnership with the Neat Group; cruises are booked in partnership with CheapTickets and Cruise.com. (Partnerships tend to change, so on Yahoo! and other sites, do not be surprised if other partners show up.) Booking any of these kinds of reservations through Yahoo! is often the same as if you were to go to those partner services directly. The convenient combination of services, plus the added information that Yahoo! provides with the reservations, makes Yahoo! Travel a very worthwhile starting place for bookings.

On Yahoo! Travel's main page, in addition to the Quick Search section for searching for reservations, you will see sections for Destinations and Hotel Guides, Interest Guides, and, of course, links and ads for travel deals. If you have a Yahoo! account and have booked anything through Yahoo!, there will be a box with links to your personal travel information (Reservations, Travel Profile, Check Flight/Gate Status, Trip Planner, Newsletter subscription, Alerts, etc.). You will also see a link to FareChase, Yahoo!'s tool for comparing prices for flights across numerous travel sites. (FareChase is covered in detail later in this chapter.) The main page also has a search box that enables you to search all of Yahoo! Travel for a destination, type of travel, deals, etc.

Search Travel, Yahoo! Travel's search box, searches the entire site—a feature that may not normally be unique but is too rare by far on travel sites. In Yahoo! Travel, this search function is especially valuable because of the range of information found within Yahoo! Travel. For example, if you search for Aruba, your search results will include a link to Yahoo!'s Visitor's Guide to Aruba, links to parts of guides that cover specific places on Aruba, links to Yahoo!'s information on individual hotels, clubs, resorts, and restaurants on the island, and links to shopping and entertainment. There are also very useful links to deals; Yahoo! search results pages kindly separate those out by placing them in the "ads" portions of the page. With the search box, you can narrow down your search by using multiple terms with a plus sign in front of them, for example *+aruba +inclusive*.

Yahoo!'s Destination Guides are extensive. Click on the name of a city from the list (or use the pull-down menu for a longer list) or click on the map to get to the Yahoo! Visitor Guide for that city. There you will find extensive information on where to stay, where to eat, and things to do. For each category, you will find descriptions and prices, plus ratings and reviews by Yahoo! users and user reviews pulled from elsewhere on the Web. You will also see a section that draws descriptive information from a variety of travel guide sites, such as Fodor's.

Yahoo! Travel's main page also has a section of Interest Guides, which leads to information similar to that found in the Visitor Guides; however, the information is accessed by selecting a type of vacation or category of interest, such as All Inclusive, Gambling, Adventure, Last Minute, Beaches, Nightlife, Families, Romance, National & State Parks, and Ski & Snow.

Yahoo!'s Trip Planner lets you create your own "guide" for your trip. With it, you can save information on hotels, restaurants, and attractions, as well as maps, your own comments, travel dates, and links to other sites. You can print your guide, share it with others, and access it over the Internet wherever you are.

Though it "farms out" the actual booking process, Yahoo! Travel puts that process together with a tremendously useful collection of facts and tools that enhance the ease with which you can make reservations decisions and plan your trip.

CheapTickets

www.cheaptickets.com

As you can tell by the name, CheapTickets focuses on finding low prices. It also deals exclusively in leisure travel (with no business services section). CheapTickets uses the same reservations software used by Orbitz (ITA Software's QPX system), and you will find that the search options for flights (and hotels, cars, and vacations) are virtually identical to what you find on Orbitz (with the exception that for flights CheapTickets does not offer the "Search one day before and after" option found on Orbitz). Despite the search similarities, however, the search results can be very different, and the "cheap" in CheapTickets can come to the fore emphatically. For a quick trip to London (same flight, same days, same hotel), the price on Orbitz was $1,582, while the price on CheapTickets was $876. Most of the time, the differences will not be that dramatic, but it can happen.

CheapTickets provides a separate tab for Last-Minute Trips. The search function and search results are the same as for the Vacations tab. What differs are the deals shown for each: The deals under the Last-Minute tab focus specifically on last-minute travel. Price Alerts on CheapTickets works exactly the same as Deal Detector on Orbitz. As with flight searches, however, CheapTickets may find alerts for the same trip that are cheaper than those from Orbitz.

The CheapTickets Cruise section is significantly more robust than its big competitors, covering 73 cruise lines (compared to nine for Travelocity, nine for Expedia, and 17 for Orbitz). CheapTickets Gold program (requiring a membership fee) offers cash-back, special member pricing, airline coupons, and other advantages.

Opodo

opodo.com

Opodo is one example of a non-U.S.-based agency site with a primarily non-U.S. audience that can also be of use to U.S. travelers. Such sites can be particularly useful when traveling *within* a particular region (Europe, in the case of Opodo). In many situations, if you are traveling to multiple cities within Europe, you may find it useful to book one flight to your first European city and then separate flights for travel within Europe. You can also sometimes save substantial money by finding an inexpensive flight to a major city and then using a separate round-trip ticket to get to your final, smaller city using a "local" airline. Opodo has separate sites for the U.K., France, Spain, Germany, Italy, Sweden, Norway, Denmark, and Finland.

Opodo, which is owned by nine leading European airlines and Amadeus (discussed later in this chapter), covers more than 500 airlines, 65,000 hotels, and 7,000 car rental locations.

Comparison Shopping Sites

There are several metasearch engines that will compare prices across dozens or hundreds of travel sites. Simply enter information about where and when you want to go; the engine then goes out to the sites of the providers and returns a list that allows you to easily find which travel sites are offering the best prices for your trip. The following four sites are easy to use, and all have a number of things in common. All of them search both airline sites and travel agency sites (such as Orbitz). All of them let you enter your departure city or airport, your destination city or airport, and the number of travelers. All display the basic information about the matching flights as long as the provider shows that information prior to purchase. The rates you see will be the same as you would initially see in a search at the provider's own site. All of these metasearch engines provide options for modifying your search after you have reached the results page. None of them sell tickets directly; instead, when you choose a flight, you are sent to the provider's site for further details and to purchase the ticket. All of them provide comparison searches for hotels and cars as well as flights.

There are some differences among these engines, however. For some, your search can contain additional search criteria and options such as one-way and multi-leg flights or searching for nearby airports. For each of them, the ways results are displayed can differ significantly. How you can modify your search from the results pages and sort your results differs as well.

One major difference to keep in mind is that they don't all cover the same travel sites, depending, among other things, on their agreements with airlines and agencies. For this reason, although the purpose of these sites is a "one-stop" comparison, you may want to use more than one of these metasearch sites to avoid missing some bargains.

SideStep
www.sidestep.com

SideStep was a pioneer in providing this kind of comparison service for travel (Figure 3.5). It covers more than 150 travel sites and provides searches for hotels, cars, flights, vacation packages, and activities.

- *Additional search options:* When searching, you can have SideStep include nearby airports, and you can specify the part of the day (anytime, early morning, morning, afternoon, evening), one-way or round-trip, and number of travelers by age.

- *Can sort results by:* Airlines, departure time, number of stops, and price.

- *Other options on results pages:* You can change dates and refine your search by departure and arrival times, number of stops, airports, and airlines. You will find checkboxes by each flight that enable you to choose flights for comparison: Choose the flights of interest and click on the Compare button, and a table is displayed that lets you easily compare the price, airline, departure time, connection time, arrival time, trip duration, meals, aircraft type, and total distance for each selected flight. Use the e-mail link on the results pages to e-mail information on selected flights (using the same check-boxes as for the Compare option).

- *Unique features:* For those who use Internet Explorer (IE), SideStep provides a downloadable toolbar (more precisely a sidebar) that provides instant access to a SideStep search. When you download it, an icon is placed on your IE navigation bar. Click it and SideStep opens in a window on the left of your screen. SideStep also offers a free weekly newsletter with current bargains.

- *Also searches:* Hotels, cars, flight and hotel, and all three, plus vacation packages and activities.

FareChase

farechase.yahoo.com

FareChase from Yahoo! is integrated into Yahoo!'s Travel site and also integrates some of Yahoo!'s other features, such as Yahoo! Messenger.

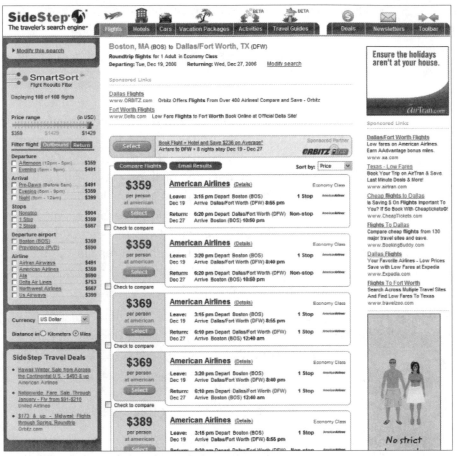

Figure 3.5   SideStep search results page

- *Additional search options:* You can search for one-way as well as round-trip tickets and use a checkbox to include nearby airports, but you cannot yet search for multi-leg or open-jaw flights, or flexible dates. (In an "open jaw" flight, segments of your trip are not connected by a flight; for example, you fly from New York to Barcelona but fly back to New York from Madrid.) Click on the More Search Options link on the main page to search by number of connections, connection time, and cabin class. FareChase stores your five most recent searches, making it easier to return to the site later and quickly check on trips.

- *Can sort results by:* Price, departure times, or return times.

- *Other options on results pages:* You can refine results by flight times, airports, airlines, or number of stops. On the results pages, you will see a list of airlines that were searched. FareChase does not search airlines that do not serve your destination city.

- *Unique features:* For each flight shown, the information can be e-mailed or IMed to yourself or someone else. The Flight Details link for each flight gives you a pop-up window with more detail for that flight. This option is convenient and can save significant time since you do not have to leave the FareChase site and go to the provider site.

- *Also searches:* Hotels

Mobissimo
mobissimo.com

Mobissimo, which the site says is Italian for "ultimate in mobility," searches more than 170 global travel sites, including dozens of low-priced European airlines. It also has one of the easiest-to-read results pages.

- *Additional search options:* As well as common search criteria, you can search for one-way tickets and cabin class.

- *Can sort results by:* Mobissimo results are arranged in columns by provider, airline, departure, arrival, number of stops, and price, and can be sorted by any of these. Just click on the column heading.

- *Other options on results pages:* You can filter results by approximate departure time. Results are shown in dollars, but a menu permits a listing change to show prices in any one of 25 currencies. A search form similar to the one on the home page is also provided on the results pages.

- *Unique features:* Mobissimo offers a free newsletter and maintains a blog.

- *Also searches:* Hotels, cars, and activities.

Kayak

www.kayak.com

Kayak covers more than 120 travel sites, hundreds of airlines, and more than 115,000 hotels. You can use Kayak at its own site, but it is also used by AOL's travel section, About.com's travel sites, and USA TODAY.com's travel section. It has convinced a number of low-fare airlines to participate, ones you may not find either on travel agency sites such as Travelocity and Expedia or on the other comparison sites.

- *Additional search options:* On Kayak's main page, you can specify round-trip, one-way, multicity (open-jaw with up to four legs), time of day (morning, afternoon, or evening), cabin class, nearby airports, nonstop, and which of your preferences profiles you wish to use.

- *Can sort results by:* Price, airline, departure time, arrival time, and number of stops.

- *Other options on results pages:* Kayak has a very sophisticated, but easy-to-use, search results page. Using "sliders," you can narrow your search by price range and arrival and departure times. You can also narrow results by airport, number of stops, and airline. For any flight listed, click on the "details" button to bring up a pop-up window that shows additional details about the flight. Results pages also display which airlines were covered in the search.

- *Unique features:* With the Kayak Buzz tool (look for the link on the main page), you can choose your destination (city and a region of the world), and Kayak Buzz will display a list of lowest fares to the 25 most popular destinations in that region.

- *Also searches:* Comparison searches are also provided for hotels and cars. The site provides searches for cruises and vacations, but with those, you must identify a specific travel agency to search.

Amadeus
www.amadeus.net

Amadeus is a Global Distribution System, like Sabre, that provides the central technology behind reservation sites. It has a consumer site of its own at www.amadeus.net, available in 11 languages, where you can get timetables and detailed flight information, including an indication of seat availability by cabin class. The site also provides information on hotels and cars, weather reports, airport guides, subway guides, destination guides, measurement conversions, a phrasebook, world dialing codes, and a world clock. As a company, Amadeus is outstanding for its behind-the-scenes work for other reservation sites. The strength of the Amadeus.net site is in its timetables and the excellent collection of travel tools. It is not a price comparison site but is an aid to identifying available flights.

- *Additional search options:* On the main Amadeus.net search page, you can search for timetables by departure and destination cities, date, time, class, airline (alphabetically), and direct flights.

- *Can sort by:* Departure time.

- *Unique features:* Good collection of travel tools.

- *Other options on results pages:* Link to current flight status and table showing which days the flight operates.

- *Also searches:* You can also get rates for hotels and cars, but Amadeus does not connect you directly with the provider.

Farecast

farecast.com

Farecast is a price comparison site, but a very unique one: It compares prices not by provider but by when is the best time to buy. Since whether you buy a ticket three months ahead, 21 days ahead, or three days ahead can affect the price tremendously, Farecast can help you decide by providing a prediction of the direction of prices, based on charts of the history of fare prices for that market. Results will show whether the fares for the trip you selected are currently rising or dropping or remaining the same, an indication of average fare change, and a confidence factor reflecting Farecast's track record for predictions for that market. It will also provide a tip as to whether to buy now or wait. Farecast is new and has started with predictions for 75 U.S. cities but has much more planned in terms of cities and features.

Bidding Sites for Airfare and Hotel

Shopping around from site to site for the best price and using fare comparison sites, such as FareChase and Mobissimo, are two ways of getting the lowest price for your travel. Another approach, which will definitely meet some people's needs but not others, is bidding for airfare and hotels. With this approach, available on Priceline and Hotwire, you specify your destination and travel dates and select a price that you are willing to pay. With Priceline, it is truly a bid in that you specify an amount and your bid may or may not be accepted. With Hotwire, you pick from a list of low fares or hotel rates. In both cases, you will not know exactly what you have gotten until you buy it. You have to actually make the purchase to find out the airline and departure times, or in the case of a hotel room, the name and exact location of the hotel. Therefore, particularly for airfares, your travel plans must be flexible to take advantage of the lower prices you might get on these sites. Do you want to have to get up at 3 A.M. to make that 6 A.M. flight, and then have a long layover to change planes? If it saves enough money, that will be fine with some travelers, but not others.

The bidding method suits some people very well and adds a bit of a challenge that some find exhilarating. If you are retired and have a very open calendar, with an adjustable daily schedule, and are a flexible person, you can do very well. If you are traveling on business, you will be less likely to find that this approach fits. There is actually somewhat of a culture of people who have invested a lot of time into the process and have developed skills and sets of rules to help them get the best deal and take some of the guessing out of the game. There are sites specifically devoted to how best to "play the game."

Tickets purchased through Priceline or Hotwire must, at present, have a U.S. departure city. However, for U.K. departures, you can use Priceline's U.K. site (priceline.co.uk).

Priceline.com
www.priceline.com

Priceline now offers both its original bidding option ("Name Your Own Price") and the option of choosing exact flights in the same way as on other reservation sites. For the bidding option, as it says on the Priceline site, "If you can fly any time of day, agree to fly on any major airline, stay in any name-brand hotel or rent from any of the top 5 U.S. rental car agencies—you can save a lot of money with Priceline!"

To search flights using either approach, specify your departure city, destination city, departure date, return date, and number of travelers. Click the Next button and the results page will show you the "Name Your Own Price" option at the top of the list (Figure 3.6). Beneath that is a list of flights with a stated price and full flight details (the "regular purchase" option).

If you choose the bidding option, you are then asked to make a choice of one or more departure and arrival airports, the price you are willing to pay, your name, whether you are under 18, and the number of children in the party who are under age 2. The price you specify is the price for the fare itself. On the next page you will be shown the total price, with taxes and fees added, information about the restrictions that apply, and forms to fill in credit card and related information. The next step is to click on the link to buy the tickets. If your price is accepted, you will receive your answer within a minute, at which point you will find out the exact flight and times. If your bid is not accepted, you can enter some alternate specifications. Since Priceline has 34 partner airlines and domestic carriers (for the U.S.), the ticket you actually get may be for a flight of an affiliate of those airlines.

Before you make the actual purchase, you will know some additional information besides the airport, city, and date information you entered: The departure time for U.S. domestic flights will be between 6 A.M. and 10 P.M., arriving no later than by 12:30 A.M. the next day; your flight may be nonstop, or you may have one or two connections each way; and layovers will be no more than three hours. Tickets are nonrefundable,

Figure 3.6   Priceline search results page

nontransferable, noncancelable, and not eligible for frequent flyer miles. (Be sure to check the Priceline site in case any of these factors have changed; Priceline is very straightforward about the restrictions and other factors you need to consider.)

On Priceline's main page, you will find links for additional search options, including one-way flights, multi-destination flights, and searching by airlines and flight times. Options are also offered for limiting your results to first or business class, nonstop flights, and unrestricted fares. The main page also allows you to include hotel or hotel and car.

With Priceline, you can also bid for hotels and rental cars (with a flight purchase). Cruises (from 17 cruise lines) and vacation-package reservations can also be made through Priceline but not with the bidding option. Priceline has an 800 number for help with tickets you have purchased, but questions regarding initial bookings are handled by e-mail.

For advice on bidding, check out the Bidding for Travel site discussed later in this chapter.

Hotwire

www.hotwire.com

Hotwire partners with airlines, hotels, and car rental agencies to help them get rid of unsold inventory at bargain prices. In some cases, prices are so low that the provider cannot advertise it on its own site. For comparison purposes, Hotwire also displays low fare and rate information on flights and rooms not from partners. As with Priceline, you can save substantial money by "buying without seeing," but Hotwire does it a bit differently. With Priceline, you enter basic information about your needs and then bid a specific amount. With Hotwire, you enter similar information, and Hotwire returns a list of possibilities with the bargain prices shown. You make a choice, purchase it, and then find out the details.

To search for a flight on Hotwire's main page, choose a Flights search, enter your origin and destination, your departure and return dates, and the number of tickets you want. (You are also provided with links to do a one-way or multicity search). Then click the Find a Flight button. On the results pages, you may see three types of flights listed: Clearance Fares, FlexSaver Fares, and Retail Fares (Figure 3.7). Flights labeled Clearance Fares can be a flight at any time of day, while FlexSaver Fares show you the part of the day (morning, afternoon, evening) when the flights will depart and return. Before you purchase tickets for either Clearance Fares or FlexSaver Fares, you will be shown the date and number of stops but not the exact time or airline. Prices shown include taxes and fees. You are ticketed as soon as you click the link to book the purchase.

If in your search you have picked a date that is during a peak travel period, Hotwire will let you know. When you are selecting dates from its pop-up calendars, Hotwire highlights peak dates, making it much easier to avoid them.

For all flights, before purchasing, you can count on the following: reserved seating (never standby); flying on a major airline (within the U.S, or between the U.S. and Canada, on United, American, Northwest, Continental, US Airways, America West, Delta Air Lines, Hawaiian, Aloha or their codeshare partners); not being on a red-eye unless it was specified on the results page; no more than one stop (unless indicated) and layovers of no more than three hours. On the other hand, though, know that you cannot cancel your tickets, get a refund, or exchange or transfer your reservation. (One caveat: Check the Hotwire site to see if the preceding information is still correct.)

Hotwire lets you search not only for flights but for hotels, car rentals, and cruises as well. You can also search for just a hotel and car or for packages that combine flights with a hotel and/or car. Also explore the Deals & Destinations tab for featured bargains. For hotels

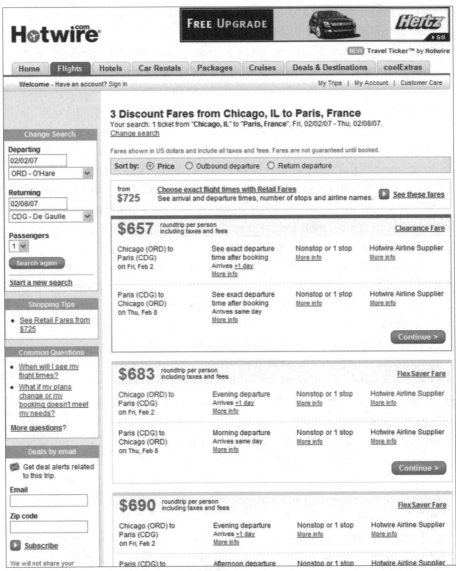

Figure 3.7   Hotwire search results page

and cars, you have a buy-now-see-the-details-later option as with flights (you will not know the name or exact location of the hotel or the car rental company until you buy). For cruises, Hotwire works like other reservation sites and does not have an equivalent to the Clearance Fares or FlexFares it offers for flights.

If you are not planning to make a reservation right away, sign up for Hotwire's Travel Ticker, which will let you know of special deals.

If you still are unsure about using a bidding site to make reservations, go the following site for advice or to participate in discussions on how to use bidding sites most effectively.

BiddingForTravel.com

biddingfortravel.com

BiddingForTravel.com is a collection of forums with the goal of promoting "informed bidding." In its introduction, it refers specifically to Priceline products, but it also has a section on Hotwire. You will find some really good advice and insights here.

Airline Sites

With all the travel agency sites out there, as well as fare comparison sites that let you search scores of airlines all at once, a reasonable question would be, "Why bother searching an individual airline's site?" There are several reasons:

- Some airlines do not allow travel agency sites and others to list their flights, and you may not find out about the lowest fare without going directly to the airline's own site. Also, some may have exclusive deals with one of the comparison sites, meaning that the airline may be covered on one but not another comparison site. These situations may be especially true for

> low-fare airlines such as Southwest, JetBlue, Ryan Air, and similar carriers.
>
> • Airlines may offer some deals directly that are not available through agencies.
>
> • The airline sites may provide benefits not available through some agencies, such as frequent-flyer bonus miles, redemption of airline certificates and coupons, and boarding passes you can print out on your own computer. Also, while you are on the airline's site, you can also check your frequent-flyer mileage balance.

There is a good article at Wikitravel (wikitravel.org/en/Discount_airlines) that discusses discount airlines and also provides links to other articles in WikiTravel that contain lists and links to discount airlines by continent. (If you are not familiar with wikis, they are Web sites similar to an encyclopedia, where anyone can contribute, edit, or add to existing articles on the site.) Make use of these articles to find discount airlines in the part of the world where you will be traveling.

So, if it is useful to go to these airline sites, why won't you see the next few pages filled with a list of airline Web sites? Because the easiest way to get to an airline site when you don't know its URL is to simply type the name of the airline into a search engine's search box. Almost invariably, the link to the airline's site will be among the first few items listed. It works even for an airline such as United with a name that's a common word. Worst case: You may have to add the word "airline" in the search box. If you still feel an urgent need for a list of airline sites, try the following:

Skytrax—Airline Web Sites
www.airlinequality.com/Airlines/Web_links.htm

Skytrax has links to more than 400 airline sites. Other uses of this site will be covered later in this chapter.

AirlineNumbers.com

www.airlinenumbers.com

AirlineNumbers.com has links and phone numbers for more than 260 airlines.

A Sampling of the Hundreds of Other Good Travel Agency Sites

There are indeed hundreds of travel sites out there, each with varying levels of "goodness." If you skipped the Introduction to this book, you may want to go back and look particularly at the section that covers some tips for evaluating travel agency sites. Just because a site is not included here certainly should not cast any aspersions on its integrity. If you run across a travel agency site for the first time and think you might want to use it to make reservations, you may want to check out some of the travel discussion groups, and particularly Epinions.com, for user reviews (see the section on Travel Discussion Groups and Forums at the end of Chapter 2).

The following are additional examples of some well-known sites and were chosen for inclusion here because of the variety in structure and appearance that they demonstrate.

Travelzoo

www.travelzoo.com

Travelzoo focuses on sales and deals from more than 500 companies—airlines, cruise lines, hotel chains, and car rental companies. Look particularly at the links to deals arranged by location and in the Last-Minute Travel section. While you are there, be sure to sign up to join the 10 million travelers who receive the Travelzoo newsletter.

Site59.com

www.site59.com

This is another good example of a site with a specific focus, in this case, last-minute weekend getaways.

LastMinuteTravel.com
www.lastminutetravel.com

Use LastMinuteTravel.com to save substantially on fights, hotels, cruises, cars, and packages by making your travel plans shortly before you leave.

Getting Even More for Your Money: Frequent Flyer Resources

Even infrequent flyers should be Frequent Flyers, that is, they should sign up for frequent flyer programs. It usually takes only a few extra moments, and you never know when your flying patterns might change and you will find yourself using a particular airline much more frequently than expected. Especially if you fly internationally, the miles can accumulate rather quickly, but there are other ways to make that happen. Way back when Trump Airlines was still around, I picked up 12,000 miles in a single round-trip flight between Boston and Washington, D.C. The airline gave a minimum of 1,000 miles for any flight and had a special promotion that awarded triple miles. Also, it guaranteed that if your flight was more than 20 minutes late, the airlines doubled your miles for that ticket. Guess what? My flight was late. Don't expect bonanzas like that often, but if you play your cards right and are a bit lucky, mileage can very quickly pile up. If you use a credit card that provides airline miles, every trip to the grocery store can get you closer to a free ticket.

FrequentFlier.com
frequentflier.com

Check out FrequentFlier.com for advice on managing and maximizing your miles, news, links directly to the frequent flyer program pages on airlines sites, descriptions of programs, links to airport sites, a forum, and a free newsletter, the FrequentFlier Crier.

WebFlyer
www.webflyer.com

WebFlyer is a company that provides a range of products for frequent flyers, including AwardGuide, AwardPlanner, and publications. On the main page of WebFlyer, a menu leads to sites for each product. One of these, the FlyerTalk site (www.flyertalk.com), provides free, quite active forums that focus on frequent flyer issues.

Free Frequent Flyer Miles
www.freefrequentflyermiles.com

Free Frequent Flyer Miles specializes in advice on how to rack up miles without even flying. It discusses credit cards and other opportunities to take advantage of special offers that will help you quickly accumulate mileage points.

Some Other Sites to Help Get You Off the Ground

In addition to sites that help you take advantage of frequent-flyer programs, there are several other sites that air travelers will find useful in planning (and taking) their trips. The following are some of the better-known sites that can assist you in having a good flight.

SeatGuru
www.seatguru.com

Before you make your seat selections, you may want to check out SeatGuru. Click on one of the 40 airlines covered by the site and then on the type of plane (or Equipment, as airline folks say). You will then see a diagram that gives you a detailed "map" of the plane (Figure 3.8), identifying good and poor seats, and the locations of galleys and

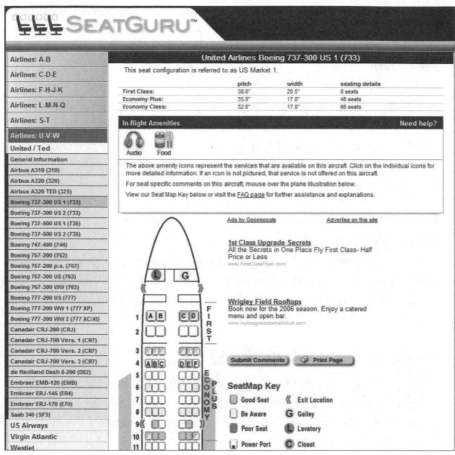

Figure 3.8   SeatGuru seating map

lavatories. Hold your cursor over a seat for more detail about leg room, storage space, seat pitch, width, video facilities, availability of laptop power outlets, and general comfort to expect in that location.

Skytrax

www.airlinequality.com

On Skytrax, you will find a variety of rankings and awards for airline and airport quality. The passenger forums are a great place to find out what customers have to say. Among many other things, you can find pictures and seating dimensions for seats by airline. You can even view pictures of various airlines' amenity kits, if the color of the toothbrush is important to you ...

OAG
www.oag.com

Though this book focuses on free information on the Web, it would be remiss if it did not at least mention the well-known OAG (which once upon a time stood for Official Airline Guide). The OAG site primarily provides information about its fee-based subscription services, such as OAG Flights, which furnishes "Online access to ALL the world's scheduled flights." On the free side, the site also offers quite a bit, including information on airlines, airports, countries, passports and visas, currency, and understanding air tickets.

There are numerous other sites that provide useful products for flyers for a fee. If you are willing to invest a bit of money, consider FlightExplorer (www.flightexplorer.com) for flight tracking and First Class Flyer (firstclassflyer.com), a publication with guidance for first-class travel.

Discussion Groups and Forums for Flyers

Several of the sites already mentioned in this chapter incorporate forums relevant to flying. Some provide very general topics, and some focus on specifics, such as frequent flyer miles. Take a look particularly at the following site.

FlyerTalk

www.flyertalk.com

FlyerTalk is a very active forum for people who want to make the best of frequent-flyer programs. The forum contains more than a million postings primarily in two categories: Miles & Points and Travel & Dining. The former set contains subforums on specific airline programs (and hotel frequent guest programs as well). FlyerTalk also provides a live chat option.

This chapter has examined major reservation sites, with a particular focus on airline reservations. While it has presented some additional sites relevant to enhancing your flying experience, you will encounter scores more reservation sites in the chapters that follow. Those sites are covered in those chapters rather than here because of their particular emphasis, specialty, or unique utility. For example, in Chapter 6, "Finding a Bed and a Meal," you will find travel agency sites that specialize in hotels. Many of those same sites will sell flights as well. As you plan your trip, make use of both the more general sites (Travelocity, etc.) and the more specialized sites covered in later chapters. Not every site available is listed here (or elsewhere in this book) but exclusion does not mean that it is not a good site. As said previously, before you spend money through a site you have never before heard of, check out the discussions groups and particularly Epinions.com to find out what kind of experience others have had in using that agency. If you have not done so already, you will soon develop your own list of sites for services and prices that best suit your very own unique reservation needs.

Train, Car, and Ferry Travel

Unless you are vacationing in your own backyard, you are almost undoubtedly going to need some ground transportation to get from one place to another. This chapter will take a look at the ways the Web can be useful in arranging travel via trains, cars, and ferries (yes, ferries are not really "ground" transportation, but since they are usually used in conjunction with a car, they are included here). The sites discussed in this chapter provide basic advice for train, car, and ferry travel; where to get reservations for these conveyances; and a variety of other tools, such as roadmap sites to help you get from one place to another.

Trains

There are, of course, plenty of reasons to take a train and a variety of trains to take. You may just need a ride from one city to another, you may want to travel within a city (e.g., on subways), or you may take one just for the pleasure of a train ride or as a great way to see the countryside and other sights. For any of those reasons or a combination of all of them, some of us just like trains. If you get a chill of excitement watching the scene from *Murder on the Orient Express* where the train is preparing to depart and all are aboard (there is a moment of near silence, then everything suddenly comes alive as the locomotive's headlight floods the screen, the theme music comes in, and the train starts to roll), then the excitement of train travel is probably part of your reason for continuing to climb aboard. Rest assured that you will not be involved in the kind of suspense Agatha Christie provided, and there will probably be no background theme music, but you can meet a variety of people, have a great ride, and hop off at a new place in life feeling relaxed, entertained, and sometimes even enlightened.

Fortunately you will not need to do the level of planning the *Orient Express* characters did, but when planning to travel by train, you may need to know about schedules, reservations, what train lines are available, and which to take. The Web can provide assistance in all these areas.

Train Schedules and Reservations

When planning a flight, finding schedules and making reservations are usually done at the same time on the same Web site. This is somewhat less frequently the case with train reservations, especially for those made abroad. On the other hand, for those traveling abroad, making reservations is simplified by the availability of rail passes that cover multiple countries. The next few pages will focus on some ways the Web makes it easy to search for schedules, make reservations, and book your seats. Rail reservations differ from most other travel reservations in another way: The biggest reservation sites (Travelocity, Expedia, and Orbitz) are of little use. Travelocity connects you to the RailEurope and Amtrak sites, Orbitz transfers you to the Amtrak site, and Expedia has no rail option at all. Going to RailEurope, Rail Canada, and Amtrak sites directly will easily provide more information and service. For other countries, you can usually go directly to the site for the railway company(ies) for that country.

Rail Passes

Rail passes are mentioned first because they, in many cases, can offer the most in a single package. Eurail passes, for example, can provide unlimited travel for a given period of time in multiple countries. (If you like some spontaneity in your travel plans, it is great to be able to walk into the Gare de l'Est, look up at the board, and get on "the next train out" to any city that sounds interesting.) With rail passes, you can cover wide territories and have great flexibility at a very low price, but consider the details before you buy. The following site from Rick Steves is a great place to start if you are considering a European rail pass. The first eight sites in this chapter are about European rail passes, schedules, and other information, and the ones that follow are examples of similar sites for individual countries (the U.K., the U.S., Canada, and Australia). For rail passes in other countries, you should find it easy to locate sites with a simple search on the name of the country in combination with the phrase "rail passes" (e.g., Japan "rail passes"). In addition to the following sites that sell rail passes, you will also find them available through hundreds of other travel agency sites.

European Rail Travel

Rick Steves' Europe—Eurail Passes
www.ricksteves.com/rail/rail_menu.htm

If you are thinking about traveling in Europe by train, start with this site. Even if you are thinking about buying rail passes in other continents, this site still can provide good advice about rail passes in general. The site includes how European rail passes work, suggested itineraries, how to read European train schedules, point-to-point ticket cost comparisons, how to choose and order your rail pass, and how to use your rail pass. You can also purchase rail passes here. As usual, you can count on Rick for good, practical, clear, and interesting information.

Rail Europe
www.raileurope.com

Rail Europe, from the Rail Europe Group (which pioneered Eurailpass), is an online travel agency owned primarily by French National Railroads (SNCF) and Swiss Federal Railroads (SBB), but it represents 35 European railroads. Through the site, you can buy passes, packages, and other rail products for 35 countries.

The Rail Passes link on the site leads to a comparison chart that helps you choose the kind of pass you need depending on your destinations. In addition to rail passes (including those with special rates for youth and seniors), you can make reservations for point-to-point tickets on regular trains, "premier" trains (high-speed, etc.), scenic trains, and night trains throughout Europe.

For point-to-point tickets, click the Train Tickets & Schedules link. The search box there will let you specify origin, destination, dates, and number of travelers (adults, children, youth, and seniors). Search results will show the train options you have (departure and arrival times, prices, etc.), and from there, you can select and purchase your tickets. Rail Europe also offers bookings for cars, hotels, and air-hotel packages.

The Man in Seat Sixty-One
www.seat61.com

For "a beginner's guide to European rail passes," click the Railpasses link on this site. This site is a labor of love created by Mark Smith, aka "The Man in Seat Sixty-One," who offers advice and information on how to travel by train and ship, primarily between the U.K. and Europe, Africa, Asia, the U.S., and Australasia. He also has pages devoted to travel within the U.K. and Ireland. Though the emphasis is on travel from the U.K. (London in particular), the pages for each of 83 countries provide useful information on train travel in those countries regardless of your trip's origin. Also, if you want to know about the "real" Orient Express, be sure to see the page on that topic.

Eurail

www.eurail.com

Eurail is owned by the Eurail Group G.I.E., which "is owned by a number of train- and ship-operating companies, referred to as the Eurail members." This site offers information about Eurail passes, sells them, and furnishes a map under the Where to Buy link that identifies agents throughout the world who can sell Eurail passes.

European Train Timetables

Many Web sites provide timetables for European trains. Many or most of them use the same underlying database and software from a company called HAFAS. Two such sites, International Train Planner and Die Bahn, are discussed here. You will see many similarities between these sites. You may find that you prefer one timetable site over the other because of the layout or amount of detail provided. For a useful explanation of how to read these timetables, take a look at Rick Steves' site (discussed earlier in this chapter), particularly at his discussion of Train Schedules: Breaking the Code (www.ricksteves. com/rail/itinplan.htm#schedules).

International Train Planner

plannerint.b-rail.be

This site, which comes directly from HAFAS, has interfaces in French, English, German, and Dutch. The Route Planner search form has options for origin, destination, date, time, means of transport (all, high-speed trains, Inter-City Express, EuroCity, InterRegional trains, etc.), connections (all, direct, direct with sleepers, direct with couchettes), and how many bicycles you will be bringing (up to three, up to 13, more than 13). The plus and minus numbers to the right of the date and time boxes are used to increase or decrease the date and time choices incrementally, or you can use the calendar to choose a date and then click the Paste Selected Date button. Search results pages show a summary of each possible train at the top of the page and extensive details for the route underneath the summaries (Figure 4.1). (Americans who have not traveled on European trains before should be pleased to see that this and other European timetables usually even provide the platform where the train will arrive. In the U.S., this information often remains a mystery until the last moment.) Click the Print View link for a printable version, and click the Connection Graphics link to see a diagram of the route for each connection. The Stops & Stations section of the site provides detailed timetables from specific stations and stops. With this site, you can plan one stage at a time. After you have seen the options for your first train, click the Return Journey or Continue Journey links for your next train.

Die Bahn
reiseauskunft.bahn.de

Although the main page is, not unexpectedly, in German, if you look closely, you will find links on the page (an inch or two down, toward the right side of the page) for English, French, Italian, Spanish, and Dutch interfaces. The site uses the HAFAS database, so it's similar to the International Train Planner site. On the main search form of the Die Bahn site, however, you can specify your return trip, intermediate stations ("via"), number of passengers (adults and children), first or second class, type of train, and whether your BahnCard makes you eligible for a discount.

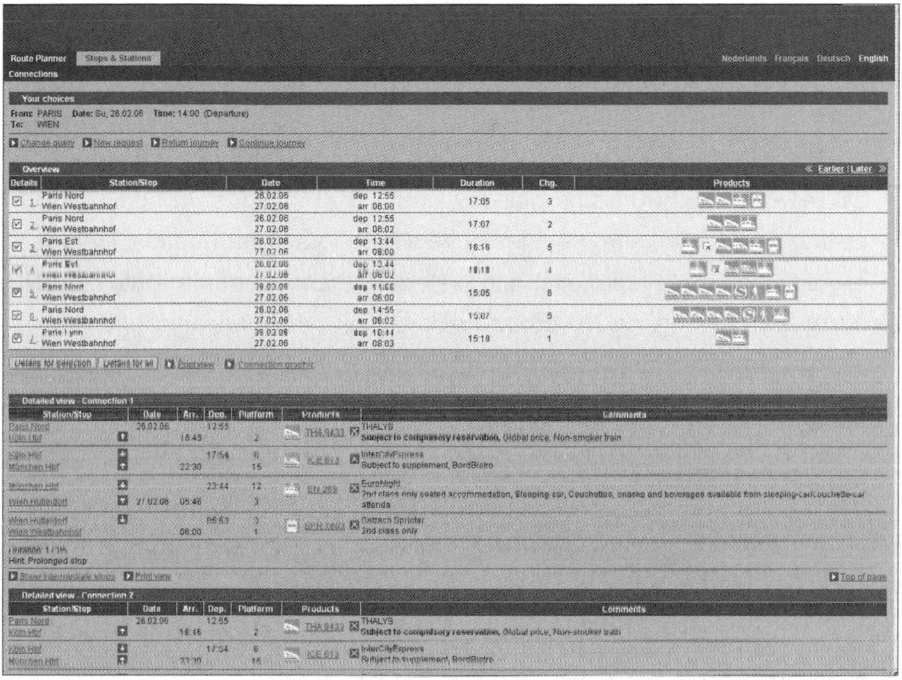

Figure 4.1   International Train Planner search results page

Railfaneurope.net—The European Railway Server

www.railfaneurope.net

This site for railway fans and train travelers provides detailed information on European trains, arranged by country. The Pictures section contains hundreds of pictures of locomotives, trains, stations, and even trolleys, funiculars, and train tickets. Much of the site, including the Stock Lists and Liveries sections, may not interest most travelers, but it will be of considerable interest if you are a hard-core train fan. Like other travel information, just observing what is going on around you on the trains and in the stations can be more fun if you can see it with a more informed eye.

U.K. Rail Travel

BritRail

www.britrail.com

BritRail provides a variety of passes that cover the U.K. network of 26 railways, 18,500 trains per day, and 2,400 stations. In addition to selling passes, the site provides quite a bit of other information, including downloadable rail maps, suggested itineraries, scenic routes, and more. By clicking on the Point-to-Point link, you can also get timetables. However, on the form that results from that click, be sure to choose Ticket & Reservation under the Types of Ticket question.

Britain on Track

www.britainontrack.com

This "official BritRail supplier" is an example of one of numerous travel agency sites that sell BritRail passes for purchase in the U.S.

National Rail Enquiries

www.nationalrail.co.uk

National Rail Enquiries is the official information service for National Rail, which is the collection of train companies that operate Britain's rail service. The site provides an easy-to-use search form that will provide routes, fares, and schedules. Purchases are not made directly through the site, but once you have selected your trains, the site will link to a choice of vendors. The site also provides extensive details on each station, printable timetables, a Train Tracker for the current status of today's trains, and details on passenger services. National Rail Enquiries lists sites with information in WAP format (for cell phones and other wireless devices) at www.rail.co.uk/ukrail/hot news/hotnews.html.

U.S. Rail Travel

Amtrak

www.amtrak.com

The heyday of trains in America has indeed passed, and there are, unfortunately, far fewer trains and stations than a few decades ago. In spite of this, Amtrak, America's passenger rail service, does have plenty to offer, both for simple transportation and for sightseeing. On Amtrak, you can see the U.S. as no other form of travel can provide, especially when traveling on trains that have Sightseer lounges. (If you are European, be prepared to temper your expectations a bit before boarding. It is no secret that Amtrak trains aren't as reliable as European trains.)

Like Amtrak itself, the Amtrak Web site also has a lot to offer (Figure 4.2). The Reservations tab on the main page lets you search easily for trains (and sort by either schedule or fare), view fares (including options and details for seats and sleeping accommodations), and purchase tickets. If you are traveling far, consider using the Multi-City option on the search page. Using that feature, you may be able to put together a more enjoyable itinerary than Amtrak suggests if you just specify your origin and destination. You can also add in some interesting layovers.

With the Schedules tab on the Amtrak home page, you can see schedules by arrival and departure city and timetables for particular trains (such as the Capitol Limited and the City of New Orleans). The Stations tab leads to information about stations and their locations, hours, facilities, and services, as well as descriptions and maps for the train routes served by that station. Click on the Hot Deals tab for special offers and discounts, including Weekly Specials that can include some very attractive discounts of up to 90 percent. In this section, you will also find links for rail passes and programs. The Traveling

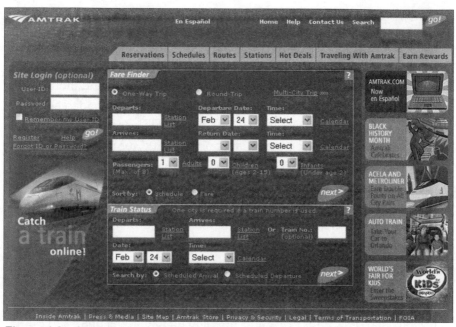

Figure 4.2   Amtrak main page

with Amtrak section furnishes extensive and well-organized information on preparing for and taking trips aboard Amtrak.

The Amtrak site's Rail Passes & Programs section (under the Hot
Deals tab) describes five Amtrak programs. The USA Rail Passes pro-
gram is for non-U.S. and non-Canadian travelers. The other rail pass
programs offered are North America Rail Pass, Rail-2-Rail (for
Southern California), California Rail Pass (for California regional
trains), and Florida Rail Pass (for permanent Florida residents).
Amtrak's Explore America Fares (for travel within one or more of four
U.S. regions) is, strangely, not available through its site.

If you are traveling from the Northeast or Midwest to Florida, consider using Amtrak's unique Auto Train to transport both you and your
car from the Washington, D.C., area (actually, Lorton, Virginia) to

Sanford, Florida (near Orlando). To get to Auto Train information, click on the Routes tab, and then under Browse by Region, click on South.

Amtrak Unlimited: Your Unofficial Source for Amtrak Information
www.amtraktrains.com

This site provides more (and *un*official) information about Amtrak, including photos of trains that Amtrak should have placed on its own site. The forums section is particularly active, with thousands of postings.

The Train Traveler
www.thetraintraveler.com

Created for the North American train traveler, this site contains articles on train destinations, editorials, questions and answers, and book reviews. It also takes you beyond Amtrak trains with its section on Excursion and Dinner Trains. The site also offers a collection of about 30 links to other train travel sites, particularly links to various associations for train travelers.

Canadian Rail Travel

The main site for Canadian rail travel is VIA Rail Canada. You also will find information on the Amtrak site for rail passes for both the U.S. and Canada.

VIA Rail Canada
www.viarail.ca

VIA Rail Canada is the primary site for information and bookings for Canadian rail travel. You will find information on schedules, fares, stations, and services, plus discounts for various categories of travelers. The site provides maps and descriptions of the Canadian railway routes, as well as detailed information and photos for features and services for each train.

Rail Travel in Other Countries

Yes, it is somewhat of a shame to lump information on rail travel for another 200 or so countries together in one brief section, but my publisher tells me that if I write a 1,000-page book, it will cost you a lot more money. Fortunately, it is very easy to get to rail travel sites for other countries through a simple search engine search. If you want to get to the site for a country's main railway(s), search for the term "railway" and the name of the country, for example, *Thailand railway*. If you want to focus on sites *about* rail travel in that country, add the term "travel" to make those sites appear higher on the search results list (e.g., *china railway travel*).

Excursions, Tours, and Scenic and Luxury Trains

Just getting from one place to another is, of course, only one reason for train travel. Even when the main purpose is getting from one city to another, train travelers still enjoy many benefits. Some trains exist primarily for other purposes, such as immersing oneself in luxury, taking oneself briefly back to the "old days" of trains, or experiencing the thrill of going up the side of a mountain at a 60-degree angle. Many of the sites already discussed will provide information on and reservations for such trains. The following are examples of sites that will get you aboard for one of these experiences.

Luxury Train Online
www.luxurytrainonline.com

This travel agency offers tours on the Orient Express, Royal Scotsman, Blue Train, Trans-Siberian Express, Al Andalus Express, American Orient Express, Royal Canadian Pacific, and Rovos Rail.

Orient-Express
www.orient-express.com

Among many other things, the Orient-Express Hotels, Trains and Cruises travel company enables you to relive the heyday of luxury train travel. Even if you aren't really planning to take one of the trains, spend some time daydreaming with the photos on this site. To learn how this Orient Express relates to the original "Orient Express," take a look at the page on this topic at The Man in Seat Sixty-One site (www.seat61.com/OrientExpress.htm) mentioned earlier in this chapter.

The Luxury Trains
www.theluxurytrains.com

The Luxury Trains site offers eight different luxury train tours to cities, festivals, and other sights throughout India.

Classic Train Journeys
www.classictrainjourneys.com

Classic Train Journeys is a travel agency that can book luxury, historic, and scenic train journeys on six continents.

Rails USA—Tourist Railroads
www.railsusa.com/links/Tourist_Railroads

Tourist Railroads is a section of the larger Rails USA site (www.railsusa.com), which is an extensive collection of links to information on all aspects and forms of railroading in the U.S. This particular part of the site has links to more than100 scenic, cog, narrow gauge, excursion, and other railways. You will also find a link (www.railsusa.com/links/Canada/Tourist_Railroads/) for about 20 such opportunities in Canada.

Railroads and Railroading Links

There are thousands of Web sites that cover travel by rail, the history of railroads, model railroading, and related topics. If you are an avid rail traveler, you might want to expand your options considerably by looking at the following site.

RailroadData.com
www.railroaddata.com/rrlinks

RailroadData.com is a collection of links to more than 5,000 railroad sites. For the traveler, there are a number of categories on the main page of the site that can lead to particular kinds of rail travel experiences. You might want to especially consider the following categories: High-Speed Trains, International, Live Steam, Narrow Gauge, Park Trains, Passenger Trains, and Tourist Railroads and Museums.

On the Road: Getting Places by Car
Road Trip Destinations

Road trip destinations are, in many cases, the same places that one can get to by plane or rail, and for finding information on those destinations, you can use the travel guides discussed in the preceding chapters. However, since travel by car or RV (recreational vehicle) can take you to more out-of-the-way locales, you might want to take advantage of other approaches, which include using search engines and visiting sites specifically addressing road trips.

There are, of course, thousands of sites that provide information on destinations to which you might want to drive. The more specific your destination, the more help a search engine can provide. To find information on small towns, specific monuments, parks, historic homes, castles, and so on, a search engine can often take you most quickly to information on the attractions. Keep your initial search simple, but specific enough, and use quotation marks for phrases, for example: *"Mount Vernon"*, *"Niagara Falls"*, *"Stratford-upon-Avon"*, *"Normandy beaches"*, *"Black Hills"*, *"Stonehenge"*, *"Blarney Castle"*, *"Wall Drug"*, and *"barbed wire museum"*.

The next several sites discuss road trips in general and specific aspects of road trips, offer particularly useful tools and content, or are examples of specific categories of road trip destinations. For the latter, keep in mind this is just a small sampling selected primarily to show the variety of sites available for specific locations that can be found by using a search engine.

RoadTrip America

roadtripamerica.com

RoadTrip America is an extensive site with a broad range of advice, articles, and links related to road trips in North America. It covers not just car travel but travel by RV, motorcycle, bicycle, and off-road vehicle. Annotated links to hundreds of sites offer information on destinations, itineraries, and special topics such as traveling with pets, and for special groups such as solo travelers, couples, disabled travelers, and international visitors. Two unique collections of articles and advice are RoadTrip America's sections on Working on the Road and how to stay connected to the Internet while traveling. The latter section introduces you to the world of Dashboarders, "individuals who use a variety of wireline and wireless devices to connect to the Internet while working and/or living on the road."

America's Byways

www.byways.org

This site from the U.S. Department of Transportation has information on 126 roads that have a particular scenic, archeological, cultural, historic, natural, or recreational interest. Browse by state or use the search box to find descriptions, photos, specific places to visit, and articles. The main description page for each byway includes maps and directions, itineraries, calendars of events, and links to further information.

Roadsideamerica.com
roadsideamerica.com

Most people can find their way to the usual tourist attractions, but not everyone can return from a road trip with the experience of having seen the world's largest replica cheese, the Museum of the American Fan Collectors, a banana museum, or a hay-sculpting contest. This site is a guide to "offbeat tourist attractions." You can browse attractions by state to work into your itinerary at least a few of the 7,000 attractions described here.

FreeTravelTips.com—Road Trip Tips
www.freetraveltips.com/RoadTrip

The Road Trip Tips section of the FreeTravelTips.com site is rather brief, but it provides useful tips for preparing for a road trip and advice on road safety.

Road Trip Driving Tours of the American Revolution
www.revolutionaryday.com

"Revolutionary War, History-Based Travel, Road Trip Driving Tours of the American Revolution" (this actually is the full title of the site) is a good example of a site that provides driving itineraries for travelers with specific interests.

Road Trip USA

www.roadtripusa.com

Road Trip USA offers itineraries for 11 outstanding trips: Pacific Coast, Hwy. 93: Border to Border, US-83: The Road to Nowhere, The Great River Road, Appalachian Trail, Coastal East Coast, US-2: The Great Northern, US-20: The Oregon Trail, US-50: Loneliest Road, US-80: Southern Pacific, and Route 66: The Mother Road. For each, you will find a general description of the route, descriptions of highlights, and links for itineraries across neighboring states.

Hear's a Journey

www.hearsajourney.com

Hear's A Journey creates and sells 90-minute audiocassettes for driving tours through Europe.

England, Scotland & Wales—A Travel Guide

my.core.com/~jcnash

England, Scotland & Wales—A Travel Guide contains a nice selection of itineraries, advice, destinations, and links scattered throughout the site. Look particularly at the Holiday Itinerary (The Tours) section for suggested tours ranging from two to 34 days.

Driving in England—Usesful Tips for the Traveler

england.visualenc.com/general/driving.html

Driving in England—Useful Tips for the Traveler is brief, but it contains some very practical tips for anyone driving in England for the first time. Find out about roundabouts before you get on one. (There is a good chance you may actually begin to prefer them to incessant stoplights.)

Travel Alberta—Scenic Road Trips

www1.travelalberta.com/en-ca/index.cfm?pageid=7

If you are headed for Alberta by car and want to see the best of what it has to offer, check out Travel Alberta—Scenic Road Trips. You will find a good selection of detailed itineraries (which you can sort by title or trip length), as well as extensive, well-organized information on a large number of other types of vacations (hiking, fishing, golf, camping, etc.) and other attractions and events. (I don't want to slight Canada's other provinces, which have similar sites. However, the Scenic Road Trips section of this site serves as an excellent example of provincial, state, and other local sites that offer information on road trips.)

Getting Around Germany—Driving

gettingaroundgermany.home.att.net/auto.htm

Although this site is actually written by a Texan, you will find a very good introduction to what you need to know if you plan to drive in Germany. Look particularly at the section on the Autobahn. This is actually part of a larger site (gettingaroundgermany.home.att.net.verkehr. htm) that contains, as well as the driving section, sections on parking in German cities and getting around Germany by other means, including flying, rail, buses, and taxis.

Car Rentals

If your driving vacation or business trip involves renting a car, there are of course plenty of company sites anxious to rent to you, including the big online travel agencies, smaller agencies, and sites for the car rental companies themselves. Particularly if you do not rent cars frequently, you may want to spend a few minutes with the following site for general advice.

FreeTravelTips.com—Rental Car Tips

www.freetraveltips.com/Cars

The Rental Car Tips section of Free Travel Tips.com provides tips in a Q&A format on topics such as getting the best deal, clubs and programs, policies, payment, reservations, insurance, refueling, and more.

Using the General Reservation Sites for Renting Cars

Almost all of the largest travel agency sites (Travelocity, Expedia, Orbitz, Yahoo! Travel, Cheap Tickets, Opodo, and others) offer car rental options, and, in some cases, you can actually save money by combining a flight reservation with a car rental. Most of the bidding and price comparison sites (Priceline, Hotwire, Mobissimo, SideStep, and Kayak.com) also offer car rental options. For a general discussion of these sites, see Chapter 3, "Reservation Sites: Flights and More." The following descriptions for the general travel agency sites focus only on what they offer for car rentals. The search options are very straightforward, with all of them asking where and when you want to pick up the car. Most will allow you to indicate either an airport, a city, or "near an address" for the pickup location. Some will offer more detailed search options, such as the kind of car you want, eligible discounts, and preferred vendors; some will also differ in what packages they offer (flights and cars, hotels and car, etc.). As you use these sites, note whether prices include taxes and fees. Car rental sections for Travelocity, Expedia, and Orbitz are covered here. Most of the other large travel agency sites are powered by one of those three, and search options and results pages will be the same (including prices) as you will find on whichever of the three sites is "behind" the search. One useful exception, Yahoo! Travel, is also included.

Travelocity—Car Rentals
www.travelocity.com/cars

Travelocity's car rental section covers 50 car rental agencies. On the main search page, the Car Type search option allows you to choose: "5 Basic Types" (economy, compact, intermediate, full-size, minivan), Economy, Compact, Intermediate, Standard, Full-Size, Premium, Luxury, Convertible, Station Wagon, Van, Sport Utility, Pick-up Truck, or Specialty. You can also specify your discount eligibility for a corporation, association (e.g., AAA), or car rental company. Links at the bottom of the search form take you to a page where you can search for one-way rentals or use coupons. On results pages, click on the preferred type of car (e.g., compact) for a pop-up window that displays a photo of the car and details about luggage and passenger capacity. Results pages show both the daily rate and total price for the rental. Click on the daily rate to see full details and special equipment options (ski rack, child seat, etc.).

Expedia—Car Rentals
www.expedia.com/daily/cars

The car rental section of Expedia includes 12 car rental companies. In addition to the usual search criteria, the search form also provides options for searching for package deals that include the car, flight, hotel, or flight and hotel. Instead of starting at an airport or city, you can select a place or a U.S. address for a pickup location. You will then be given a choice to have Expedia find cars within one, two, five, or 10 miles of that location. You can also indicate on the search page any discount code you have for corporate, contracted, special, or advertised rates and your choice of a car rental company. Click on the Additional Options link to specify additional special equipment you may need. On the search results pages, you will see results only for Expedia's six preferred vendors, unless you specify a particular car rental company. The default view on results pages is a list by preferred vendors, but you can also switch to a Car Size View or Car Price View. For each, a link will display photos, make/model, and passenger capacity for each car.

Orbitz—Car Rentals

www.orbitz.com

Orbitz offers car reservations from 16 companies and packages for flight–car and hotel–car combinations. Orbitz's Matrix Display at the top of results pages shows a nice compact comparison of price, vendor, and size options, with more detailed information shown under that. Click on the company name or car size links to see just the options for that category. Click on total cost to view details for that specific choice. By default, results are shown for Economy, Compact, Midsize, Standard, and Full-Size cars. Click on the View More Car Types link to view Premium, Luxury, Convertible, Van, and SUV choices, and then click on Select to see details for a particular choice.

Auto Europe

www.autoeurope.com

Contrary to the title, Auto Europe covers more than just Europe, serving as an agent for multiple car rental companies (e.g., Avis, Europcar). It provides car rentals for more than 4,000 locations in 47 countries and separate search interfaces for each of those countries, as well as an international site.

Yahoo! Travel—Car Rentals

travel.yahoo.com/?qs=c

Car rentals on Yahoo! Travel are powered by Travelocity, and you will find the search options and results pages are basically the same, with one significant exception: The main car search page has a link for More Car Search Options. Click on it to select car type and get checkboxes for 28 options, such as Premium SUV, Luxury SUV, Specialty Sports, Luxury Wagon, or Extra Special Car (that one is for a Jaguar XJ8 or similar car). You can select up to five types for your search. On that page, you can also specify up to five car rental discount memberships.

Bidding and Price Comparison Sites for Cars

Priceline—Car Rentals

tickets.priceline.com/rentalcars

Priceline offers rentals from five major car rental companies and, as with flights and hotels, you can either bid on a rental ("Name Your Own Price") or search for a car in the same way as with the sites just discussed. For details on Priceline bidding procedures, see Chapter 3.

Kayak—Car Rentals

www.kayak.com/s/index.jsp?tab=cars

With Kayak, you can do a comparison search on a variety of sites, covering approximately 10 car rental companies. On results pages, you can sort the results by Price, Agency, or Car/Class. A slider allows you to narrow or broaden results by price range, and checkboxes let you limit results by car class (type), rental agency, and options (air conditioning, automatic transmission, and unlimited mileage).

SideStep—Car Rentals

www.sidestep.com/car/search_result.do

SideStep's car search covers multiple travel sites, with options for about 10 car rental companies. Results can be sorted by estimated cost or agency. Click on Select to go directly to the car rental site.

Mobissimo—Car Rentals

www.mobissimo.com/search_cars.php

Mobissimo likewise covers about 10 car rental companies that it finds on the travel sites it searches. Results can be sorted by Provider (travel site), Rental Company, Car Type, or Price.

Car Rental Companies

Especially if you have a membership in a particular car rental company's frequent traveler program, you may want to go directly to the company's Web site. If you don't remember the company's URL, you can probably find it quickly by putting the company name into a search engine. If you would like a list of car rental companies in a particular country or state, try the following Yahoo! Directory site. If you want to find car rental locations in or near a specific city or town, try Google Local (local.google.com) or Yahoo! Local (local.yahoo.com; Figure 4.3), and enter the phrase "car rental" and the location (for example, *car rental Portland ME*). If you are looking for cars in the U.K., substitute "*rental*" with "*hire*" in your search.

Yahoo! Directory—Automotive > Rentals

dir.yahoo.com/Business_and_Economy/Shopping_and_Services/
Automotive/Rentals

The main listing in the automotive rental section of the Yahoo! Directory has more than 100 companies, including well-known car rental companies, plus a few for specialty, luxury, and exotic cars. However, many more are accessible by clicking on the Regional category near the top of the page. From that link, you can browse companies by country (68 countries), U.S. states, or region (Caribbean, Central America, and Europe), or by categories for Adaptive Technology Vehicles, Motorcycles, Recreational Vehicles, and Trucks. In some cases, you may find substantial savings by going to a "local" car rental agency in the country where you'll be traveling.

RVing: Recreational Vehicles

Recreational vehicles (RVs) are more typically referred to outside the U.S. as "caravans." They can be thought of as an interesting cross between camping and motels, between staying in your own comfortable

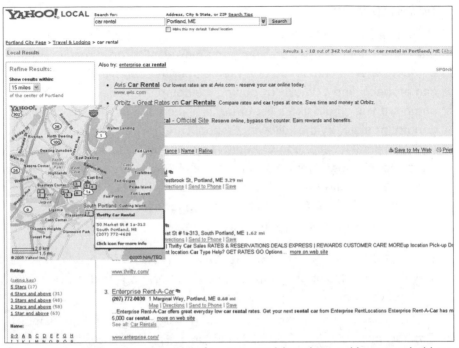

Figure 4.3   Yahoo! Local search for car rental locations, with cursor held over map and location icon

surroundings and getting out to new surroundings, and between comfort and "roughing it." But RVing is more than what is reflected in those dichotomies. It is a unique experience, not just a variety of camping and not just a compromise. It can be a "lifestyle." The following sites provide general information, advice, and how to find places to park overnight. As with many other topics covered in this book, what you find here is a small sampling of what the Web offers. For extensive collections of links on the topic, see the RV Links and RVNetLinx sites that follow. For more on the camping side of things, including additional campsite directories, see Chapter 7, "Adventure, Outdoor, and Educational Travel."

NewRVer.com

www.newrver.com

RV Travel

rvtravel.com

Both of these sites—NewRVer.com and RV Travel—are produced by RVbookstore.com. NewRVer.com should be your first stop, even if you don't fit into the "*new* RVer" category. It includes nearly 100 articles on buying, maintaining, using, and enjoying an RV, ranging from fairly general articles such as "New to RVing, Rent First!" to specific topics such as "How to Back Up a Trailer" and "The ABCs of Camping with Pets." RV Travel is similarly rich in articles, from the free newsletter by the same name, and those with a focus on "News, Information and Travel Advice for RVers."

RV Links

www.rv-links.com

RV Links bills itself as "The Best Collection of RVing and Camping Links on the Web," and that is very possibly true. Its collection of annotated links covers a very broad range of topics and issues involved in traveling and/or living in an RV, arranged in categories such as Boondocking (living in an RV "without using RV parks and utility hookups"), Budget RVing, Camping, Resorts, Clubs, Communications, Cooking on the Go, Destinations, Forums, Fulltiming, Pets, Publications, the RV Market (buying, selling, leasing), Safety, Maintenance, and more. If you really want to get into RVing (or already have) and want to find out what the Internet offers, check out this site.

RVNetLinx

www.rvnetlinx.com

This collection of RV-related links may be the other contender for the title of "best collection of RV links." The site contains annotated links for a variety of RV categories, even including a category for RV

Humor. The Campgrounds section contains links to RV campgrounds throughout the U.S. and Canada. Some sections are not actually links but actual pages of information, such as the very useful glossary that you will find under RV Terms and Types of RVs. For a list of places to rent RVs that goes beyond the U.S., Canada, and the U.K., check out the Rentals section of the site.

GORP

gorp.away.com/gorp/activity/rv.htm

The GORP site, which is discussed in more detail in Chapter 7, has a Driving/RVs section that merits mention here because of its useful articles on RVs and even moreso because of its collection of recommended drives and trips for RVers (and regular drivers as well).

Go Camping America

www.gocampingamerica.com

Go Camping America is the official site for the National Association of RV Parks and Campgrounds. Use the Find a Park link to find a list of RV parks and campgrounds by state, including a description, location, phone number, e-mail address, and facilities for each listing. The site also has travelers' tips, activities for kids, a message board, and a Links section with several RV-related sites.

Woodall's

www.woodalls.com

Woodall's, which is discussed in more detail in the Outdoor section of Chapter 7, is long recognized as a source of information for camping, RV tenters, and variations on those categories. Using the Advanced Search option on the main page, you can search its RV campgrounds database by state or province and city, 50 amps availability, accommodations for big rigs, allowance of pull-throughs, fishing, swimming, Internet access, laundry, year-round availability, and extended-stay campgrounds. Reservations are made by contacting the provider directly. To use the directories on the site, registration is required (it's free). The Woodall's site also provides articles, RV and camping links (under Links), and the very active Open Roads Forum, which contains more than 2 million postings. (Look for it under Communities.)

UK Camp Site

www.ukcampsite.co.uk

UK Camp Site contains a directory of campsites, a directory of caravan-related and camping-related companies, and a very active collection of message boards. The campsite directory (Camp Site Search), which is searchable by name, town, or county, includes thousands of sites, with the location, description, reviews, map, link to its site, and an e-mail "enquiry" form for each one. You will need to sign up for some information, but registration is free. The directory also has an Overseas Campsites link for campsite listings in the Channel Islands, France, Germany, Northern Ireland, Ireland, Spain, and a small collection for other countries.

The Caravan Club

www.caravanclub.co.uk

The Caravan Club requires a paid membership to access the complete site, but if you are caravanning in the U.K., you may want to seriously consider signing up, not just for the information found on the site, but because of the access to "private" caravan parks and other benefits. Though the Caravan Club may or may not agree with the comparison, Americans might think of this as an AAA for U.K. caravanners. The directory of Caravan Sites and Parks found on this site is available without a membership.

ACSI Eurocampings

www.eurocampings.co.uk

ACSI Eurocampings provides information for more than 8,000 campsites throughout Europe.

Road Trip Tools

The sites just discussed are tools for the traveler, providing information, advice, and descriptions for destinations, itineraries, and the like. There are also a number of sites that offer help with a variety of other tasks and provide information to get you where you want to go.

Road Maps

Although a number of sites offer road maps and driving directions, the sophistication of these has been increasing rapidly, with sites offering a lot more than just maps and directions. Though you will probably want to have a regular road map with you, the maps you can get from the Web include not only the map, but also your itinerary and driving directions, plus driving distances and time, and even estimated travel cost. All the map sites that follow provide the following features:

- Maps of specific locations you select
- Driving directions with step-by-step directions and exact distances for each step
- Capability of zooming in and out and moving the viewable area of the map to the North, South, East, or West
- A link for a printable version of the map

Most sites allow you to save addresses you enter so you can use them again without retyping, and almost all provide a link that will send the map or directions by e-mail. Beyond those common offerings, choices vary tremendously from one map site to another. Some will let you add additional points of interest to the map (services, attractions, etc.), reverse directions (for returning home), chart a route that avoids toll roads, specify multiple destinations, send maps and directions to a cell phone or PDA, display current traffic problems, and so on.

Which map site(s) you choose to use will probably depend on what countries they cover and what features appeal to you. If continental Europe is your destination, your options include MapQuest, MapBlast, Yahoo! (U.K. & Ireland version), Via Michelin, and Maporama. If you are headed to Eastern Europe or the Middle East, then Via Michelin, Maporama, and Yahoo! (U.K. & Ireland version) will be the best. If you are headed to a fairly small country, you may want to start with Maporama or the U.K. version of Yahoo! since these two sites include driving directions for 62 and 49 countries, respectively.

MapQuest

www.mapquest.com

MapQuest provides driving directions for the U.S., Canada, and 12 European countries. It also has road maps for 217 other countries, but the amount of detail for those may be somewhat limited. MapQuest also provides a link to request a map by latitude and longitude.

When you request driving directions, as with the other map sites, individual steps of the itinerary will be displayed. For each step, there is a Map link which, when clicked, will show a more detailed map for that particular step. A Reverse Route link will produce driving directions for your return trip. Click on the Avoid Highways link on the directions page to stay off highways. Maps and driving directions can be forwarded to an e-mail address or PDA, and driving directions can also be sent to cell phones. You can also find types of businesses (e.g., French Restaurants) at or near a particular U.S. location by using the search box on the Maps page.

MSN Live Search—Maps

maps.live.com

The Maps section of MSN's Live.com utilizes MSN Virtual Earth to provide driving directions and draggable maps of North America, Australia, most of Europe, and some of Asia. For some locations, traffic situations are shown on the map. Maps, but not driving directions, are available for additional countries. For directions, you can specify that your route be the shortest time or the shortest distance, get reverse directions, and send results by e-mail or to a mobile device.

Google Maps

maps.google.com

Google Maps provides maps and driving directions for the U.S., the U.K., Canada, China, France, Germany, Italy, Netherlands, and Spain. As a part of the Google Local service, it also provides the capability of adding yellow-pages-type data to the maps it produces. One of the ways both Google and Yahoo! stand out from some other maps services is that you can use your mouse to drag the map to a new position in any direction (instead of clicking on a direction and having the page refreshed, as with other maps sites). To get a map, you can either use dragging and the "zoom" bar on the map to focus on your location, or you can enter the name of the place in the search box. You can enter a city and country (*Edinburgh Scotland*), a specific address (*1600 Pennsylvania Avenue Washington DC*), or even a specific place or business (*Bloomingdales New York NY*).

For driving directions, click on the Get Directions link and fill in the boxes. On the results page, if you click on any of the itinerary steps, a "bubble" will open on the map showing detail for that step (Figure 4.4). In the corner of the map, you will also notice links for Satellite and Hybrid views. Click on Satellite, and the map will be replaced with an actual satellite image with the route superimposed. Click on the Hybrid link to add place names, streets, street names, route numbers, and landmarks to the image. Taking it one step further, if you need to find a camera shop, click on the Find Businesses link next to the search box, and a box will appear next to the location box. Then, enter *cameras* in that box, click Search, and locations of camera stores will be added to the map. Click on the location "balloons" for details.

Yahoo! Maps
maps.yahoo.com

Yahoo!'s main U.S. site has driving directions for only the U.S. and Canada. However, if you go to any of Yahoo!'s international sites, such as the UK & Ireland site (uk.yahoo.com), you will find maps and driving directions for many other countries. The UK & Ireland site, for example, includes maps for 49 countries. (Links to Yahoo!'s international sites are found near the bottom of Yahoo!'s main page.)

On Yahoo!'s main (U.S.) site (as with Google), the maps are draggable, making it easy to move the map in various directions. For driving directions, Yahoo! saves locations you have previously entered, and you can enter multiple stops. (As soon as you have entered your first destination, Yahoo! provides another box for the next destination.) Links are also available for reverse or for round-trip directions. On the directions results pages, hold the cursor over any step to see that leg of the trip highlighted on the map. Click on a step to see a small map with detail for that step. With the Find on the Map option located beneath the directions, you can have Yahoo! show Community Services (ATMs, banks, gas stations, etc.), Entertainment & Shopping (amusement parks, malls, golf courses, etc.), Restaurants & Bars

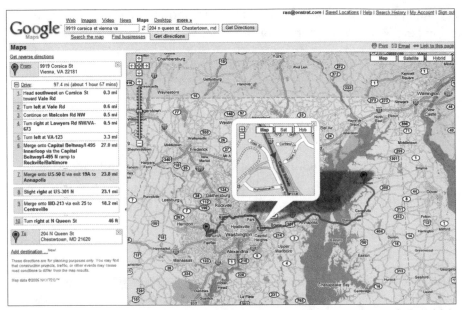

Figure 4.4   Google Map display with bubble showing one step of the driving
directions

(Chinese, seafood, etc.), and Travel & Transit (airports, hotels, parking, etc.). Choose what you want to see by using either the search box or the categories, and the matching locations will be identified on the map by numbered callouts. Click on each one for details. Current traffic reports are also shown on the map, and you can send maps to your mobile phone or e-mail them. Driving directions are available on the main Yahoo! Web site, as well as on mobile phones at mobile. yahoo.com/dd.

Yahoo! Maps—UK & Ireland
maps.yahoo.net

From Yahoo!'s U.K. site, you can get maps and driving directions for 49 countries. For maps, hold your cursor over a place for more information about that place. A Proximity box beneath a map allows you to add a variety of services and attractions (garages, parking, tourist information, hospitals, petrol stations, churches, etc.) on maps (maps for specific places, not the driving directions maps). Maps can be manipulated using the tool icons shown on the map (Figure 4.5). Using those icons, you can go back and forth to previous map views, zoom in and out, turn dragging on or off, and even maximize your screen view. You can also take advantage of another feature not available on many other map services: You can click the Measure tool icon, click on successive points on the map, and then get measurements between the points you selected. Settings options shown beneath driving directions maps let you choose the shortest or fastest route, compact or detailed descriptions for the steps of the itinerary, display of miles or kilometers, degree of roadway use you prefer (avoid, less, normal, more), and modes of transportation to avoid (toll roads, roadways, ferries, and train ferries).

Rand McNally

www.randmcnally.com

The Rand McNally site offers maps and driving directions for only the U.S. and Canada. When selecting maps or routes, the site saves recently used addresses, and in addition to the usual origin and destination information, the Advanced Options allow you to view concise (fewer) steps or standard (more) step detail, fastest or shortest route, and distances in miles or kilometers. On directions pages, you will see an overview map of your entire trip, steps for the route, and a map of the destination by default. On the directions search page, there are options to view just the text for the directions or a version that shows the overview map, the steps, the destination map, and detailed maps for each step. A checkbox option on the search pages will let you see cumulative mileage with each step. The zoomable and movable (by

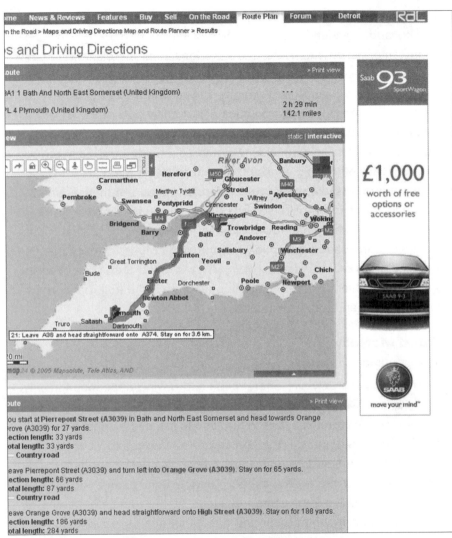

Figure 4.5   Driving directions at Yahoo! Maps—UK & Ireland

compass direction) version of the map is not immediately shown on the results page. Instead, you must click a link below the map to see the "adjustable version." The site provides a number of useful extras, especially if you register (it's free). You can save your trip plans and driving directions and return later to edit them if you want. The TripMaker Planning Tool also allows you to include stops along the way for activities and places to stay. With Rand McNally's Things to Do option, you can specify a location, how far you are willing to drive from that location (5, 10, 25 miles), and the kind of activity you are interested in (Fun & Games, Outdoor Adventures, Arts & Culture, History & Heritage, Sports & Recreation, Local Highlights), and the site will compile a detailed list of possibilities. The Mileage Calculator even charts mileage between two locations without driving directions. Additional services, such as road construction reports, are available for a subscription fee.

ViaMichelin
www.viamichelin.com

ViaMichelin provides maps and driving directions for 43 countries. When you request driving directions, click on Options, then on the Customize Your Route link to add stopovers to your route. You can also choose either the route recommended by Michelin, the quickest route, the shortest route, a preferred motorway, or a toll-free highway, and you can have distances shown in either kilometers or miles. You can even have ViaMichelin estimate the cost of your trip. (You specify approximate fuel consumption and fuel price.) If you enter a departure date, the site will even calculate the estimated time of any scheduled roadwork. The ViaMichelin site also provides weather and traffic reports (the latter only for Great Britain). The site is available in English, French, Spanish, Italian, Dutch, and German. By registering (it's free), you can save maps, itineraries, addresses, and information on hotels, restaurants, and tourist attractions. For the latter three items, the free registration also provides access to content from the long-established and highly regarded Michelin Guides. Once you have signed up, you can easily search for tourist attractions listed in *The Michelin Green Guide*. Itineraries and maps can be saved and sent by e-mail.

Maporama
maporama.com

Maporama supplies driving directions and maps for a greater number of countries than any of the other sites discussed here, with driving directions for 62 countries and small maps for 217 countries. Once you have identified the map or route you want, the results pages enable you to add additional stops and features and then have the itinerary recalculated (Figure 4.6). You can display maps in three sizes, customize your itinerary by choosing units in either miles or kilometers, select the fastest or shortest route, specify your driving pace (slow, moderate, or fast), and choose whether to take toll roads. Click on the "with intersections" checkbox if you would like small maps displayed for each intersection of roads in your itinerary. You can also have the Maporama interface appear in your choice of 26 languages. The My Maporama feature enables you to save your maps and itineraries. For itineraries and maps of France, you can also have maps display real-time traffic information. On the main page, instant maps are available for 73 airports. Maporama can also be accessed from your mobile phone (wap.maporama.com) or PDA, and maps and itineraries can be downloaded to your PDA.

Other Road Trip Tools

The following tools will help you find the cheapest gas, drive safely, plan short day trips, and keep the kids so occupied with games and activities in the car that they'll be saying, "Darn, we're almost there."

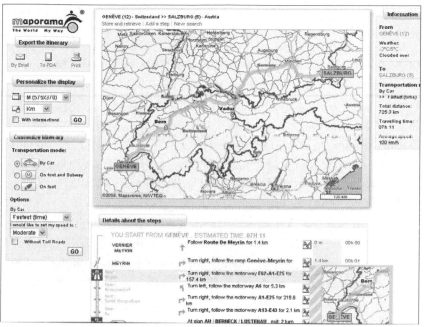

Figure 4.6   Maporama results page

AAA Fuel Price Finder

aaa.opisnet.com

The AAA Fuel Price Finder compares gas prices at 85,000 gas stations in the U.S. Look for the Fuel Finder link under the Safety & News tab on the AAA main page. Search by state and city or ZIP code, and specify stations within a three-, five-, or 10-mile radius.

GasBuddy.com

www.gasbuddy.com

GasBuddy.com is a combination of more than 170 GasBuddy gas information sites in the U.S. and Canada. To view your locality, either click on the map or search for a specific ZIP code. Once you're on the

GasBuddy sites for your state or province, you can search by brand and location.

U.S. Department of State—Road Safety Overseas
travel.state.gov/travel/tips/safety/safety_1179.html

This site provides basic information of interest to people driving outside the U.S., including information on safety, security, international driving permits, and general tips.

Hotels.com—Road Trips
www.hotels.com/roadtrip

If you are looking for some ideas for a fairly short road trip, this section of Hotels.com is a great place to find interesting destinations based on the length of time you are willing to drive, the compass direction, or a combination of the two. Simply enter your ZIP code, choose the time (one to six hours), and/or the direction, and Hotels.com will compile suggested destinations, along with a description of each (from Rough Guides) and a form to use to search for hotel reservations.

MomsMinivan.com
www.momsminivan.com/index.html

MomsMinivan.com features "101 Car Travel Games & Road Trip Ideas for Kids." The game descriptions are clearly written with useful details, as well as illustrations and, in some cases, "printables," such as car bingo cards.

National Traffic and Road Closure Information
www.fhwa.dot.gov/trafficinfo

The National Traffic and Road Closure Information site from the Federal Highway Administration doesn't actually contain traffic or road closure information, but it does contain great collections of links for information on weather, road, and traffic conditions. You will find collections of links on these topics for each state and on a national level.

Ferries

Yes, this section on ferries could easily have been included in Chapter 5, "Cruises: Ships, Barges, and Boats." But it is in this chapter because ferries serve a different purpose from the vessels discussed in the cruise chapter and because ferries are typically part of a longer "overland" trip. Unlike cruises, ferries are primarily for getting from one point to another, and the ferry you take will probably depend on where you are headed. (However, you really don't have to be going anywhere—ferries can also make a great day trip.)

Maps (either printed or from the map sites just discussed) will often lead you to the name of the ferry or water taxi you need and the departure and arrival ports. A simple search engine search on the names of the ports or countries and the term "ferry" may be a good start (e.g., *England Ireland ferry*), and there is a good chance that search will lead to a site that provides timetables and other information, including the ability to make reservations and purchase tickets. The following sites offer another way to get that information, or if you just want to have the experience of a ferry trip, they can help you decide on a ferry crossing the Mersey, to Staten Island, the Star Ferry, or elsewhere. Hundreds (or maybe thousands) of sites provide information on ferry and water taxi routes. The small sampling that follows includes two sites that cover ferry information for many countries. The first one, along with others in the section, offers details on two of the world's busiest ferry localities (the English Channel and the Northwest U.S.–British Columbia area), and the last three sites discuss smaller ferry localities.

Dan Youra—Ferry Guide
www.youra.com

Though the main focus of the Youra Ferry Guide centers on Washington State and British Columbia, it is also a guide for ferries worldwide, or at least for ferries in more than 25 countries. The site contains more than 60 links to ferry company sites in Europe and Asia and more than 75 sites in North and South America and the Caribbean. Sites are listed by country and by state in the U.S.

AFerry.to
www.aferry.to

This site is an online ferry travel agency through which you can find timetables and fares (and purchase tickets) for more than 160 ferry routes worldwide. The site also has maps and driving directions for more than 200 ferry ports.

Brittany Ferries
www.brittany-ferries.co.uk

Brittany Ferries, according to its site, was formed in 1972 "largely in order to transport cauliflowers and artichokes from Roscoff to Plymouth." But it now has become "the leading maritime carrier on the Western and Central Channel." The site provides not just routes, timetables, and bookings but also accommodations and holiday packages for France and Spain.

Ferrybooker.com
www.ferrybooker.com

Unlike the Brittany Ferries site, which is a site for a specific ferry line, Ferrybooker.com is an example of a travel agency site specializing in ferry travel and providing bookings for multiple lines. In addition to ferries, the site covers bookings for the Eurotunnel, hotels, and cars. In the site's Planning section, you will find guides to ports and regions served by the ferries (and the Eurotunnel) and brief but useful advice on driving abroad.

UKIreland-Fastlinks

www.ukireland-fastlinks.com

The UKIreland-Fastlinks site is a quasi-governmental site that provides timetables, fares, and booking for 17 ferry routes between the U.K. and Ireland. On the site, you will also find information on each of the ports and how to get to them by car, bus, or rail.

NY Waterway

www.nywaterway.com

NY Waterway offers information on the variety of ferry services available to and from Manhattan, including commuter ferry and bus services, sightseeing cruises, ferry and bus charters, and specialized ferry cruises, ranging from baseball to Broadway cruises.

NCDOT Ferry Division

www.ncferry.org

For a ferry ambiance that is very different from the NY Waterway services, head to North Carolina. The NCDOT Ferry Division site comes from the North Carolina Department of Transportation and supplies information on eight ferry routes in the state.

Ferryboats in Istanbul, Turkey

www.turkeytravelplanner.com/WhereToGo/Istanbul/Transport/
IstanbulFerry.html

This site is included here not just for geographic diversity but as an example of a useful ferry resource that can be found fairly deep within a larger travel site, in this case, Turkey Travel Planner (www.turkeytravelplanner.com). Sites like this one for specific ferry locations can usually be found easily with a search engine (search for *Istanbul ferries*).

Discussion Groups and Forums for Train, Car, and Ferry Travel

All the general discussion groups covered in Chapter 2 provide useful information, advice, and commentary on train, car, and ferry travel. The following sites include examples a bit more focused on traveler discussions of these topics. Each is a part of a site that was discussed earlier in this chapter.

On Track On Line Forums

www.on-track-on-line.com/forums

The On Track On Line forums cover rail travel in the U.S., Canada, Europe, and Asia. The forums are active, with more than 35,000 posts. Although you can read messages and search without registering, you must register (it's free) to post messages (and take advantage of online chat, polls, private messages, etc.).

RoadTrip America—The Great American RoadTrip Forum

www.roadtripamerica.com/forum

As indicated by the title, most messages on this site are about U.S. road trips. You can search and read messages without registering, but (free) registration is required to post messages. Messages are categorized into 12 topics, each with multiple threads, within which you will find advice and information on the RV lifestyle, scenic drives, camping, vehicle preparation, cooking on the road, and book reviews. The forum is active, with more than 25,000 posted messages. You can communicate with the group and send private messages to other forum members.

Amtrak Unlimited Forums

forums.amtraktrains.com

Amtrak Unlimited Forums contain more than 4,000 topics and more than 60,000 messages under the categories of Amtrak Rail Discussion, Commuter Rail Discussion, Model Railroading and Computer Games, Travelogues/Trip Reports, and Miscellaneous Rail Discussions.

Woodall's—Open Roads Forum

www.woodalls.com/cforum

The Open Roads Forum on the Woodall's site is a very active online community for RVers, with nearly 3 million posts in the following categories: Recreational Vehicles, Camping, General Forums, Technical Resources, Locations, and Other Discussions.

UK Camp Site—Information Forums

www.ukcampsite.co.uk/chatter

This forum covers both caravanning and camping, primarily in the U.K., but with some content related to those activities elsewhere. It is very active, with more than 1.5 million posts on more than 75,000 topics in 12 main categories. You can browse without registering, but (free) registration is necessary to search for messages, read campsite reviews, and access other benefits.

RV Travel—Forum

forum.rvtravel.com

RV Travel has 34 message boards in five main categories: Forum News, RV Discussion, On the Road, and Rigs. For some, but not all, of the boards, registration is required to post messages. It is an active forum, with more than 9,000 posts.

Cruises: Ships, Barges, and Boats

In case you haven't noticed, cruises have become one of the most popular forms of vacation travel in the past few years. If you talk to any of your friends, chances are they will readily regale you with their cruise stories. If you haven't taken a cruise and don't have your own tales to tell, you don't have to feel left out. The Web can quickly remedy that situation. As with other forms of travel, the Web has resources to help you find the cruise that suits you, purchase tickets at the best price, and get advice and information to make the best of your cruise experience. For reservations, you will find cruise options on the big reservation sites (Travelocity, Orbitz, etc.) and find many reservation sites that specialize in cruises and even specialize in particular kinds of cruises. You will also find a number of sites that provide advice on cruising, and when you get back, you can add your own advice and stories. (Be sure to talk about the food.)

This chapter will help you identify the resources that will be of help in planning and purchasing your cruise. It will provide suggestions on how to best take advantage of the sites and will acquaint you with the range of sites that cover the many available cruise options (cruises on the big cruise ships, river and barge cruises, sailing ship cruises, and others). The chapter will look at the kinds of cruises on which you can spend a lot of time, if you wish, "just relaxing" and letting the ship's crew do the work for you. Though they can be great vacations, we won't get into either renting boats or "cruising," which refers to buying your own boat and living and traveling on it for extended periods of time. As they say, that's a whole other story.

The Cruise Experience: Kinds of Cruises

Cruises are, of course, not for everyone, and it is not my purpose to evangelize the unconverted and get everyone "on-board." If you have never taken a cruise and have decided that the last thing you would ever want to do for a vacation is go on a cruise, you can certainly skip to the next chapter. However, since travelers tend to be open-minded, you might first want to consider two facts: (1) Large numbers of people who said that they would never want to take a cruise have done so anyway and come back anxious to take their next cruise, and (2) all cruises are certainly not the same. A barge on the Rhone has appeal to people who couldn't care less about five days in the Caribbean.

In general, there are a half-dozen or so main categories of cruises, each with their own unique experiences (and myriad sites for each category). These may include standard cruises on the big cruise lines, cruises on smaller and mid-size ships, cruises on sailing ships, river and barge cruises, and day cruises.

As mentioned before, ferries could have logically been included here in this chapter, but because ferries most typically are taken by people who are driving, the topic is instead included in Chapter 4, "Train, Car, and Ferry Travel." Take a look at that chapter for details about routes, reservations, and other information on ferries.

After looking at the following sites to get cruise advice and then examining cruise reservation options available on the big reservation sites, we'll take a look at some specialized sites for cruise reservations and for information on each of the more common categories of cruise types.

Cruise Guides and Advice

CruiseMates: The Complete Online Cruise Guide and Community

www.cruisemates.com

As the site says, "CruiseMates is an independently owned and editorially unbiased 'Internet Cruise Magazine and Cruise Information Guidebook' offering accurate and up-to-the-minute cruise information and providing a place for cruise enthusiasts to meet." That description is modest compared to what you will actually find here. Beginning cruisers and old hands will find more than enough to make this site their "first port of call" when planning a cruise. The site is arranged in six main categories: News & Features, Ship Reviews, Cruise Shopping, Message Boards, Interactive Features, and About Us (Figure 5.1).

In the News & Features section, you will find news about the cruise world and access to hundreds of magazine-type articles written by the CruiseMates staff. Cruise News covers everything from ship refurbishments to new cuisines. Ship Features does not contain details about the features aboard ships but rather feature articles on topics ranging from "A Transatlantic Crossing" to "Best of the Bathrooms." Most feature articles are about individual cruise lines or individual ships. In the News section, look for the More Information pull-down menu. In addition to Bargains, a news archive, and a Search Cruisemates site search, the menu offers information on CruiseMates Cruises, which are group rate deals selected by CruiseMates and led by a CruiseMates staff member. For the very cautious, the More Information menu also links to Vessel Sanitation reports on more than 150 ships from the U.S. Centers for Disease Control. (Check to see if the kitchen's sanitizing rinse temperature has acceptable ratings.) Under the News & Features menu (or under the Cruise Guide links on the left of the page), you will find sections for information and advice

Figure 5.1   CruiseMates main page

for the following categories: First-Time Cruisers, Single Cruising, Family Cruising, Kids & Teens, Gay/Lesbian Cruisers, Consumer Affairs, Ship Articles, Ship Reviews, Before You Go, Onboard the Ship, Ports of Call, Best of Cruising, and Humor & Opinions. The first five sections provide articles and advice, as well as message boards that focus on a particular topic.

Under the Ship Reviews section, you will find detailed reviews and descriptions of both cruise lines and individual ships written by the CruiseMates staff. You can also read travelers' reviews, submit your own reviews, and participate in an ongoing poll. The Ship Itineraries link in this section shows which cruise lines and which ships are headed for which destinations. You can browse by either cruise line, destination region, or which cruises sail from which ports. The Theme Cruises link is likewise an easy-to-use compendium of upcoming cruises that cater to passengers with special interests. Theme cruises will be discussed later in this chapter, but this portion of the CruiseMates site is an excellent place to begin to grasp the amazing variety of special programs offered by cruise lines, from acupuncture to film to wine.

There is lot more on this site. Browse through the menus for message boards, cruise bargains, chat, user-contributed photos, cruise trivia, and more. Don't miss the Cruise Links section, where you will find links to cruise line sites and cruise-related sites. Finally, consider signing up for the free CruiseMates Newsletter.

About.com—Cruises
cruises.about.com

The Cruise section of About.com is another good place to get background information, advice about cruises, articles, news, and reviews. The main part of the page features articles, including cruise news, articles on cruise destinations, and reviews of specific cruises, cruise ships, and cruise lines. A menu on the left-hand side of the page categorizes the site's other resources: Essentials, Cruise Offers, Topics, Buyer's Guide, and Tools.

In the Essentials category, you will find articles on basics such as planning your first cruise, packing, and choosing destinations. The Cruise Offers category has links to sites for travel agents or cruise lines with special offers.

The Topics category is perhaps the richest of the lot, with subsections for cruise lines, destinations, photos, planning, reviews, and Web cams. There is also a cruise glossary and a subsection for news and press releases from cruise lines and other sources. A Getting There subsection offers information on ports of departure, airports, and hotels. Other subsections of Articles & Resources lead to articles on cruise themes, activities, travel gear, and more. The Cruise Lines subsection has more than 250 articles conveniently arranged by the type of cruise line (Large Ship Cruise Lines, Mid-Sized Ship Cruise Lines, Small Ship Cruise Lines, Sailing Ships, River Ships and Barges, Freighter Cruises, Adventure Cruise Lines, Yacht Charters, and Classic Cruise Ships).

About.com also offers a free weekly e-mail newsletter to keep you up-to-date on cruise news and ideas.

CruisePage.com
www.cruiseserver.net/travelpage/cruiselines

CruisePage.com, which is a part of the TravelPage.com site, provides information on cruise itineraries (11,000 of them), reviews of ships, cruise news, photos, and forums. The main page has a useful list of cruise lines categorized by style—Deluxe, Premium, Mass Market, Budget, River, Specialty, and, for historical purposes, Former Cruise Lines and Classic Liners and Cruise Ships. (The latter even includes a page for the *Titanic*. If you are still a bit unsure about cruising, skip that page.) Click on a cruise line for the contact information page, the Web site for the line, and a list of its ships. Then click on a ship for a detailed description and review of the vessel. This site is definitely one of the best on the Web for reviews of ships. The reviews, which are written by CruisePage staff, are extensive, frank, and well written.

Some other features CruisePage.com offers are:

- Book a Cruise – Behind CruisePage.com is a travel agency to help you (by e-mail and by phone) select and book a cruise. The Cruise Search portion lets you find cruises by date, price, length, cruise line, and destination.

- Photo Gallery – There are lots of places on the Web (especially cruise line sites) where you can find pictures of ships, cabins, etc., but on this site you can view hundreds of photo albums created by travelers. You can browse the albums by category, or you can search by keyword for a place, ship, or other features. Seeing what catches other people's eyes can nicely supplement official photos of ships and their facilities.

- Cruise Talk – CruisePage's forum is large and active, with more than 150,000 postings arranged in 12 categories. For more about this forum, see the Discussion Groups section at the end of this chapter.

- Cruise News – This section furnishes news articles about what is happening on particular cruise lines, ships, and cruises, and in cruising in general.

In addition to those sections, you will find a variety of additional links under the Reviews, Community, Industry, and other menu sections on the left of the CruisePage.com page. Some links you may particularly find of interest are Port Information, Inspections Scores (those CDC reports), Shipyards, Ship Cams, Special Needs, Potpourri, and Freighter Travel. Use the Ship Cams section to check out the Webcams for your cruise ship, and then arrange to be there at a particular time so you can wave to friends or family back home. (Yes, maybe a bit hokey, but that's the way some of us happily are.)

CruiseDiva.com
cruisediva.com

Created by travel writer and "cruise diva" Linda Coffman, this site provides articles and practical advice on a range of topics, including packing, planning, ports, ships, cruise lines, cruise news, and more. Check out the Hot Tips Archive for useful advice on odds and ends.

World Cruise Guide (WCG)
www.cruise.travel-guides.com

The title may be a bit overstated for what you will find here, since the site is more of a city guide, but the site is useful for getting a quick overview of what to see, buy, and eat in the world's most popular ports of call.

Cruise Reservations

There are literally thousands of travel agencies on the Web that can help you choose and book a cruise. Since it is obviously impossible, with not even desirable, to cover all of them here, most of this chapter will be devoted to the biggest, best-known sites for booking cruises, and examples of various kinds of other sites where you can book cruises—sites from cruise lines themselves and sites that cater to specialty cruises. In general, plan on doing quite a bit of browsing on the Web. In addition to visiting the sites discussed here, try fairly general searches such as *Mediterranean cruises* to uncover some of the hundreds of excellent mid-size and smaller travel agencies.

Cruise reservation sites (online travel agencies) differ in the kinds of options they provide for browsing through cruise information and for searching for cruises that match your particular needs, inclinations, and pursuits, or even eccentricities. (If you don't have any of the latter, consider getting some. It will make life more fun, particularly if you find some that will annoy your children.)

Most cruise reservation sites will provide a search by combinations of destination, departure date, and length of cruise. Depending on the site, you may also be able to specify departure port, price, cruise line, ship, and other factors. Which factors are searchable may help you decide which reservation site to use. For example, you can save the cost of airfare by leaving from a port near your home, which means that being able to quickly identify the nearest port may be very important in your search.

For all reservation sites, look for statements about what is and is not included. Prices shown may or may not include booking fees, taxes, port fees, and other government fees. Prices stated are usually per person, double occupancy, and you will almost undoubtedly have to pay an additional fee for single occupancy.

Cruise Reservations on the Big Travel Agency Sites

When using one of the big reservation sites (Travelocity, Expedia, or Orbitz), be aware that you are not searching all cruise lines—a lot of them, but not all. These sites may have elements in common, but each also has unique features and deals. On their main pages, all provide featured deals different from those you will find on the other sites. Each site has advanced search features and combinations of search features that differ from the others' (Table 5.1). All the sites also provide reviews, some of which are written by travel critics and some by fellow travelers. (Here, as elsewhere, when reading travelers' reviews, keep in mind that there are people who will never be pleased and

Table 5.1   Cruise Search Criteria Available in Expedia, Orbitz, and Travelocity

	Expedia	Orbitz	Travelocity
Destination	✓	✓	✓
Departure Date	✓	✓	✓
Length of Cruise	✓	✓	✓
Cruise Line	✓	✓	✓
Departure Port	✓		✓
Ports of Call		✓	
Price		✓	✓
Ship		✓	✓
Senior Rates	✓	✓	
Residency	✓	✓	
Quality Rating	✓		

whose only goal in life seems to be to find fault.) All these reservation sites have toll-free numbers to put you in touch with actual travel agents who will be glad to help you.

Because of the differences in which cruise lines are covered, special deals, search options, and additional information provided, in most cases it will be worthwhile to try your search on more than one travel agency site. Together, these sites cover about 20 major cruise lines, so, particularly if you are looking for smaller, specialty, or non-Western cruises, do not rely totally on the following three big travel agency sites.

For all of these sites, the pages that mention specific cruises or specific ships will offer descriptions of the vessels and lots of photos. Typically, there will be links that provide details on public areas, state-rooms, deck plans, and itineraries. Remember the cliché about the value of pictures. Doing some window-shopping using the photos can really give you a good idea of what to expect on board.

Travelocity—Cruises
travelocity.com/cruises

Searching for Cruises on Travelocity

Travelocity provides a search of 11 cruise lines. In addition to the common search options, when searching for cruises on Travelocity, on the main page you can search by ship, and by clicking the More Search Options link on the main cruises page, you can also specify a desired price range and departure port. You will also notice on the main page that for departure port you can have Travelocity "Also search nearby ports." For departure dates, you can specify a month, particular day, or range of dates. (Travelocity also powers the cruise search on the Frommers.com site, so if you search for cruises there, the results will be essentially the same as on Travelocity.)

Search Results from Travelocity

Results pages will give you a list of matching cruise options and radio buttons that allow you to sort results by price, special offers, ship rating, length, and cruise line (Figure 5.2). A checkbox next to each cruise lets you compare up to four cruises shown in the results. Click on the cruises of interest, and then click the "Compare Now" link. The result will be an excellent chart where you can easily compare such things as vacation length, ports of call, prices, and departure dates. For each result, click on "More Information" for details about that cruise. The Continue link will move you in the direction of selecting and booking that particular cruise.

If you searched by cruise line on the main page, you will be shown a sailing calendar that nicely lays out sailings by destination and month.

Other Cruise Options from Travelocity

On almost all Travelocity cruise pages, you will find a menu for Cruise Tools, which provide an entirely different level of useful cruise information, including the following:

Figure 5.2   Travelocity cruise search results page

- Cruise FAQs – This link takes you to answers for nearly 400 frequently asked Travelocity questions. Use the pull-down menu at the top of the page to narrow the list to search 60 FAQs related to cruises. First-time cruisers, especially, will find the time spent here very worthwhile. The answers include information on what to wear, tipping, luggage, and much more, even links to driving directions to the cruise terminal.
- Cruise Finder – Links to the Advanced Search page.
- Customer Service – Provides general Travelocity support (not cruise specific).
- Featured Articles – Links to about a dozen articles related to cruising
- First-Time Cruisers – Links to more articles and FAQs.
- Gay/Lesbian Travel – Provides information about gay/lesbian-oriented deals and destinations.
- Group Online Form – Request information on travel for a group requiring eight or more staterooms.
- Luxury Cruising – Find deals for the well-heeled, or those who aren't but want to splurge.
- Sail from U.S. Ports – Identify sailings from a specific U.S. port.
- Traveler Reviews – Find out what others have said.

Another great feature is the Ship Finder link, found near the top of Travelocity cruise pages. It provides a very handy chart that compares ratings, service entry dates, number of specialty restaurants, availability of Internet cafés, and movie theaters for each ship from the 13 lines Travelocity covers. The chart also includes links to deck plans for each ship.

Expedia—Cruises
www.expedia.com/daily/cruise

Searching for Cruises on Expedia

A cruise search on Expedia covers nine cruise lines (compared to 11 for Travelocity and 86 for Orbitz). On the main cruise search page, you will find a selection of cruise options by destination, month of departure, and cruise line. A checkbox also lets you check for any discounts based on state of residency (U.S.), as a senior (55 or older), and as a previous cruiser. Click on Additional Options to qualify your search further by length, star rating, and departure port. Toward the bottom of the main page is a section labeled "Cruise Line Deals," which contains links to ads for cruises on a few additional cruise lines that are not included in an Expedia cruise search.

Search Results from Expedia

On the search results pages, you will find radio buttons that allow you to sort results by price, cruise length, or cruise line (Figure 5.3). The default sort is by Expedia Picks, which include special promotions such as shipboard credits (basically coupons that can be applied to money you spend on board) or upgrades.

Click on either the name of the cruise on a results page, for example, "7-night Caribbean-Western (Galveston roundtrip)," or the picture of the ship to get further details, including the itinerary, availability, and descriptions of ports of call. On those pages, you will also find links to descriptions of Cabins, Decks, and Amenities, as well as Reviews and Photos.

Other Cruise Options from Expedia

The All About Cruising menu on the Expedia pages contain links to the following:

Figure 5.3   Expedia cruise search results page

- Why Cruise? – A brief overview of what cruising has to offer
- Cruise Line Reviews – Profiles of cruise lines, including links to profiles of each line's ships and the sailing calendar for each
- Cruise Calendar – Sailing calendars for 18 cruise lines
- Ship Info and Reviews – Reviews for more than 180 ships
- Ports-of-Call – How to get around and what to see and do in 180 ports worldwide
- Cruise Protection Plan – Information on how you are protected when you purchase a cruise through Expedia

Expedia also offers a free newsletter to alert you to special cruise offers, including last-minute deals.

Orbitz—Cruises
cruises.orbitz.com

Searching for Cruises on Orbitz

With Orbitz, you can search for cruises across 86 cruise lines. On its main page, you will find options for Destination, Cruise Line, Ship, Departure Port, Departure (month and year), and Cruise Length. Another window lets you identify whether any travelers are 55 or older. (Orbitz can arrange special discounts for senior travelers.) A Sort By menu allows you to sort your results by price, online booking, cruise line, destination, trip length, and other criteria (Figure 5.4).

Search Results from Orbitz

Search results can be sorted by Cruise Line, Rating, Price, Length, or Date. Select cruises of interest, then click on "View and compare selected." A table will appear where you can easily compare pictures of the ships, itineraries, price, ratings, and special promotions.

Other Cruise Options on Orbitz

As well as searching for cruises on the Orbitz main cruise page, you can use the Browse All Cruise Deals link (or similar), which offers easy browsing by destination, cruise line, or interest. The latter presents lists by U.S. ports, cruises for singles, couples, and families, premium cruises, exotic destinations, and luxury cruises. Orbitz cruise pages also have an "Information on cruising" menu for additional information in the following categories:

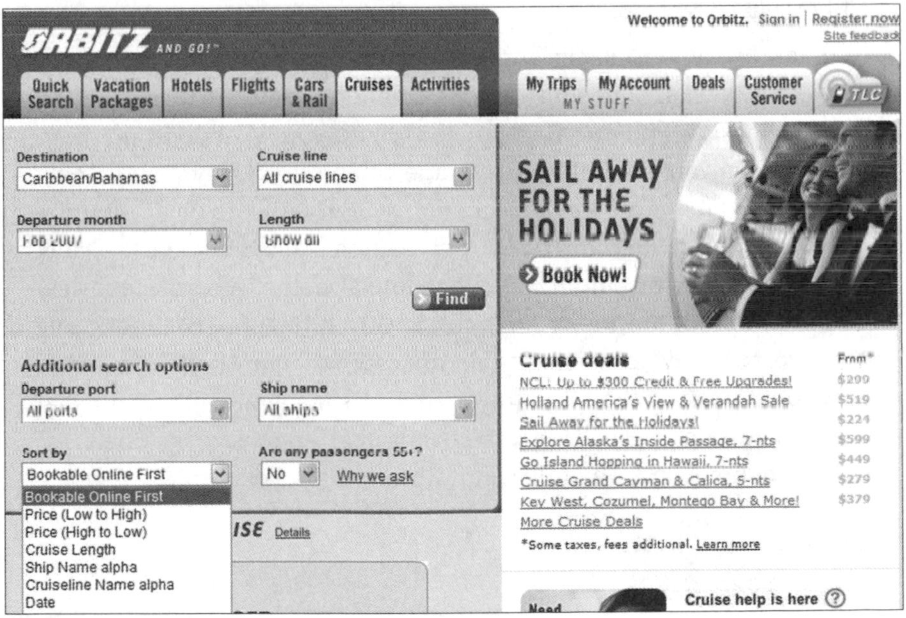

Figure 5.4 Orbitz cruise search page

- First-Time Cruisers – Provides a quick overview of the benefits of cruising, plus links to information on cruise lines, their ships, and their sailing calendar.

- Cruise FAQs – A very brief listing of answers to questions on charges, packing, insurance, passports, tipping, and more.

- Ports of Departure – A chart with which you can identify sailings by port, length, price, etc.

- Cruise Lines – Brief descriptions of 60 of the cruise lines covered by Orbitz. For each, if you click on the logo, you will be taken to a list of deals from that line.

Last-Minute Cruise Reservations

If you are able to climb aboard at the last minute, or at least with only a few weeks' notice, there are tremendous savings to be had. As a matter of fact, you can find cruises where you will spend no more per day than you would for an average-priced hotel room, and meals and entertainment are included in the deal. Discounts of 75 percent and specials for less than $50 per day can actually happen. How about a 14-day cruise from Barcelona to Galveston with an oceanview cabin on one of the major lines for $599? It happened. (I seriously considered delaying finishing this chapter for that one.) If you look around on most of the large travel agency sites, you will find special last-minute deals. Plus, there are sites that specialize in deals for near-term bookings. The following two are examples.

Vacations To Go
vacationstogo.com

Vacations To Go lists literally hundreds of cruises with deep discounts that depart in the next three months. You will have to register (it's free) to use the listings. Once you have registered, click on the 90-Day Ticker link for a list by region (Figure 5.5). Click on the column headings to sort cruises within each region by length, sailing date, departure port, cruise line and ship, ship rating, price, or percent saving. The Find a Bargain link takes you to a page where you can search by region, month, line, ship, length, ports of call, and departure port. If you click on Custom Search on the Find a Bargain page, you will find what may be the most powerful cruise search engine out there. From that page, you can search multiple regions, specific date ranges, minimum and maximum cruise lengths, price range, multiple cruise lines, ship rating, size of ship by maximum and minimum number of passengers, multiple ports of call, and multiple departure ports. You can also specify that you want to see the least expensive oceanview, bargain balcony, or cheapest suite.

The menu on the left side of the Vacations To Go page enables you to find special deals for the following categories: Age 55+ Rates, Grand Voyages, Group Cruises, Inaugural Cruises, Interline Rates, Military Rates, Past-Passenger Rates, Police/Firefighter Rates, Hosted Singles Cruises, Singles Discounts, Teachers' Rates, and Theme Cruises. The site also has a useful offering of general information on cruising, cruise lines, and cruise ships. Actual booking arrangements are handled by phone or e-mail. Don't disembark from this site without registering to get its newsletter.

LastMinuteTravel.com

www.lastminutetravel.com/PageCruiseSearch.aspx

LastMinuteTravel.com covers not just last-minute cruises but also flights, hotels, cars, and more. The cruise section covers seven cruise lines, visiting just about all parts of the world, and you will find some very good bargains.

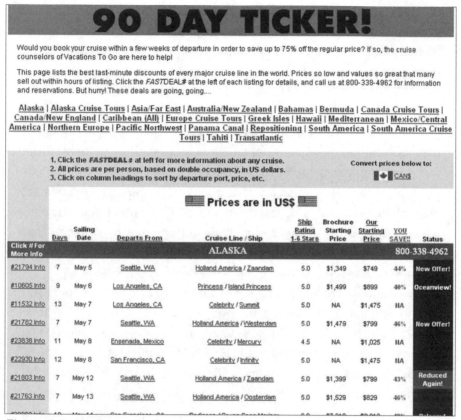

Figure 5.5   Vacations To Go 90-Day Ticker

Sites for Major Cruise Lines

As you would guess, each of the major (and minor, for that matter) cruise lines has its own Web site. So why would you want to go to a cruise line's site if you can use the reservation sites we just discussed? Because among other things, you may find some special deals that the travel agency sites did not uncover. You are also likely to find some details that the other sites did not include, on topics such as frequent-cruiser programs, packing, boarding, excursions, and frequently, lots more photos. Even if you have already booked your cruise elsewhere, visit the cruise line's home page to learn more about planning and what to expect.

Often, the easiest way to find a cruise line's site is to do a simple search in a search engine (i.e., if you want to find the site for "Princess Cruises" search for "*princess cruises*"). Capitalization doesn't matter, but put the name in quotation marks to make sure you get that exact phrase.

However, if you want to have a nice list of links to many cruise lines, all in one place, the Tutto Crociere site has one of the best lists.

Tutto Crociere: The Cyberspace Cruise Magazine— Cruise Lines, Ferry Operators, Freighter Cruises, River Cruises, Casino Cruises, Tall Ships Cruises— Official Web Sites
www.cybercruises.com/cruiselines.htm

In addition to a number of other useful lists and resources, the Tutto Crociere site contains links to more than 200 cruise lines, ferries, etc.

Getting Competitive Quotes for Reservations

One way to take advantage of multiple travel agency sites is to use the CruiseCompete site.

CruiseCompete.com
www.cruisecompete.com

With CruiseCompete, you can search for cruises from 27 cruise lines, then select a cruise and have up to 100 travel agencies provide quotes for that cruise. To use the CruiseCompete.com site, you must register. After you submit your request for quotes, you will be notified by e-mail when the quotes are submitted by the travel agencies. As well as searching, you can also browse through 75 categories (regions, cruise lines, specialty categories, and holiday specials).

Cruises on Smaller and Specialty Ships and Lines

The big reservation sites will typically lead you to the big cruise lines. Depending on your tastes and destinations, big may not always be best. If you are looking for the widest range of activities, services, and menus on a single ship, you may indeed need to look at the largest ships. However, smaller ships provide a very different environment and ambiance, and a lot of other differences as well. Emphasizing the "differences" aspect, these lines often focus on specialty cruises. Sometimes the specialty is just the geographic area they cruise, but the specialty sometimes focuses on activities and special interests or on the type of vessel (for example, windjammers). When looking for theme cruises, though, we often end up back at the big cruise lines.

As with finding sites for major cruise lines, the easiest way to find sites for these smaller and specialty cruise lines is by doing a simple search in a search engine. If you are an oenophile, try a search on *wine cruises*, or you can be more specific, for example, *danube wine cruises*. (In both instances, search without quotation marks. You do not want to insist that those words be together in that precise order.) If your interest is quilting, you may be surprised how much you can find out just by searching *quilting cruises*. In some cases, you will be led to sites for specific cruise lines or to travel agencies with a particular focus.

Because of the great variety in terms of ship size, geographic specialization, themes, and other specialties, it can be difficult to come up with neat categories to use for discussing these. Also, since there are thousands of sites with these various focuses, it is impossible to cover all of them here. So, as in other places in the book, I will provide a sampling and place them in somewhat arbitrary categories in order to give a reasonably good idea of what is out there and what is possible.

Smaller Cruise Lines

For an extensive list of smaller cruise lines, take a look at the Tutto Crociere list previously mentioned (www.cybercruises.com/cruise lines.htm).

Theme Cruises

The easiest way to find a theme cruise matching your interests may be to use a search engine (e.g., search for *yoga cruise*). If you want to just browse through the possibilities, the first three sites that follow can provide lists of theme cruises. The final two in this section are examples of specific offerings. The first of those, Geek Cruises, is one of the best-known theme cruise specialty sites, and the second is an example of a geographically-based theme cruise.

CruiseMates—Theme Cruises, Special Programs & Events
www.cruisemates.com/articles/itineraries/theme.cfm

CruiseMates, which was discussed earlier in detail, has a page that offers an excellent compendium of theme and special cruises arranged by cruise line with a detailed description of each type of cruise.

CLIA (Cruise Lines International Association)— Special Interest Guide to Theme Cruises
www.cruising.org/planyourcruise/guides/theme.cfm

From the CLIA theme cruise page, you can pick from 27 categories (Figure 5.6). Ten of these categories are for specific music genres

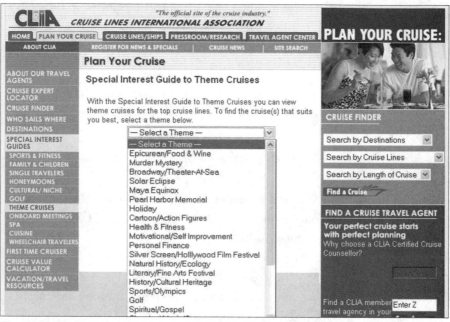

Figure 5.6   CLIA Special Interest Guide to Theme Cruises

(Big Band/Swing, '50s Sock Hop, etc.), while the rest range from Cartoon/Action Figures to Personal Finance. Once you have chosen a CLIA category from the list, you will be shown a list of cruise lines that offer such cruises. When you click on one of the links, you will be taken to the main page of the cruise line, so you may have to dig around on the site a bit to find the specifics (or just call the cruise line's 800 number).

About.com—Cruises—Lifestyle— Special Interest and Theme Cruises
cruises.about.com/od/lifestylethemecruises

This section of the About.com Cruises site provides a variety of articles and links to other sites on theme cruises, as well as articles and links to cruises for specials groups (senior cruises, nude cruises, etc.—no category for nude senior cruises yet).

Geek Cruises—Education That Takes You Places
www.geekcruises.com

With Geek Cruises, you can combine fun and learning on high-tech conference-style cruises to Alaska, Hawaii, the Caribbean, and Europe.

Holland America Line—Alaska Inside Passage Cruises
www.hollandamerica.com/dest/dest.do?dest=A&region=G

On Holland America's Alaska cruises, you can explore the state's glaciers and other unique sights.

River and Barge Cruises

Many of the sites and lists mentioned earlier in this chapter contain information on river and barge cruises. So whether it's the Mississippi, the Volga, or the Yangtze, you are likely to find a cruise that will take you along that river. If you are looking for ideas about where to cruise, start with the following sites. If you know where you want to go, you may want to start with a search engine search (e.g., *rappahannock river cruises*). For some of the larger river cruise lines, you may want to go directly to their sites to see what they offer. Before you book, though, check out some travel agent sites to see if they offer better discounts than the "brochure" prices.

Tutto Crociere: The Cyberspace Cruise Magazine— Cruise Lines, Ferry Operators, Freighter Cruises, River Cruises, Casino Cruises, Tall Ships Cruises— Official Web Sites
www.cybercruises.com/cruiselines.htm

Already mentioned in regard to its list of cruise lines in general, Tutto Crociere's list contains links to 30 river cruise lines.

About.com—River Cruise Lines and Barge Cruises
cruises.about.com/od/rivershipsandbarges

The River Cruise Lines and Barge Cruises section of About.com contains links to around 20 river and barge cruise lines.

Barges in Europe
www.bargesineurope.com

On the Barges in Europe site, you can browse through information on barges in France, England, Ireland, Scotland, Holland, Germany, Belgium, and Italy.

Oceancruises.com—Cruise Directory: River Cruises
www.oceancruises.com/cruise_directory/cruises/river.htm

Oceancruises.com's River Cruises directory gives brief descriptions for 15 river and barge cruise lines.

Major River Cruise Lines

As you look for river cruises, there are two major lines that you will undoubtedly encounter: Viking River Cruises and Uniworld River Cruises.

Viking River Cruises
www.vikingrivercruises.com

Viking has a fleet of 17 ships that ply the rivers of Europe, Russia, and China.

Uniworld River Cruises
www.uniworld.com

According to Uniworld, it offers "more itineraries on more rivers aboard more ships than any other travel company" in Europe, China, and Russia.

Sailing Ships

If the sound of the wind humming in the rigging, the taste of salt air, and maybe a bit of nostalgia for the ships of yore appeal to you, there are still opportunities for you to spend a few days "before the mast." And unless you want to, you won't actually have to scrub the decks, polish the brass, or climb that rigging. The range of options for sailing cruises is broad, from the large "tall ships," which carry more than 100 passengers (such as Windstar, with 148 passengers, and a staff of 90), to mid-size vessels with a few dozen passengers to smaller vessels. I guess you could even include a one-hour rental of a sailboard, but we won't stretch it that far.

If you are considering a sailing cruise, a good first stop on the Web might be the cruise section of About.com for some useful articles and links. For reservations, searches on the big reservation sites may uncover only one sailing ship line, Windstar, so if you want a range of options, you will need to go to one of the smaller travel agencies or to the sites for the cruise lines themselves. Since many of the smaller lines (often single ships) are limited geographically, you might want to do a search engine search such as *sailing ship cruises maine*. If you want to do a search that is less likely to miss some sites, try *cruises australia ("sailing ships" OR windjammers OR "tall ships")*.

**About.com—Cruise Lines with
Sailing Ships—Windjammers**
cruises.about.com/od/sailingships

The Cruise Lines with Sailing Ships section of About.com includes a number of articles about sailing cruises and a list of links to sailing cruise lines and travel agencies.

Sailing Ship Adventures
www.sailingshipadventures.com

The Sailing Ship Adventures site provides a cruise search that includes more than 40 vessels and allows you to search by destination, vessel, length of cruise, and time frame. Click on the Spotlight Voyages link to browse by type of cruise: Navigation & Seamanship Training Voyages, Tall Ship Races & Events, Diving Cruises, Holiday Voyages, Educationally Themed Voyages, Singles Voyages, and more. For each ship, the site provides photos and details.

SmallShipCruises.com
www.smallshipcruises.com/allsailboats.shtml

As evident from the name, SmallShipCruises.com is a travel agency that specializes in cruises on small ships, including sailing ships. The site provides information on more than 45 sailing ship lines. Bookings are handled by phone.

Windjammer Barefoot Cruises
www.windjammer.com

One of the best-known and largest sailing fleets, Windjammer Barefoot Cruises has two four-masters and two three-masters that cruise through the Caribbean carrying from 64 to 122 passengers.

Windstar Cruises
www.windstarcruises.com

Windstar Cruises has four ships (four- and five-masters that are officially "motored-sail-yachts") providing luxury cruises in the

Caribbean, the Americas, Europe, the Greek Isles, plus transatlantic voyages.

Star Clippers
www.starclippers.com

The Star Clippers line offers "casual elegance" aboard its three ships, with cruises in the Caribbean, the Far East, the Indian Ocean, and the Mediterranean, as well as transatlantic voyages. The largest, the *Royal Clipper*, is the largest fully rigged sailing ship in the world.

Luxury Cruises

For those of us who were not brought up with maids and butlers running around, most of the cruises mentioned in this chapter might be considered "luxury." There are, however, cruises that emphasize true luxury.

Silversea
www.silversea.com

Silversea is one of several cruise lines where the emphasis is on luxury. Both *Condé Nast Traveler* and *Travel + Leisure* have repeatedly named Silversea the best small ship cruise line and travelers' reviews seem to emphatically agree. Passengers are pampered by amenities: all-inclusive (including gratuities), large suites (not just cabins), premium wines, 24-hour room service, five-star personalized service, and more.

Day Cruises

Cruises do not have to be long; they can be as brief as an hour or so. Particularly if you are visiting cities, these "cruises" can be a nice way to see a city from a different perspective and really relax while you are doing so. Most large cities with a harbor or river will have companies providing boat tours. To find tours of interest, check out the city guides in Chapter 2, or you can do a simple Web search, such as *sydney harbour tours* or *new york city boat tours.*

Cruise Travel Agencies

If you would like to see a list of about 400 travel agencies that specialize in cruises, look at the Tutto Crociere—Cruise Travel Agencies Web site.

Tutto Crociere: Cruise Travel Agencies Web Sites
www.cybercruises.com/travelagencies.htm

Tutto Crociere lists more than 400 cruise travel agencies in alphabetical order with a very brief description of each.

Cruise Webcams

See it live (or almost live). More and more ships and ports are providing Webcams so that you can see what is happening at the moment. Some are really "live," refreshed constantly, and some are almost live, refreshed every minute or so. You will find links to these in some guides, particularly About.com (cruises.about.com/od/cruisecams) and Cruise Addicts (www.cruise-addicts.com). But for a site with the primary purpose of putting you in contact with Webcams, check out Kroooz-Cams.

Kroooz-Cams
www.kroooz-cams.com

Kroooz-Cams provides easy access to Webcams on more than 70 ships, in most cases from cameras on the bridge, looking out over the bow, but also from other places on the ship, often the stern (aft-cams) or the Internet café (so you can wave to you friends while you are online). Kroooz-Cams also lets you view more than 75 "port-cams" from ports around the world (and throws in a collection of links to information on the port). You can see for yourself if the sun is up in Sorrento or if the surf's up in Maui.

Cruise Discussion Groups and Forums

In addition to general travel discussion groups covered in Chapter 2, check out the following for opinions from other travelers on cruises, cruise lines, cruise destinations, and other cruise-related topics.

CruisePage.com—Cruise Talk

cruisepage.com

To get to the CruisePage.com forums, go to the main CruisePage. com page and click on Cruise Talk. The forums contain more than 180,000 postings arranged in 12 categories: Cruise Lines, Cruise Ships, Cruising 1.0, Ocean Lines and Classic Cruise Ships, Ferry Travel, Mid-Ships Lounge, Technically Speaking, Ports of Call and Destinations, Young Cruisers Forum, Crew's Quarters, ShipMates, and Alternative Cruises. You can also search the forums. Note that the search box (displayed on the upper left of most pages) searches the entire site, not just the forums. To search just the forums, click on the search *link*. This will take you to a page where you can search by keyword, date, and words in the subject or in the entire message and limit your search to one of the 12 categories. If you have seen messages from a particular member that you find useful, you can also search by the member's registration number.

Cruise Addicts Forums

www.cruise-addicts.com/forums/index.php

The Cruise Addicts Forum is big, with more than 1 million postings (Figure 5.7). Forums are divided into Cruise Lines, Cruise Addicts

Onboard—Roll Calls (Cruise Addicts members touching base with other members who will be with them on upcoming cruises), Special Interest Cruising (Family, Honeymoon and Wedding, Singles, River Cruises), Cruise Discussion Topics (First-Time Cruisers, Scuba and Snorkeling, Cruise Fashions, Teen Cruise Addicts, Cruise Air, Hotel Tips and Reviews, Cruise Ship's Casinos and Gambling), Cruise Addicts Group Cruises, and Ports of Call. The search box on the forums page searches the entire Cruise Addicts site, including the forums.

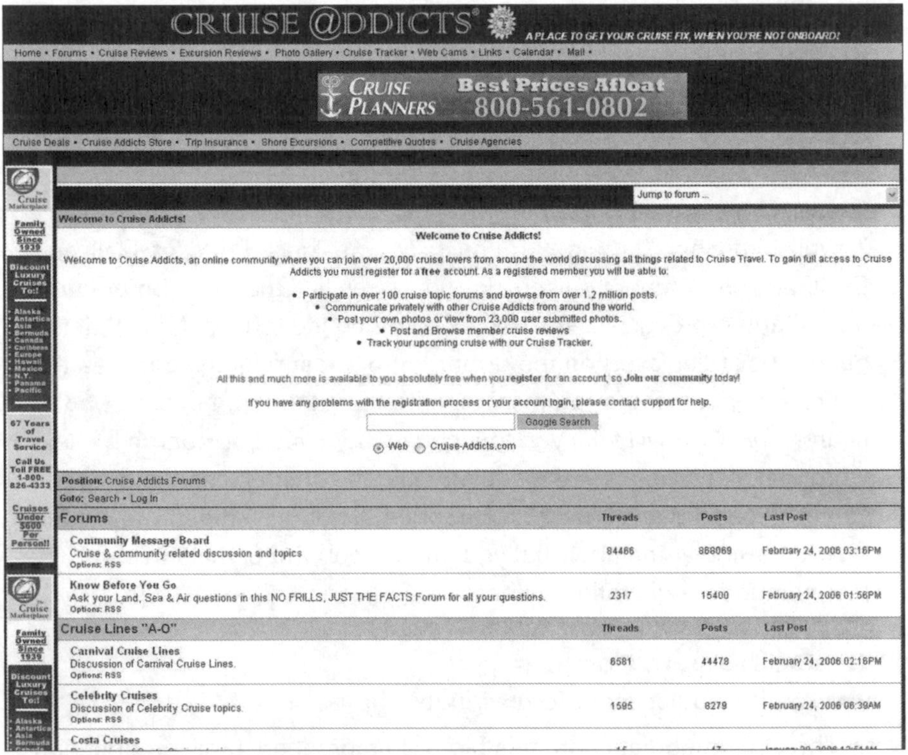

Figure 5.7 Cruise Addicts Forum

Finding a Bed and a Meal

For a typical traveler, the basic necessities are food, lodging, and transportation. The previous chapters have covered transportation, so now it's time to find a place to sleep and something to eat.

Lodging

Whether you use the Web or other means to find a place to sleep, you will probably start by already knowing, or asking yourself, what role your lodging is to play in your vacation or business trip. In some cases, the answer may be "anyplace in a reasonable location that is clean, cheap, and has a comfortable bed." In other cases, you may be looking for a resort hotel with a broad range of amenities, recreation, and on-site events. Or your answer could be anywhere between those two extremes. In any case, your criteria for lodging will, to at least some degree, determine what Web sites will be most useful to you. The general travel agency sites (Orbitz, Expedia, Travelocity, etc.) will get you fairly "regular" hotel accommodations and may save you money by packaging a hotel with a flight (or other service). Other sites will get you similar rooms, but their emphasis will be on discounts. If you are a frequent traveler who accumulates "frequent guest" points, you may want to go directly to a specific hotel chain's site. If you are looking for charm in a comfortable, friendly, laid back surrounding, there are sites for inns and bed-and-breakfasts (B&Bs). If you want the hotel to *be* your vacation, other sites can find the best resort for you. If "cheap" is your overarching criterion, there are also sites that will get you to a hostel or even "get thee to a convent." The following sites are grouped along those lines. There are also relevant sites that will not sell you a hotel room but will provide advice and lodging information. As it goes when searching other travel services on the Web, investigate several of these lodging sites. Various sites will emphasize search criteria, provide different kinds of background information on your options, and often offer you exactly the same accommodations at significantly different rates than other sites. For some of the following categories, only a small sampling is provided here, but the examples given are intended to give you a taste of what is available. For example, an Irish example is given for "farmhouse holidays," but search engines can find similar farmhouse holiday sites in different countries.

Background Information on Lodgings by Country

Though the categories of lodging establishments (hotels, hostels, etc.) are fairly similar from country to country, the names (B&Bs, pensions, etc.), procedures, and policies may differ considerably. If you are traveling abroad, check the following sections at the Frommer's and Rough Guides sites for a good understanding of what to expect and the options available. The following two sites are also helpful for acquainting you with lodging terms that you may encounter in only certain countries (for example, in France there are *gîtes d'étape* and refuge huts).

Frommer's—Destinations
www.frommers.com/destinations

Frommer's provides an excellent overview with very good detail about the kinds of accommodations available in a country, the terminology used, how they differ, what to expect, how they are rated, and more. To get to this information, go to the Destinations section of Frommer's and click on the continent; then in the list of links for countries (not cities), choose the country. Under the Complete Guide section, look for Planning a Trip and then the Tips on Accommodations.

Rough Guides—Travel
www.roughguides.com

In Rough Guides, to get a good overview of accomodations by country, click on the Destinations tab, and then on the link for the particular country. For each country, look in the Basics section for an Accomodations link. You will typically find an overview of what that country offers in terms of types, availability, and cost of accomodations. Usually, there will be links to more detail on the specific varieties of lodging available. For Mexico, for example, there are links for further details for campsites, hammocks and cabañas, and youth hostels. For Egypt, there are details for hotels, hostels, and camping. Austria's page provides information for hotels and pensions, mountain huts, hostels, camping, private rooms, and farmhouses.

Major Hotel Reservation Sites

There are a number of well-known sites on the Web that specialize in hotel bookings, generally covering hotels throughout the world. Some sites even provide a map showing where the hotels are located, making it easy to book a hotel near the spots you want to visit. The major differences among all of these sites are the number of hotels and countries they cover, the criteria by which you can search, the ways in which you can sort results, the amount of detail provided about each lodging, whether a map showing the location of the hotels is provided, and photos. (You can probably feel a lot more comfortable making a choice if you have seen not just the front of the hotel, but pictures of rooms, the lobby, and other areas of the hotel.)

Hotels.com

www.hotels.com

With access to more than 70,000 properties worldwide, Hotels.com, an operating company of Expedia, provides reservations for a range of accommodations and "specializes in providing travelers with accommodations during sold-out periods." Hotels.com guarantees its rates "to be the lowest rate you can find." (This does not necessarily apply to every hotel on Hotels.com, but the site clearly identifies those to which the guarantee does not apply.)

The main page of Hotels.com provides tabs to search for Flights, Condos, B&Bs, Vacation Packages, Groups, Deals, and Destinations & Interests. The search form on the main page can search for hotels by city, but you may want to take advantage of additional search criteria by clicking on the search for Amenity & Landmark. With this feature, you can search by City, Landmarks (for the particular city), Property Type (All Types, Hotels, Vacation Home or Condo, Bed & Breakfast, Suite, Resort, or All Inclusive), Amenities (Business Center, Fitness Center, Pets Allowed, etc.), as well as check-in and checkout dates, number of rooms, and number of adults and children (Figure 6.1). A Search by Address link takes you to a similar form, where you can search by a specific address. (If you give a city and state, be sure to put a comma after the city, or it won't work.)

On search results pages, results are listed by "Hotel.com picks" or closeness of the match to your search criteria, but links will also let you sort results by hotel name, star rating, and price. A "narrow search results" section enables you to specify price range, amenities, and proximity to landmarks. You will notice a checkbox next to each listing.

Figure 6.1 Hotels.com Search by Amenity & Landmark form

Click on the hotels you're interested in, and then click on the
Compare link for a chart comparing the hotels you selected. Take
advantage of the link on results pages to "See these hotels on a map."
Hotel.com's motto is "We know hotels inside and out," and when you
click on the name of a hotel on a results page, the site usually lives up

to that motto. For each hotel, you will typically find a detailed description and list of services, photos, virtual tours, guest reviews, maps of location and nearby attractions, and details of rooms and rates.

The search for flights and vacation packages on Hotels.com is done through Expedia. The search for suites, condos, and B&Bs is the same as the Amenity & Landmark search, but the appropriate types of properties are already selected. If you have not yet decided on your destination, the Destinations & Interests tab leads to a page where you can browse by location or interest (family fun, romantic get-aways, etc.).

All-Hotels

www.all-hotels.com

All-Hotels provides a reservation service for accommodations at 120,000 luxury, chain, and discount hotels in 12,000 locations around the world. It provides both a Quick Search option (where you can specify your destination, arrival date, number of nights, and number of adults, and request a hotel chain) and a directory where you can specify a city or browse by continent, country, and city.

Search results can be sorted alphabetically or by "all-hotels specials," lowest price, or luxury hotels. For each hotel, you will typically find a one-paragraph description, a list of features and amenities, and photos. When browsing geographically with the directory, you can narrow your results by budget hotels, standard hotels, luxury hotels, or discount hotels.

All-Hotels also offers hotel–flight packages, promotions and deals, a multiple-room search, and a section on discount hotels.

PlacesToStay.com

placestostay.com

PlacesToStay.com covers 16,000 hotels in 5,000 destinations in 160 countries. According to the site, it "features the largest portfolio of independent properties anywhere online," and through the site, you can take advantage of special rates that have been negotiated with these properties.

You can search by the usual specifications of destination, dates, and number of people, and results can be sorted by price, rating, location, and name of the property. On results pages, click on the name of the hotel to see a detailed description of the hotel, directions, and a photo.

Quikbook

www.quikbook.com

Though the number of cities and hotels that Quikbook covers is small compared with other hotel reservation sites, it has unique features that many travelers will find attractive. On Quikbook's main page, the search form provides a hotel search in 49 U.S. and Canadian cities and allows you to specify your desired destination, arrival date, number of nights, and number of adults and children. The very useful Neighborhood menu lets you select a specific section within a city. (If you are looking for destinations not in the U.S. or Canada, use the Destination pull-down menu to choose See More Cities or click on the Rest of the World link. This link will take you to Quikbook's partner site, Hotel Marketplace, which covers more than 55,000 international hotels.)

Using the links found in the Shortcuts box on the main page, you can identify hotels with a variety of features or amenities, including complimentary Wi-Fi, smoke-free rooms, Airport Hotels, All-Suite Hotels, Boutique Hotels, Complimentary Breakfast, Convention

Center Hotels, Health Club (full-service), Hip Hotels, Historic Hotels, Pet-Friendly Hotels, Restaurants (highly rated), and more than a dozen others.

On search results pages, click on the name of a hotel to see a detailed description, features and amenities, ratings, photos, and a link to a map showing the hotel's location. You will also notice that many hotels are labeled "Book Now, Pay Later." For these, the room will not be charged to your credit card until you check out of the hotel (as would typically be the case if you booked through the hotel directly). Bookings made through Quikbook are guaranteed to be the lowest available price or Quikbook will match the competing price. (For details, read the FAQ section of the Quikbook site.)

ASE (Accommodation Search Engine)
ase.net

ASE's hotel search is actually a search of other accommodations sites. With this approach, it provides access for reservations at 150,000 hotels, B&Bs, and hostels worldwide. The amount of information about a particular accommodation will vary since for some results, you will be taken to information directly from one of those provider sites and in other cases, you will be taken to a page created specifically for ase.net.

You can either search by country, city, and U.S. or Canadian state or province or browse by location. For either approach, the results pages provide radio buttons to narrow your results to Hotels, B&B/Hostels, or Self-Catering facilities. Your search capabilities can be considerably enhanced by using ase.net's Preferences tab to indicate your preferences for a certain price range, the importance of a central location, the kind of accommodation (Chain Hotel, Independent Hotel, B&B, Hostel, Self-Catering, or Chalet), and the Facilities and Activities available. A Languages tab lets you specify results be shown in one of five currencies and one of six languages. The Search by Chain option on the main page allows you to browse geographically for listings from more than 100 chains.

hotelguide.com
www.hotelguide.com

hotelguide.com does a comparison search of multiple hotel reservation sites, including Hotels.com, TravelWeb.com, Bookings.net, hotel.de, and WorldRes.com. It covers 100,000 hotels in more than 200 countries. To take full advantage of the site's search capabilities, click on the Detailed Search link on the main page. You can search not just by destination, dates, and number of guests, but by facilities, star rating, hotel type, and name.

Hotel Reservations on the Big General Travel Agency Sites

The largest general reservations sites (Expedia, Orbitz, Travelocity) include a hotel bookings section and provide discounts for combining a hotel with a flight and/or car rental. Combinations can often result in significant savings. (On a recent three-day trip to Vienna, Austria, I saved more than $200 by combining flight and hotel reservations.) All offer special prices they have negotiated with hotels they cover. Keep in mind that these sites are travel agencies, and the listed hotels tend to be from hotel chains—do not look here for small, independent hotels, inns, and B&Bs. Though the hotel pages for each of the three sites look different, they have a number of things in common, including:

- To get to the hotel search form from the site's main page, click on the Hotels tab. That will take you to the main hotel page, which includes the hotel search form and also special hotel deals, hotel deals by city, and, sometimes, "last-minute" deals.

- All provide the standard hotel search capabilities (destination, dates, number of guests, and number of rooms), and if you click on a link for additional search options, you can specify hotel name, hotel chain, ratings, and proximity to a specific (U.S.) address.

- All let you narrow your search by hotel amenities (restaurant, pool, room service, pets allowed, etc.). For Expedia, this option is available on the search results page. For Travelocity, it is on the Hotel Advanced Search page.

- As a search result, all offer a list of hotels that match your criteria and display basic information about each. From that results list, you can click on the name of a particular hotel to get more details.

- On results pages, all provide options at the top of the list to sort results by price and Picks (Best Values) and sometimes by other factors (distance, hotel rating, etc.).

- On results pages, all provide (for larger cities at least) a pull-down menu or a map to find hotels in certain sections of the city, nearby suburbs, or nearby cities.

- All provide extensive property descriptions, including lists of amenities and features. You will almost always find several photos and often a video or panoramic view of rooms and public areas.

- All provide maps showing hotel locations.

- All have a vacation section to help you choose and book resort vacation packages.

Rather than repeat the common features just described, the following summaries for the three sites point out unique and useful features of their hotel offerings. In addition to the agencies discussed, most other large travel agency sites, such as CheapTickets.com and OneTravel.com, also offer hotel reservations. If one of those is among your favorite agencies, check it out. The sites covered in the Hotel Price Comparison Sites section provide ways to quickly compare hotel prices from numerous agencies.

Travelocity—Hotels
travelocity.com/hotels

Travelocity guarantees the lowest prices for more than 20,000 of the hotels it covers, and you can maximize your savings by combining a hotel with a flight. All three big general travel sites let you specify hotels with certain amenities, but Travelocity provides the longest list of amenities (24 options), from which you can select up to three. Among the options are free breakfast, free high-speed Internet, free local calls, beachfront property, and kitchenette. The Amenities options are accessible on the Hotel Advanced Search page by clicking the Search by Address, Points of Interest link on the main hotel search form (Figure 6.2).

Results listings can be sorted by Travelocity Picks, Price, Ratings, Hotel Name, and City Name; each listing shows the daily rate for your trip for different room types. In the listing for each hotel, there are links for AAA's rating of the hotel, traveler reviews, a map, and a list of amenities.

Expedia—Hotels
www.expedia.com/daily/hotels

Expedia's hotel search provides access to more than 60,000 hotels worldwide and offers ways to save money by combining hotel reservations with a flight, a car, or both. On results pages, you will see hotels listed in the default Hotel List View, but tabs are available for a

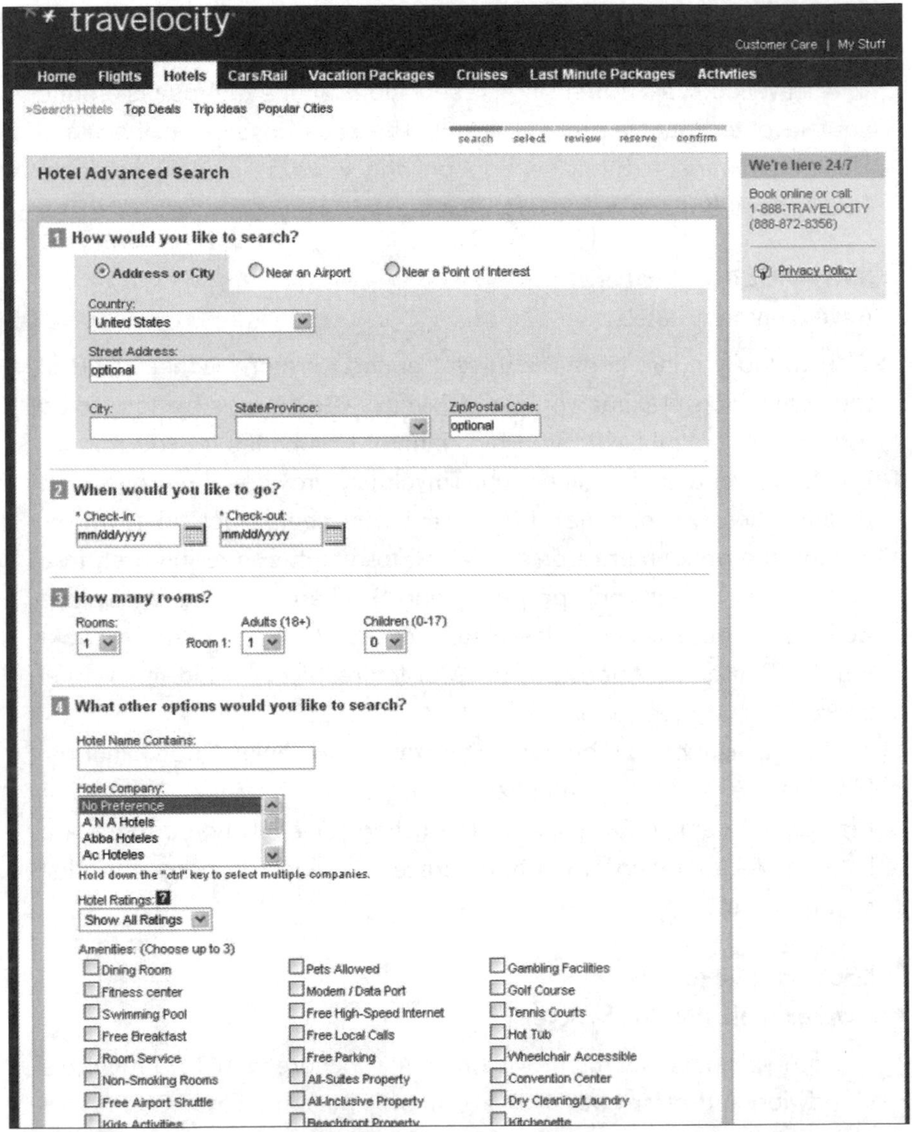

Figure 6.2   Travelocity hotel advanced search page

Hotel Map View and, in some cases, an Area Map View. The Hotel Map View adds a map with a zoom feature above the listings for hotel locations (Figure 6.3). (Color-coded dots on the map indicate hotel availability for the dates specified in your search.) Next to each of the hotels in the list is a checkbox. Check those of interest, click Update Map, and only the hotels you checked will appear on the map. The Area Map View, which is available only for some large cities, shows neighborhoods. Click on one to see a description of the neighborhood with a link to a list of neighborhood hotels.

For any of the views, results lists can be sorted by Expedia Picks, Price, Hotel Name, City, or Hotel Class. For each listing, you will see a chart with the rate for each day of your trip for different room types and special rates. The Narrow Your Search link on listings pages takes you to a list of amenities to fine-tune your search. (The number next to the amenity shows how many hotels in your current listing have that amenity.) When you click on a hotel name for a detailed description, you will find numeric traveler ratings for Hotel Service, Hotel Condition, Room Cleanliness, and Room Comfort. A Traveler Reviews link will take you to recent traveler reviews.

Orbitz—Hotels
www.orbitz.com/App/ViewHotelSearch

Orbitz is not specific about how many hotels it covers but says the number is in the "tens of thousands." As part of a search, you can save money by combining a hotel reservation with a flight or a car. On search results pages, Orbitz defaults to a listing by Best Values first but offers tabs to sort the results by lowest price or by star rating. For those listings labeled Low Price Guarantee, Orbitz guarantees that its prices are the lowest available.

For larger U.S. cities, Orbitz's Neighborhood Matrix Display will appear at the top of results pages with a map of neighborhoods and

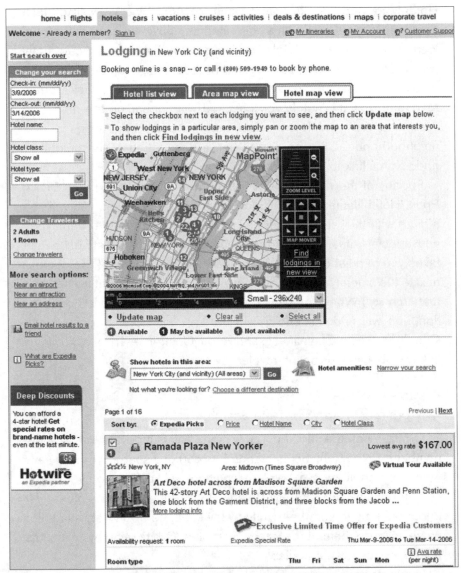

Figure 6.3   Expedia hotel search results page (in Hotel Map View)

a table showing the lowest prices (by star rating) for hotels in each neighborhood (Figure 6.4). For smaller U.S. cities, similar tables may show the lowest rates for hotels at various distances from the city (e.g., within two to five miles).

Last-Minute and Other Discount Hotel Sites

LastMinuteTravel.com—Hotels

www.lastminutetravel.com

In addition to providing savings on last-minute flights, LastMinuteTravel can also provide savings for last-minute hotel reservations around the world. You can get some excellent deals, but read the details regarding refunds (as with any discount site). Also, when you book really last minute arrangements (like for *tonight*), be sure to note, before making the final step of booking, whether the reservation is a "confirmed" reservation or is "on request." The latter means that the hotel has not confirmed the reservation yet.

LateRooms

www.laterooms.com

LateRooms offers rates up to 70 percent off the regular price for 50,000 hotels worldwide. Choose a country, then a city, and then select a hotel from the list. When you click on the Details link, you will be given details for the hotels and a table with the various prices for each of the next few days. (You really see how much the last-minute booking can save!) You can book online (or call) to guarantee your reservation with a credit card, but you don't actually pay until you check out of the hotel.

Priceline.com—Hotels

www.priceline.com/hotels

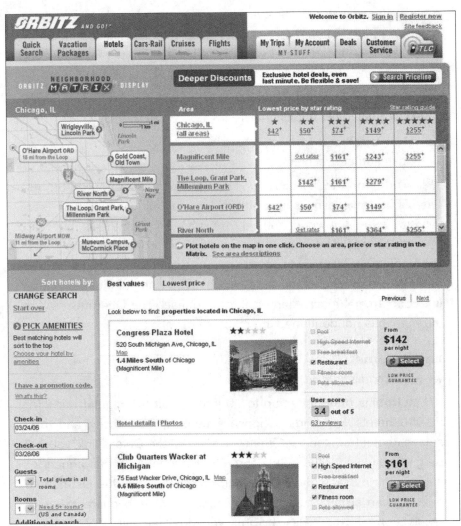

Figure 6.4 Orbitz Neighborhood Matrix Display

Priceline's overall bidding approach was discussed in Chapter 3. The benefits and procedures for booking hotels are basically the same as for booking flights. As with flights, Priceline offers the bidding option ("Name Your Own Price") and the option to choose an exact hotel as on other reservation sites. To use the bidding option, choose a city and dates, then, in most cases, the neighborhood(s) and a quality level (star rating), and then name your price. A review of your request is shown, along with the total price, including taxes and fees. Enter your credit card information, click on Buy My Hotel Room, and you will be notified immediately if your price is accepted. If not, your credit card is not charged.

Hotwire—Hotels

www.hotwire.com/hotel

Hotwire partners with hotels (and airlines and car rental agencies) to help them get rid of unsold inventory at bargain prices. Like Priceline, you are bidding "blind": You do not find out what the actual hotel is until you have purchased the room. With Hotwire, you enter the city, neighborhood, dates, desired class of hotel, and similar information, and Hotwire returns a list of possibilities with the prices. You choose from the list, make your purchase, and then find out the name and exact location of the hotel.

Hotel Price Comparison Sites

The first four sites that follow, which were also discussed in detail in Chapter 3, cover hotels as well as flights. For all, search results can be sorted by various criteria (price, star rating, distance from the city center you specified, etc.). On results pages, SideStep, FareChase, and Kayak provide panels that let you request specific results by further modifying criteria such as price ranges, neighborhoods, etc. With FareChase and Kayak.com, you can view the locations of hotels on a map.

SideStep—Hotels
www.sidestep.com/hotel

The hotel section of SideStep covers more than 90,000 hotel properties. On results pages, you can sort by SideStep Picks, Price, Star Rating, or Hotel Name, and you can also modify your search by Price Range, Stars, Neighborhood, and Amenities (Figure 6.5). From the results lists, you can select specific hotels to compare side-by-side in a table format.

Kayak—Hotels
www.kayak.com/?tab=hotels

Kayak's hotel search covers 147,000 hotels. On results pages, you can sort by Price, Stars, Hotel Name, and Distance. You can also modify your search by Price, Stars, Neighborhood, Distance (from a specific landmark), Property Type, and Hotel Name and Brand. Kayak shows matching hotels on a map.

FareChase
farechase.yahoo.com

Search results for a hotel search on FareChase are shown on a map; the results list can be sorted by Popularity, Price, Name, and Distance. Search results can be modified by hotel name, neighborhood, Hotel Class (stars), Price, Bed Type (king, queen, etc.), and amenities.

Mobissimo—Hotels
www.mobissimo.com/search_hotels.php

Mobissimo's hotel search covers 139 travel sites. You can sort results by Provider (the travel site on which the rate was found), Hotel, Rating (stars), and Price.

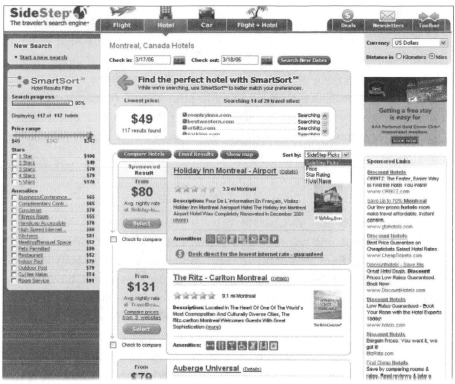

Figure 6.5 SideStep hotel search results page

BetterBidding.com

betterbidding.com

BetterBidding.com provides forums that include tips and discussions for using Hotwire and Priceline. The Winning Bids forum includes reports from users disclosing what hotels they actually received as the result of winning bids. (For the two sites, you do not know what hotel you will get until after you have bid and committed yourself.) The purpose is to give users of the two sites a better idea of what hotels they might receive with a winning bid.

Hotel Chains

If you are collecting frequent traveler points from a particular hotel chain, you may want to visit the hotel's own site for special deals. You may also want to use of the hotel's site to find the address and phone number of its hotel in the city where you are headed. A search engine will probably be the quickest way to get to the main site of a hotel chain. Searching by the name of a chain (e.g., *hilton* or *accor*) will usually get you to their home page easily.

Locating Hotels Using Google Local and Yahoo! Local

Both Google and Yahoo! are busy increasing their coverage of local information and have added a "local search" to their sites for various countries. For some of these local versions, you can specify location and type of business or name of a business and have the locations shown on a map (Figure 6.6). For other countries, the local version is presently often just a "yellow pages" lookup, which still can be useful for locating hotels in a certain city. For both Google and Yahoo!, the first full integration of local yellow-pages-type information with maps has been used for the U.S., Canada, the U.K., and some other countries. Try Yahoo! Maps (maps.yahoo.com) and Google Maps (maps.google.com for the U.S. or local.google.ca for Canada) to find hotels in a particular city.

B&Bs, Inns, Gîtes, Cottages, and More

As wonderful, luxurious, and comfortable as big chain hotels can be, the word "charm" is not usually associated with them. If you like charming, you may prefer to stay in a B&B or an inn. B&Bs, which are usually in a converted home, have a very small number of rooms and serve up both breakfast and conversation (if you want it), with plenty of amenities to make you feel at home. Inns, which have more rooms,

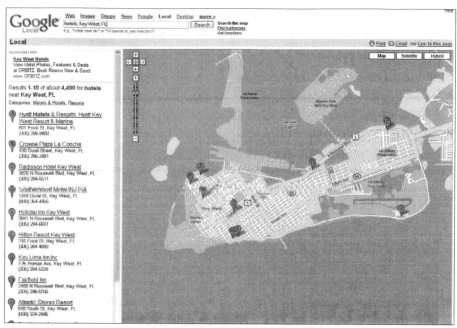

Figure 6.6   Hotel search on Google Local

including a lobby and dining room, can also be charming and almost certainly make you feel more "at home" than a Hilton or a Hyatt.

The following B&B and inn sites are a small, select sample. The first three sites cover a large number of countries. The remaining examples offer options for specific countries. While there are probably hundreds of helpful B&B and inn directories on the Web, fortunately for the traveler, there is a lot of redundancy, and the same establishment will often be listed in many directories. So you may not have to search many directories to find a perfect spot. Be aware that many sites have a rather generous interpretation of B&Bs and inns, and many of the listings in those sites will be for full-fledged hotels.

Most of the following B&B and inn sites do not book rooms directly for you, but they will provide an e-mail form so you can send a reservation request to the innkeeper. (They also provide phone numbers for contacting the property directly.)

About.com—Bed & Breakfasts
bandb.about.com

If you have never partaken of a B&B, this section in About.com may be a good starting place. Though the site tends to blur the distinction between B&Bs and inns, it provides some good background information and advice. The forum on the site, which is moderately active, could be a good place to ask questions about B&Bs.

BedandBreakfast.com
www.bedandbreakfast.com

On BedandBreakfast.com, you can either browse the directory or search using the search box for lodging listings in more than 110 countries. In addition to B&Bs, it includes "country and urban inns, guest houses, lodges, cabins, historic hotels, small resorts, guest ranches, and farmhouse accommodations." You can find B&Bs by browsing using the map, by using the destination search box on the home page, or by using the Search tab. With the Search tab, you can search by several criteria, including inn name, innkeeper name, special needs, amenities, etc. Online reservations can be made for B&Bs in 15 U.S. cities, and for others, there is an e-mail form to send a reservation request to the innkeeper. You can also purchase gift certificates directly from bedandbreakfast.com, which are accepted at more than 3,300 B&Bs across the U.S. The site has a moderately active collection of message boards and a newsletter.

TheInnkeeper.com

www.theinnkeeper.com

TheInnkeeper.com offers access to the same categories of lodgings as BedandBreakfast.com and includes listings for more than 90 countries. The Quick Search box on the main page lets you search by location, and you can use the map to browse or search by keywords, city, region, or amenities with the Advanced Search tab. The keyword option searches the description, amenities, distinguishing features, property name, city, and state.

Bed & Breakfast Inns ONLINE

www.bbonline.com

Bed & Breakfast Inns ONLINE lists 5,200 B&Bs worldwide. For U.S., Canadian, and Mexican establishments, you will find a description, pictures, rates, contact information, and links to the sites. For other countries, you will find the name, location, and link to the site. Look on the main page for links to B&Bs and inns that are in the mountains, kid-friendly, pet-friendly, or handicap accessible, have accommodations for horses, and host weddings.

iLoveInns.com

www.iloveinns.com

iLoveInns.com is a directory of 19,000 U.S. and Canadian B&Bs. Use the search box to search by location or name, or click on the Find an Inn tab to search by location, postal code, innkeeper name, inn name, leisure activity, or interest or to browse by region. For most inns, extensive details and pictures are provided, along with an e-mail form to send a reservation request directly to the innkeeper.

Town and Country Homes

www.townandcountry.ie

This site for the Town and Country Homes Association includes more than 1,300 B&Bs approved by the Irish Tourist Board. The Book or Request Now search on the main page allows you to search for available B&Bs by location and by date. The Full Accommodation link takes you to a page where you can search the entire database of homes, and then once you find a particular home, you can check for available dates. With the Activity Holidays tab, you can find B&Bs that cater to guests who want a walking, cycling, fishing, or golfing holiday.

Irish Farmhouse Holidays
www.irishfarmholidays.com

The Irish Farmhouse Holidays site has more than 300 choices for farmhouse B&Bs and self-catering holiday facilities. With the search form on the main page, you can search by County, Town, Type (B&B or self-catering), and Facilities. The site also offers a collection of useful links about travel in Ireland. (Although it wasn't a part of the promised amenities for my own family's trips to Ireland, our farmhouse stays where our kids played with their kids made for some of our most memorable moments.)

Self-Catering Holiday Cottages—The Cottage Guide
www.cottageguide.co.uk

The Cottage Guide is a directory of self-catering holiday cottages in England, Scotland, Wales, and Ireland. It lists more than 6,000 properties, "including farm houses, country houses, town houses, apartments, log cabins ... and even a few railway carriages!" On the main page, you can search by location and number of guests (from "2 or more" to "16 or more"). An advanced search page offers searches for availability within the next few weeks and by features and facilities. For each listing, you will find location, rates, phone numbers, links to the owner's site, photos, and extensive descriptions. An e-mail form is provided for contacting the owner for reservations.

Gîtes de France

www.gites-de-france.fr

Gîtes de France, the official site for the Gîtes de France organization, has 56,000 member establishments, including B&Bs (*chambre d'hôtes*), self-catering *gîtes,* children's *gîtes*, holiday and stopover *gîtes, chalets-loisirs*, farm campsites, *gîtes* that cater to the disabled, and *gîtes* for fishing, riding, winter holidays, or at vineyards or in nature parks. For an excellent explanation of what Gîtes de France offers and how it all works, see the links for accommodations options and the Know More section of the site. It may take a couple minutes to understand the navigation of the site. The Rural Gîtes tab takes you just to self-catering accommodations. The Select a Bed and Breakfast link takes you to a database of 8,500 B&Bs. Be aware that even if you selected the English version of the site, you may be on a French-only page within one or two clicks.

Gite.com

www.gite.com

Compared to the Gîtes de France site, Gite.com is tiny, with around 170 selected properties, including traditional gîtes, self-catering cottages, apartments, and villas throughout France. Searching is straightforward, and as you browse through search results, you can add choices you are considering to your personal "short list" for later comparison. The site also lists last-minute and other special offers and it provides, in its Plan Your Trip section, an excellent collection of information for the foreign traveler to France, including maps, background, and definitions, arranged into categories of history, dining out, activities, traveling, and shopping.

Luxury Accommodations

Not that B&Bs and inns can't be "luxurious," but if your main aim is to indulge and pamper yourself, be waited on like royalty, and spend some of that surplus cash that you've been trying to get rid of, there are sites that will be very happy to help you out.

The Leading Hotels of the World
www.lhw.com

The 400 hotels covered on the Leading Hotels of the World site include small luxury hotels, resort hotels, and larger five-star, world-famous hotels. In case "getting rid of money" is not one of your goals, the site also has a selection of special offers. Extensive detail and photos are provided, and rooms are booked directly through the site. The Leading Hotels of the World, Ltd. Co. also owns Leading Spas of the World (www.leadingspasoftheworld.com) and, for those who are willing to settle for a mere four-star hotel, LuxRes (www.luxres.com).

Small Luxury Hotels of the World
www.slh.com

The Small Luxury Hotels of the World site allows you to make online reservations for more than 360 hotels in 60 countries. On the main page, you can search by hotel name (or part of a name), select from a list of hotels, or search by country or hotel type (Beach Resorts, City Center, Country House, Eco-reserve, Game Lodge, Golf Resort, Private Island, Ski Resort, Spa Resort, Sports Resort, or Waterfront). By using the Advanced Search link, you can narrow your search to include specific features, sports facilities, and special needs services that are available. The Regional Information link leads to a browsable map with descriptions of regions and cities as well as links to the small luxury hotels in those locations.

Relais & Chateaux

www.relaischateaux.com

Relais & Chateaux is the site for an association of select hotels and restaurants with more than 400 properties in 50 countries. For the hotels, the average size is 25 rooms. Both rooms and tables can be booked online, and the site offers theme packages for Esprit Golf, Spa & Beauté, Fine Dining, Family, Culture, Sports, Oenology, and Weddings.

Hostels

While luxury hotels may be near one end of the spectrum, at the other end are hostels, which are still generally regarded as clean, safe, and very inexpensive. There are a number of sites that offer information on hostels internationally, and many sites that provide hostel information for just one country.

Hostelworld.com

www.hostelworld.com

With Hostelworld.com, you can search for and book from a database of 10,000 hostels in 75 countries. On the main page, you can search by country, city, and dates, and the Advanced Search option lets you search by kind of property (Hostels, Budget Hotels, Guesthouses, Apartments, and Campsites) and by features (hostels that include breakfast, have 24-hour reception desks, or provide linens, a bar, or Internet access). Search results can be sorted by availability, price, name, or rating, and a detailed description and photos are provided for each property. In the site's Community section, you will find travel diaries (you can also start your own), message boards (but they are not particularly active), and advice from Travel Gurus (for various cities). The InfoZone section offers country guides, very nice printable pocket guides, suggested itineraries, lists of events and activities, travel tips, and more.

Hostelling International

www.hihostels.com

Hostelling International comes from the International Youth Hostel Federation (IYHF), a nonprofit organization that represents more than 90 Youth Hostel associations and 4,000 hostels from more than 80 countries. From the Book Now section of the home page, you can search, book, and pay for rooms. You can search by country, city, and date; results include a description of the hostel, one or more photos, phone numbers, directions, and a map. With the Group Bookings option, you can book groups of 10 or more. As with many hostel sites, this provides extensive descriptions of what hostels are all about and what to expect. On the site, you will find information on Hostelling International's FreeNites program, in which frequent stayers can earn points for free nights.

Hostels.com

www.hostels.com

On Hostels.com, you can search for (or use a map to browse) 10,000 hostels worldwide. It also provides a guide to All About Hostelling (a guide to hostels), City Guides, Travel Tales, and Message Boards.

Resorts

Resorts, in the context of travel, actually have a couple different meanings. "Resort" can refer to a specific establishment (e.g., Sandals, The Greenbrier, or Walt Disney World), or it can refer to a specific town or area (e.g., St. Moritz, Vail, Baden-Baden, or Cancun). Resorts, of course, are often categorized by type of activity (beach resort or ski resort) and by the payment method (all inclusive or a la carte). The more you already know about where you want to go, the easier it will be to get yourself there. On the other hand, if you don't know where to go or whether you want a dude ranch, a spa, or a beach vacation, you have more work ahead of you, but also the pleasure of a lot more daydreaming. If you are in the "undecided" category, consider optimizing your time on the Internet by doing the following:

- Use the Vacations section of the general travel agency sites, such as Travelocity, Orbitz, Expedia, and Yahoo! Travel, to get some ideas and identify some typical options for where to go.

  Expand the possibilities with some of the following resort specific sites (or similar sites).

- Take advantage of discussion groups and sites (particularly Travelocity, Expedia, and Yahoo! Travel) that provide reviews of individual hotels.

- Once you have decided on a specific activity, place, or hotel, go bargain hunting. Go back to the general and resort-specific sites referred to earlier in this chapter to see exactly what they offer. Use a Web search engine to find smaller travel agency sites that may have special deals for that location. Also, if you have decided on a specific resort hotel, look at the hotel's own site.

Travelocity, Expedia, and Orbitz all provide packages that include flights along with your resort hotel cost. The three sites differ in terms of the browsable resort categories. If you are looking for a beach vacation, for example, you may want to start with Expedia or Orbitz. Expedia has a section for deals on beach vacations and also sections for ski vacations, last-minute vacations, and all-inclusive vacations;

Orbitz lists deals for beach, all-inclusive, last-minute, luxury, romance, and ski vacations; Travelocity has deals for ski holidays. You can browse by destination for major resort areas on all three sites.

Once you have narrowed your focus, use a Web search engine and search for such things as *maui resort* or *golf resort*. If you want non-U.S. travel agency sites and destinations, replaces the term "vacation" with "holiday" in your search.

As you will quickly find, plenty of travel agency sites specialize in resorts. Most are for a specific hotel chain or specific hotels or cover specific geographic regions. The following is an example of one of the broader-reaching sites.

Resort Vacations To Go
www.resortvacationstogo.com

Resort Vacations To Go is a highly endorsed site that provides reservations for resorts in North America, Britain, continental Europe, the Bahamas, Bermuda, and Hawaii. It is easily browsable, with sections for all-inclusive vacations, the Bahamas, Bermuda, Canada, Europe, Hawaii, Mexico, and the U.S. Specialty sections include the following resort categories: Adults-Only, All-Inclusives, Casinos, Golf, Honeymoons, Kids' Programs, Spas, and Weddings. With its 90-day ticker, you can browse for deals in the next three months, or the search form on the main page will let you search by location and for any date. It also offers charter specials for some destinations.

Vacation Rentals

This category overlaps with some of the other categories of accommodations already discussed. I felt it was worthwhile, though, to devote some attention to sites that focus on rentals that are typically of a week or more, are self-catering, and have more of a "home" environment, whether a house, apartment, condo, etc. To some extent, these sites might be viewed more as "real estate agent" rather than "travel agent" sites. Because of this, if you are focusing on a particular country or region, you may want to "think local" and try a search engine search on something like *holiday rentals tuscany* or *vacation rentals vail*. If you are looking for a longer-term relationship, you may want to consider "time shares," but that's definitely getting into real estate more than travel. Also see the sites listed earlier in the "B&Bs, Inns, Gîtes, Cottages, and More" section since many of those include vacation rental properties such as cottages and other self-catering properties.

Rentalo
Rentalo.com

With more than 100,000 property listings in 15,000 locations around the world, Rentalo offers listings including B&Bs, hotels, and other types of accommodations. For each property, you will find extensive detail, photos, a form to contact the owner, and, in many cases, a very convenient availability calendar for the property.

CyberRentals
www.cyberrentals.com

At CyberRentals.com, individual owners have placed ads for more than 22,000 vacation properties around the world. You can browse for properties by using the map or search by location and date. For each property, a description and photos are provided, along with information and forms for contacting the owner. Reservations are made directly with the owner rather than through CyberRentals. The main page also has a section to browse for beach, ski, golf, or lake vacations.

10k Vacation Rentals
www.10kvacationrentals.com

10k Vacation Rentals offers thousands of rentals around the world, including "condominiums, private vacation homes, beachfront hotels, oceanfront villas, mountain lodges and all other types of vacation rentals." Detailed information is provided either right on the 10k Vacation Rentals site or through a link to the site for the particular property. In either case, reservations are made directly through the owner or agent.

VacationSpot.com
www.vacationspot.com

VacationSpot.com, owned by Expedia, offers rentals around the world; however, outside the U.S., many properties are hotels rather than homes, apartments, etc. In the Vacation Ideas section, you can browse for properties that emphasize golf, skiing, water sports, hiking and cycling, or gaming and shopping. Most properties found on this site are in North America or the Caribbean.

ResortQuest—Vacation Home Network
www.resortquest.com

ResortQuest includes rated vacation properties mainly in the southeastern and western U.S. and in British Columbia in Canada. Ratings are done by ResortQuest employees.

Trading Homes: Home Exchange Vacations

Home exchange, also known as house swapping, is an opportunity to get lodging almost for free. For those not familiar with the concept, you arrange to live in someone else's house for a specified time in return for letting them stay in your house (usually for that same period). You will find good descriptions of the process on most of the following sites. The whole process is more complicated than a standard rental, but if done right, it can be both interesting and economical.

There are many agencies on the Web that can make this happen for you. Typically you can browse an agency's site for free to view properties available for swapping. However, to swap, you need to have your own home listed, which requires a fee-based membership in the agency. Consider the following sites as examples, not necessarily as the best sites for your own situation. Do some searching on the terms "home exchange" or "house swapping" along with the name of the country or locality in which you are interested.

INTERVAC
intervac-online.com

INTERVAC has been in the home-exchange business for more than 50 years, and its database has thousands of homes for exchange in more than 50 countries.

HomeExchange
www.homeexchange.com

HomeExchange has more than 14,000 listings in more than 100 countries, and as well as arranging for house swaps, you can arrange for "hospitality exchanges," where the two parties take turns hosting each other.

HomeLink International
www.homelink.org

With more than 13,000 listings, HomeLink International claims to be "the world's largest home exchange network," providing home exchanges for more than 50 years.

International Home Exchange Network
www.ihen.com

Even though you will need to join (for a fee) in order to have your home listed on the site, International Home Exchange Network allows you, on your own and for free, to make arrangements for a home swap with homes you find on the site.

Seniors Home Exchange
www.seniorshomeexchange.com

Seniors Home Exchange is an example of a home-exchange site for a specific clientele: seniors. As well as home exchanges, you can also arrange for hospitality exchanges.

"Specialty" Accommodations

There are thousands of hotels, B&Bs, and other lodging establishments that provide particularly unique, interesting, and sometimes even bizarre settings and offerings. (Your neighbors will never know unless you tell them.) The first site that follows provides a collection of a variety of such hotels. The others are examples of particular categories of such "specialty" hotels.

Unusual Hotels of the World
www.unusualhotelsoftheworld.com

Unusual Hotels of the World has brought together a great collection of certainly-not-usual hotels. With this site, you can arrange to stay in a former prison, a hotel made entirely of ice, a rainforest treehouse, underwater, or in a building resembling the body of the world's biggest beagle. Reservation inquiries are made by means of an inquiry form on the site.

Castles on the Web
www.castlesontheweb.com

Castles on the Web is a collection of information and links on all aspects of castles. The Accommodations section links to more than 100 sites that offer lodging in castles.

Paradores

www.parador.es/english

The Paradores site is a starting place for staying in Spanish paradores (government-run country hotels), which are often in castles, monasteries, or other historic buildings.

Agritour

www.agritour.net

The Agritour site is the result of the agritourism movement in Italy and puts you in touch with 1,200 Italian farms where you can spend your vacation. Booking arrangements are made by e-mail.

Lighthouses with Overnight Accommodations

www.lighthouse.cc/links/overnight.html

At first glance, you may think this site is just about lighthouses in New England. But when you look closer, you'll see the Lighthouses with Overnight Accommodations page links to accommodations in more than 150 lighthouses in 25 countries.

Iglu-Dorf

iglu-dorf.com

Way back as a child when you first heard about igloos, if you were blessed with any imagination at all, you probably spent at least a few minutes wondering what it must be like to live in one. Finally, here's your chance. Iglu-Dorf will rent an igloo to you or your group; however, it will be in the Alps, not in the Arctic. Also, unlike the Arctic igloos you imagined as a kid, along with these igloos you will get a hot tub and an order of fondue.

Hotel Reviews

Many sites just covered provide reviews of hotels, some done by professional reviewers, some by travelers themselves. For opinions of individual travelers, also check out the various travel forums. In addition to reading the reviews found on those sites, make good use of the following sites, which focus specifically on reviewing hotels.

HotelChatter

www.hotelchatter.com

HotelChatter is an Internet magazine that includes hotel reviews, news, tips, gossip, and deals for hotels worldwide. In addition to the stories by the magazine editors, you will find messages posted by readers.

HotelShark

www.hotelshark.com

HotelShark, which gathers opinions from both professional travel writers and "guest" reviewers, has reviews on hotels from more than 30 countries. HotelShark has the following companion sites: BnBShark.com, EstateShark.com, FarmShark.com, HorseShark.com, RanchShark.com, RVShark.com, SeatShark.com, SpaShark.com, TruckShark.com, among others. Links to those sites are found at the bottom of the HotelShark main page.

And Now, About That Meal

Among travelers, planning for and expectations about meals are as varied as the planning and expectations for lodging. For budget travelers, the alimentary aim may be to avoid restaurants as much as possible and buy a sausage at the Wurststand, some Chou Do Fu at a night market, or a tart at the patisserie or pick up a bottle of local wine. Millions have happily picnicked their way through a country, "living off the land." On the other hand, dining (not just "eating") at some of the world's best restaurants may, in fact, be the main purpose of a trip. In any case, enjoying the local cuisine—whether in Chicago or Caracas—can be an essential, enjoyable, and memorable part of almost any trip. The Internet offers lists of restaurants, locations of restaurants, reviews of restaurants, and reservation services for restaurants. For those for whom three or four meals a day do not provide enough contact with calories, the Internet can get you on a food tour or into a cooking school. The sites in this section provide information on dining options and how you can find them.

However, don't forget the possibilities that can be found using Web search engines, particularly if you are looking for restaurants in a specific city or town. Try a search such as *restaurants Barcelona*, or *restaurant reviews Barcelona*, or *dining guides madrid*. You might also try searches such as *"best restaurants" bangkok* or *"top restaurants" london*. If you wish, be specific about the type of restaurant, such as *thai restaurants montreal*.

Dining Overviews and Restaurant Lists Found in Travel Guides

The following two general travel guides can provide a general overview of the kinds of restaurants in a particular city, local foods, and more. Both also provide a lengthy list of recommended restaurants. Other general guides, such as ViaMichelin (www.viamichelin. com), provide lists of restaurants, but the following two guides also include a broader overview of what you will find in restaurants and cuisine in each city.

Wcities

www.wcities.com

If you are looking for information on eating (and drinking) in a large or medium-size city, Wcities is an excellent place to start. This site features extensive descriptions of the dining and drinking establishments for each city as well as a look at the types of restaurants, cuisines, and special local dishes. You may also find information on local eating customs and ceremonies and what sections of the city (or suburbs) to go to for various cuisines, styles, and ambiance. To get to the Dining guides, click on the Change City link, choose your city, and look for the Dining link on the left of the city's page. From there you can use various browsing categories to locate a list of restaurants. For each restaurant, you may find a description, location, phone, reviews, and links to a map and to the restaurant's site. You can take advantage of the Wcities Travel Bag feature to save information on selected restaurants and easily print out the guides. Wcities guides are available for mobile devices at go.wcities.com.

Fodor's Restaurant Reviews

www.fodors.com/reviews/drevselect.cfm

Though substantially shorter than the Dining and Drinking guides found in Wcities, for each city covered in Fodor's guides, you will find a Dining Overview telling you what kinds of restaurants and dishes to expect and often some related tips. To get to these, click on the Restaurants tab on Fodor's main page, and then browse to find the city. When you get to the page for a city, look on the left under Restaurants for the Dining Overview. Click on Restaurants to get Fodor's list of restaurants for that city, and click on the name of a restaurant to get a description, address, phone number, and a Diner Rating (rated by Fodor's users). You can sort the restaurants by name, price, location, cuisine, or rating score.

Web Sites Specifically About Restaurants

If you want to prepare ahead of time to make sure that your choice of restaurants is not just based on serendipity or on a hotel concierge's recommendation, the Web has innumerable sites designed to guide you to restaurants of good repute that serve the kind of food you like. The following sites offer extensive lists to choose from and/or shorter lists of the most highly recommended restaurants. In some cases, the recommendations and ratings come from "authorities" such as professional restaurant critics, but in many cases they come from the comments and votes of more ordinary restaurant goers. (For restaurants where you find only one single, glowing, "everything's perfect" review, consider the possibility that it may have been written by the restaurant's owner.) Most of the following sites cover restaurants internationally. Many allow you to add your own review of a restaurant. For other suggestions for restaurants in specific countries, take advantage of Wcities and Fodor's as well.

Restaurants.com
www.restaurants.com

Restaurants.com is a very rich restaurant guide with a broad range of categorized and detailed listings as well as ratings for restaurants around the world. Though the main page of Restaurants.com emphasizes the U.S., the site goes much further than that, covering more than 50 countries. Even for the U.S., the site has much more than the main page leads you to believe. The navigation of the site is a bit puzzling, but if you click in enough places and use the search boxes, you will find restaurants even for small towns.

For some countries, you are provided with a further geographic breakdown (states, provinces, territories, or neighborhoods). Restaurants.com also enables you to not just search by city but to narrow your search to any one of a broad range of cuisines, by nationality and style. You can further narrow your search to find restaurants that have won awards, provide banquet services, offer gift certificates, have take-out, or have their menus or reviews on Restaurants.com. When you get down to the actual list of restaurants, you will find their phone number, location, type of cuisine, and symbols for the criteria just mentioned, plus clickable symbols for those restaurants with an available map, Web site, or reservation booking option online (Figure 6.7). Other symbols indicate price range for the restaurant, whether the restaurant provides a delivery service, and whether it participates in United's Mileage Plus program. Not all restaurants are rated (by Restaurant.com's users), but for those that are, you will see numeric ratings for food, service, ambiance and overall. Click on the What They Are Saying link to get to reviews. If the name of the restaurant is clickable, you'll find a more detailed description and much more information about what the restaurant provides.

Dine.com
dine.com

According to its Web site, Dine.com is the "largest online restaurant review site," with more than 180,000 restaurants listed and more than 250,000 reviews. The site covers only U.S. and Canadian restaurants, and the Browse by Location button permits you to browse either by state (or province) or by type of restaurant. There are more than 150 types of restaurants to choose from, including dozens of national cuisines and dozens of other categories, including drive-in, Asian Fusion, dim sum, juice bar, potatoes, and vegan. With the search button, you can search by Restaurant Name, Dine.com Stars (based on reviews), Review Words, Restaurant Type, City, State, or ZIP code. When you search by ZIP code, you are then given an option to further refine your search by type of food. Whether browsing or searching, the first list of matching restaurants will show the rating, name, type, address, and phone number. Click on the name of a restaurant to see

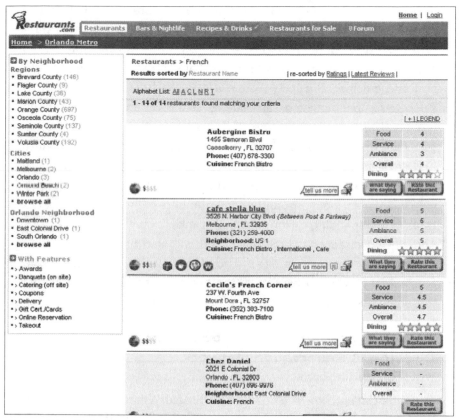

Figure 6.7   Example of a listing by city and category on Restaurants.com

more details and reviews. Dine.com's free membership will get you a newsletter and a personalized hotlist of restaurants you select.

Restaurant Row—World's Largest Dining Guide

www.restaurantrow.com

Restaurant Row contains listings for 170,000 restaurants in more than 13,000 cities and towns in more than 82 countries. The preponderance of restaurants covered here are in the U.S. (for example, there are only 345 U.K. restaurants and only 42 restaurants listed for Spain). The database is extensively searchable, and the main page provides boxes for searching by city or ZIP code or restaurant name. There are also links for five other types of searches: Simple (by location and cuisine), Proximity (within a specified distance from a U.S. ZIP Code, plus cuisine, ambiance, features, and entertainment), County (U.S. counties, cuisine, restaurant name), Neighborhood (for 22 U.S. cities), and Advanced (location, cuisine, ambiance, feature, and entertainment). All searches except for the Neighborhood search have the option to exclude fast-food restaurants. Search results provide the names, locations, and phone numbers of the matching restaurants and, depending on the restaurant, links to menus, maps, reviews, and driving directions (U.S. only). You will also find a link to make reservations (there is a fee). The "Top 10 by City" section of Restaurant Row provides lists of the top 10 rated restaurants by city. For some restaurants, you can purchase discount certificates.

GlobalDining.com—Global Restaurant Directory & Reservation Network
www.globaldining.com

GlobalDining.com is a restaurant directory that contains tens of thousands of restaurants from more than 40 countries. Sign up and the main page will be personalized for you with a list of your favorite restaurants. Use the Restaurant Finder menus on the main page to search by country, U.S. state, or ZIP code. At the city level, you will find a pull-down menu for narrowing your search by cuisine and a box to search by restaurant name. For each restaurant, you will find the address and phone number, and for some you will find a more detailed description and reviews. Restaurant information from GlobalDining.com is also available for mobile devices (wap.global dining.com).

Epicurious—Essential Restaurant Guide
www.epicurious.com/restaurants/erg

Epicurious.com is known primarily for its recipe collection, but it also has a Restaurant section that contains guides (its "essential restaurant guide") for 26 of the world's major cities and regions. For each region, Epicurious provides an overview, and for the cities, identifies recommendations for high-end restaurants, budget restaurants, hot spots, and local favorites. The America's Best Eats tab in the Restaurant section leads to articles such as *Gourmet* magazine's annual restaurant guide (U.S.) and numerous "Top 10" choices for where to get the best food, from bakeries and barbecue to pancakes and pie. Epicurious also has a forum, which is well-used to both comment on restaurants and to ask for suggestions about where to eat, etc.

GAYOT.com—Restaurants
www.gayot.com/restaurantpages

Though André Gayot's site, GAYOT.com, has expanded beyond a restaurant guide to encompass other aspects of travel, the heart of the site is still the restaurant guide, where you will find well-written reviews by professional restaurant critics. The Restaurant Search will lead you to reviews of restaurants in all U.S. states and 16 other countries. The site also has a significant collection of other restaurant-related information beyond reviews. Note particularly the Food Terms section, which provides lists of food terms for the following cuisines: French, Italian, Spanish/Latin American, Asian, Japanese, Thai, and Hawaiian.

Distinguished Restaurants of North America (DiRōNA)
www.dirona.com

The Distinguished Restaurants of North America (DiRōNA) site contains a list of more than 800 gourmet restaurants in the U.S.,

Canada, and Mexico that have received the DiRōNA Award of Excellence. On the site, you can search by name, location, and cuisine. Descriptions are minimal, but there is a link to the restaurant's site for most of the entries.

city-eating
www.city-eating.com

This site started as a guide to London restaurants but now provides reviews (both from the owners of the sites and from readers) for restaurants in more than 40 cities around the world. A main feature is city-eating's list of Top 30 Restaurants in the World, as determined by votes from readers.

Restaurants.co.uk
www.restaurants.co.uk

Restaurants.co.uk covers more than 25,000 restaurants throughout the U.K. Using the Advanced Search link, you can search by combinations of name, town, postcode, county, and cuisine. Search results pages will show the list of matching entries, with the name, location, and phone number, plus links to reviews and a map. (Reviews are not available for all restaurants.) If you notice a restaurant's name is underlined, click on the name for considerably more detail about the restaurant. The site also provides a link to browse for restaurants by county and town.

Worldpress.org—Travel and Dining
www.worldpress.org/travel.htm

Unlike most of the preceding sites, Worldpress.org does not provide extensive restaurant listings, but its Travel section regularly includes selected articles on top restaurants, such as, "World's Top 50 Restaurants 2005" and "Best Restaurants in New York City."

Restaurants Addressing Specific Needs and Tastes

Many of the restaurant sites just covered provide search options that enable a traveler to identify restaurants serving a particular kind of food. In some instances, though, it is more efficient to go to a site that focuses only on specific food requirements or preferences. The following are examples.

zabihah.com—Your Guide to Halal Eating
www.zabihah.com

This site has information on 3,841 halal establishments and contains 18,000 reviews. ("Halal" refers to meat slaughtered according to Muslim law.) The database is searchable by continent and country, and for the U.S., Canada, and the U.K., by state, province, and region, respectively. You can also search by keyword for names of restaurants. Search results also have tabs that lead to a list of grocery stores for that location. From results lists, click on the name of the restaurant for a page with further details and reviews. Click on the Halal Airline Meals link for a list of airlines that serve halal meals. A mobile version of the site is available (www.zabihah.com/mobile).

Shamash—Kosher Restaurant Database
www.shamash.org/kosher

The restaurant section of the Shamash site features a database of more than 2,600 kosher restaurants in 50 countries. From the main page, you can search by restaurant name, location, and category (meat, dairy, vegetarian, and pareve).

KosherDine.com
www.kosherdine.com

With the KosherDine.com site, you can browse lists of kosher restaurants by continent, country, and city (for larger countries).

Results display the name, address, phone number, and, in some cases, the type of cuisine, kosher category, price range, additional kosher information, and a link to the restaurant's site.

HappyCow's Vegetarian Guide to Restaurants & Health Food Stores
www.happycow.net

HappyCow's Vegetarian Guide to Restaurants & Health Food Stores contains information on more than 6,000 vegetarian or "vegetarian-friendly" restaurants worldwide. To browse the list, click on a continent on the first page, then on the country, and, for larger countries, the city. On country and city pages, at the top of the page, you have a choice of seeing "100 [percent] vegetarian restaurants only" or vegetarian-friendly restaurants. For the U.S., a Map link enables you to see the restaurant locations on a map. You can also search by keyword using the Search link on the home page. Listings show the name of the restaurant, the location, phone number, categories of service (Lacto, Vegan-Friendly, Organic, International, Gourmet, Fast-Food, Buffet, Take-Out, etc.), price range, and a brief description (sometimes type of food, hours, credit cards accepted, etc.). If the name is underlined, click on it to visit the restaurant's site. For all listings, there is a link to read or add reviews, but you will find reviews for only a portion of the restaurants listed. While you are on the site, look around. Beyond restaurants, there is a lot of additional vegetarian-related information on travel, raw food, health, humor, etc., along with a Discussion Forum with a variety of topics.

VegDining.com
www.vegdining.com

VegDining.com has listings for more than 1,000 "fully vegetarian" restaurants around the world. From the main page, you can search by city or browse by continent and country (and then, in some cases, by city, region, etc.). Listings are very brief, usually showing just the name, address, and phone number. In some cases, there will be a link to brief comments from site visitors.

World-Wide Sushi Restaurant Reference
www.sushiref.com

Though generally not consumed for religious, ethical, or health reasons, sushi has gained a very large following in recent years. For that reason and also because it is an example of a "cuisine-specific" restaurant directory, the World-Wide Sushi Restaurant Reference deserves attention. With this site, you will be able to quickly find your way to sushi almost anywhere in the world. Though the site has related information on sushi etiquette and sushi terminology, the most substantive part is a directory of around 3,000 sushi restaurants worldwide. You can get to the listings either through the geographic directory or the alphabetical index. The lists for a particular city provide the names, addresses, and phone numbers for each restaurant, plus a More Information link for detailed information from site users. Users are encouraged to update information about any of the restaurants.

Roadfood.com
www.roadfood.com

Roadfood.com is a unique restaurant site and a potentially very helpful one if you are a traveler along U.S. (and some Canadian) highways. The site contains descriptions, reviews, and even photographs of the food in more than 1,000 "local" restaurants—really a "taste of America." In addition to the listings themselves, the Forums section features more good information about a wide range of roadside foods.

Food and Wine Tours

If eating good food and drinking fine wine is not just a *part* of your planned trip but the main reason for going, there are many sites offering information about tours that focus on food and wine. If you want to be part of the process and take home added cooking skills, the Web provides information about thousands of opportunities to attend cooking schools. The following are a few examples of the many sites that will get you on your way. Especially since food and wine tour services tend to be fairly "local," explore further with specific search engine searches, such as *wine tours australia* or *cooking schools Tuscany*. For cooking schools, make use of the three general resource guides for specialty travel (InfoHub, TouristClick, and Specialty Travel Index) discussed in Chapter 8, "Sites for Special Groups and Special Needs."

ShawGuides—The Guide to Recreational & Wine Schools

cookforfun.shawguides.com

The Guide to Recreational & Wine Schools from ShawGuides is an excellent resource for locating "recreational" cooking and wine schools around the world. On the site, you will find more than 3,000 upcoming cooking and wine programs from more than 900 providers. Use the search box to search for a particular cuisine or type of cooking, a particular destination, or for that matter, any word that you think might be part of the course description. The Search by Date link takes you to a search form where you can specify a range of dates, focus (e.g., Baking-pastry, Wine, Mexican), location, and keyword. You can also browse using the geographic links on the main page. On search (or browsing) results pages, click on the name of the course or company for a page containing a detailed overview of the offering and a link to the provider's site. A newsletter is available that will provide you with new listings and a calendar of classes.

Food & Wine Trails

www.foodandwinetrails.com

Food & Wine Trails is a travel agency that offers 40 tours annually to France, Italy, Spain, Austria, New Zealand, and California (Napa/Sonoma). The agency also offers food and wine cruises. Click on the Chef Guides link to get biographies of tour leaders.

Tour de Forks—Uncommon Epicurean Adventures

www.tourdeforks.com

Tour de Forks's tours to Sicily, Sydney, Melbourne, and Tasmania offer food, wine, cooking classes, demonstrations, and face-to-face meetings with produce growers and winemakers. (The name of the site itself deserves some kind of award.)

The International Kitchen

www.theinternationalkitchen.com

The International Kitchen bills itself as "the leading provider of cooking school vacations to Italy, France and Spain since 1994" and offers tours of from two to seven days, as well as one-day cooking classes.

Cuisine International

www.cuisineinternational.com

Cuisine International can get you behind a student's apron in schools in Italy, France, Spain, Portugal, England, Greece, Morocco, or Brazil. Click on the Schools section for a list of schools, then the map, and then on the image next to each listing for details, dates, and prices. Also check out the People section for bios of instructors. So you can start practicing at home, the site also provides a sampling of recipes from the schools.

Online Restaurant Reservations

Many of the restaurant sites provide booking capabilities for all or some of the restaurants they list. There are some sites devoted specifically to reservations, including the following three. To state the obvious, though, if you found a restaurant in one of the restaurant directories or elsewhere online, you probably found the phone number, and the phone often works beautifully for reservations.

OpenTable
www.opentable.com

On the OpenTable.com site, you can book reservations for 6,000 restaurants in the U.S., the U.K., Canada, Singapore, Hong Kong, Japan, and Mexico (though there are relatively few restaurants listed for the last three countries). From the main page, click on a country or U.S. state. From the next page, select a specific restaurant or a locality, a cuisine, a price range, the date and time range, and specify the number of guests. OpenTable will reply with a list of matching restaurants and available times. To complete the reservation, you must be signed up with OpenTable, but reservations are free.

We8there.com
www.we8there.com

We8there.com is a restaurant review site that focuses specifically on the quality of restaurant *service*. Many restaurant sites have reviews for some of the restaurants covered, but this site is all reviews and ratings, contributed by readers. Coverage is mainly U.S., but it also includes reviews of more than 150 restaurants in other countries. You will also find B&B, hotel, and motel reviews. Mobile access is available at we8t.com.

Getting a Head Start on Reading the Menu

If you go into a restaurant in a foreign country and don't speak the language, there is an increasing chance that an English menu may be available. This is both good news and bad news: The good news is that you will know what you are ordering; the bad new is that the restaurant to some degree caters to tourists (even that's not necessarily "bad," but it does mean that you may not experience a truly "local" meal, ambiance, and crowd). If you can't read the menu, there is always at least a work-around—whip out something to help you translate the terms. If you have a good guide, it may even include a glossary. Or before you leave home, go to one of the following sites and print out a list of food terms. If you don't understand the local alphabet or character set, then just hope the waiter speaks a language you can understand.

GAYOT.com—A Guide to International Food Terms
www.gayot.com/restaurants/menusavvy_main.html

GAYOT.com, which was previously discussed as a restaurant directory, also contains a section that provides a handy glossary for menu terms for the following languages: French, Italian, Spanish/Latin American, Asian, Japanese, Thai, and Hawaiian.

Gastronomical Dictionary
www.todine.net/dictionary.html

The Gastronomical Dictionary contains individual pages for each of 15 categories of foods and beverages. On each page, you will find the equivalent terms for Italian, English, French, Spanish, and German. If you want to "take it with you," you will probably want to print out all 15 pages.

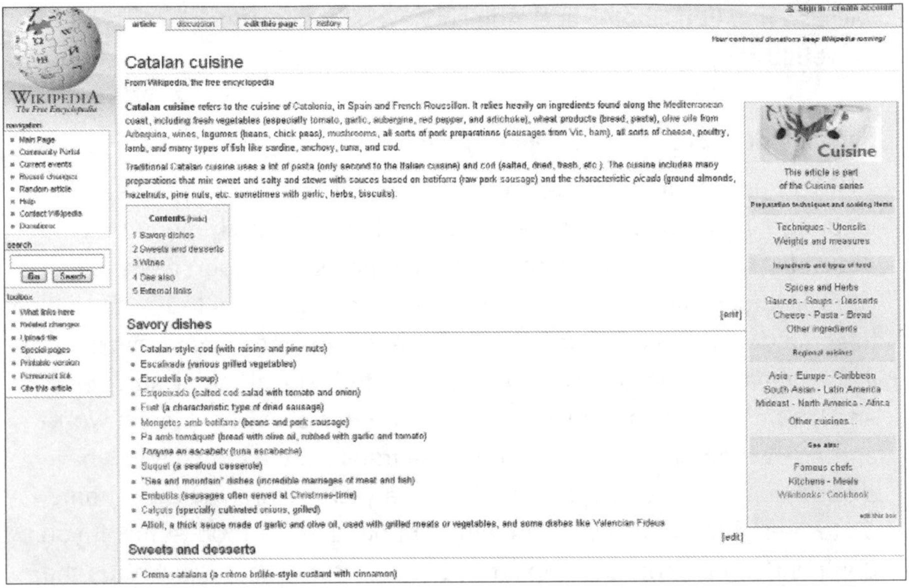

Figure 6.8   Cuisine article from Wikipedia, including a list of food terms

Wikipedia

wikipedia.org

If the other two sites don't address the language you need, try Wikipedia. On the home page, search for phrases such as *Croatian cuisine.* You won't always find such an article for the language you need, but in many cases you will. Many of the national cuisine articles in Wikipedia contain lists that will serve as a food glossary (Figure 6.8).

Hotel and Restaurant Discussion Groups and Forums

To get other travelers' opinions and suggestions for hotels and restaurants, check out the general travel discussion sites discussed in Chapter 2, "Travel Guides Online." TripAdvisor.com is particularly useful for finding travelers' opinions of hotels. From the sites discussed in this chapter, make use of the forums included in the following:

HotelChatter
www.hotelchatter.com

HotelShark
www.hotelshark.com

About.com—Bed & Breakfasts —Forums
bandb.about.com/mpboards.htm

Epicurious—Forums
www.epicurious.com/forums

HappyCow's Vegetarian Forum
www.happycow.net/forum

Roadfood.com—Forums
www.roadfood.com/forums

Adventure, Outdoor, and Educational Travel

A typical traveler may think of travel as just for relaxation, for the joy of sunbathing on a tropical beach, or for seeing the sights of a city. But for many, travel means going beyond the ordinary, pushing their own personal envelopes, and treating the body and mind to a totally new experience. For those travelers, the mention of "travel" may conjure visions of climbing in the Himalayas, taking a cruise to Antarctica, going to Peru for a course on pre-Columbian culture, or helping to excavate prehistoric settlements on Mallorca.

Some travelers might even think the phrase "adventure travel" is redundant, since, in one sense, almost any travel (even business travel) can be thought of as an adventure. The same could be said about the phrase "educational travel." (Also, if you think about the outdoor aspect, it is difficult to travel without going "outdoors" to at least some degree.) This chapter will look at Web sites that emphasize one or more of those concepts, sites that get you off your beach chair and out of the museum and get both your mind and body cranking faster.

If you didn't recognize it immediately, those three travel goals—adventure, outdoor experiences, and education—overlap considerably. Likewise, so do the sites that discuss them. In the following pages, many sites that are included in one of those three categories could easily fit in at least one other category, and for each category, there are hundreds of sites that could be included in this chapter. The ones chosen for inclusion are here because they are better known, exemplify a particular type of site, or are just plain interesting. Some are travel agencies, and some are sites that bring together the offerings of hundreds of travel agencies and tour providers. Some cover a broad range of adventures, while others are specialized. Regardless of the category in which they are found and regardless of the particular reason for their inclusion, this selection of sites will hopefully increase your awareness of the possibilities for fun, adventure, excercise, health, and learning. As you examine the Web sites, look particularly at the detailed categories the sites themselves use. Most provide more than two dozen categories and subcategories of vacations, and the categories they use vary considerably. If you are interested in cycling vacations, look for sites that provide such a category rather than those that include cycling under another category. If the site has bothered to create such a category, it probably has given considerable attention to such activities. Also, with the tremendous varieties of adventure, outdoor, and educational trips, this chapter can provide only a sampling. The sites that follow, and the categories they use, put you only one additional click away from lots of information on just about any type of adventure, outdoor, or educational vacation you are seeking.

Adventure Travel

There are a variety of sites that focus on adventure travel, and a number of others include substantial sections on the topic. How they define "adventure" can differ considerably, from simply getting away from the mundane to "soft adventure" to exhilarating yet exhausting trips where you have a good chance of earning some worthwhile scratches and bruises. In this section, you will first encounter a site for articles providing an overview and guidance for pursuing adventure travel. The next two sites are brief journeys back to two familiar general online travel guides where the overall flavor is adventure. The remaining sites are guides, travel agencies, and tour providers where the main thrust is adventure, but from a variety of angles.

About.com—Adventure Travel

adventuretravel.about.com

If your last five vacations were spent on a beach and you've decided that you are ready for something a bit more exhilarating but aren't quite sure where to head, the Adventure Travel section of About.com is a good place to get a feel for some of the possibilities that adventure travel holds. The scores of articles here range from acquainting you with basic adventures (e.g., snorkeling basics) to tips on getting started with some not-so-basic adventures (e.g., learning to skydive). In addition to the "getting started" articles, you will find collections of articles on Travel Essentials, Water Adventures, Outdoor Adventures, Destinations, Haunted Adventures, Ecotourism, Extreme Adventures, Adventure Flight, Winter Adventures, Historical Adventures, and Adventure Trade Resources. The latter section will put you in touch with a variety of trade organizations involved in adventure travel.

Rough Guides

www.roughguides.com

Although Rough Guides was discussed in some detail in Chapter 2, it's worth mentioning again since the general flavor of Rough Guides is "adventure." In Rough Guides, you will be led to adventure that is off-the-beaten track and explore destinations and sights that many travelers may have never heard of.

Rough Guides in general tends to address the adventure side of travel more than other general guides do. Use the Destinations section to identify unique and exciting stops where just being there is unarguably an adventure in itself.

Lonely Planet
www.lonelyplanet.com

Lonely Planet was also discussed in Chapter 2 and also leans toward less-visited locations. Under its Destinations section, click on a country and then look under the See and Events sections to find adventure in less-traveled locations.

InfoHub Specialty Travel Guide
www.infohub.com

InfoHub's subtitle is "The Ultimate Source of Inspiring Travel Ideas." Although "ultimate" is quite a claim, the site furnishes an impressive compendium of 14,000 vacations in more than 150 destinations for 100-plus different special interest categories. You can browse by location and through categories such as Arts & Crafts, Bicycle Tours, Culture & History, Eco & Wildlife, Hiking & Trekking, Hunting, Naturist, Paddling & Rafting, Railway Trips, Scuba Diving, Spiritual, and Sports (Figure 7.1). Subcategories include such adventures as Caving, Dogsledding, Llama Trekking, Egyptology, Gambling, Volcano Tours, Camel Riding, and Yachting. For each vacation, InfoHub provides details of the vacation (itinerary, dates, activities, etc., and information on the tour provider, including the provider's other offerings). Reservations are not made through the site, but a link will take you to a page for requesting a brochure from the provider.

iExplore
www.iexplore.com

iExplore is a travel agency for "adventure and experiential travel," with thousands of tours at guaranteed low prices. Use the Trip Finder

Figure 7.1   InfoHub Specialty Travel Guide

section to search by region (continent), country, and activity, the latter with 22 categories, including outdoor, culinary, cultural, ecotours, and safaris, among others. While you are on the site, take advantage of the Community section, which contains 300,000 traveler reviews and 225,000 photos. On iExplore, you can also ask other users questions and find a travel buddy (e.g., "Looking for traveling companion for trekking/cultural trip to Bhutan in October"). The content of the Travel Guides section of iExplore comes from Columbus Guides.

National Geographic Adventure Magazine

www.nationalgeographic.com/adventure

The National Geographic Adventure online magazine is another good site for an introduction to the possibilities for adventure travel. The site has articles, article excerpts, great photos (of course, since it's from *National Geographic*), and even video. The site also can also get your travel juices flowing with its lists of adventure trips, which are displayed by destination (continent) and by category (Active/ Adventure, Family, Photography, Private Jet/Air, Rail Journeys, Small Ships, and Land Journeys). For the trips listed, you will find descriptions, prices, and a link to the site of the company that provides the trip.

Gordon's Guide

www.gordonsguide.com

The Gordon's Guide site is designed to bring travelers together with more than 700 "adventure and active travel" companies. One of the main sections of this site is Travel Categories, which consists of four main categories and more than 50 subcategories. One of the many good aspects of the Gordon's site is that the first travel category focuses on adventure and active travel for *families* and includes 33 subcategories, such as Cattle Drives & Working Ranches (*City Slickers* lives!), Houseboat Rentals, Jungle Lodges, Wagon Train Vacations, Safaris, and more. The other main travel categories are Resort Destinations & Vacation Rentals, Special Interest Travel, and Featured Adventures. The Special Interest Travel section provides subcategories ranging from Corporate Team Building to Paintball & Skirmish Adventures. Browsing the Travel Destinations portion of Gordon's will lead you to adventures in 100-plus countries. Whether you find your way by category or by destination, for each offering you will typically find extensive detail, photos, and a form to fill out to contact the provider.

Specialty Travel Index

www.spectrav.com

Specialty Travel Index, from the publisher of *Specialty Travel* magazine, is an index to the specialty and adventure tours provided by more than 400 tour operators around the world. Select a destination and interest/activity from the pull-down menus on the home page, and Specialty Travel will provide a list of tour operators with opportunities that match. For each provider, you will get a brief description and contact information (o mail, phone number, and Web site). The Activity/Interest menu lists more than 300 categories.

World Expeditions

worldexpeditions.com

World Expeditions, which got started in 1975 as a Himalayan trekking company, focuses mainly on very active vacations (mountaineering, canoeing, trekking, etc.) but also offers some more sedate adventures, such as day walking and culinary touring. You can browse through the opportunities by using the Regions of the World, Types of Adventures, Charity Challenges, Community Project Travel, and Deals tabs near the top of the page, or you can use the search form on the main page. The Advanced Search form lets you search by Region, Country, Activity, Grading (introductory, moderate, challenging, etc.), and Dates. On the Activity menu are 24 activity categories, including Camel Riding, Community Project Travel, and Over 55 Adventures. For each adventure, the site provides a general description, dates, costs, activities, grading, and duration, but further details and bookings are handled by e-mail, mail, or fax. World Expeditions has separate sites for Australia, the U.S., the U.K., New Zealand, and Canada.

G.A.P Adventures
www.gapadventures.com

   G.A.P Adventures is a tour operator that specializes in off-the-beaten track, "unique, small group outdoor adventure travel experiences" with an emphasis on cultures, sustainable (environmentally low-impact), responsible tourism (Figure 7.2). Using the search form on the main page, you can search by location, activities (Culture/History, Cycling, Diving, Kayak/Canoe, Rafting, Trekking, Wildlife/Nature, Yacht/Sailing), and trip styles (Basix, Original, Comfort, Active, Family, Gourmet, Independent, Expedition, Volunteer, Overlands, Exploratory). "Basix" tours combine independent travel with a guided tour; the Original style includes tours that emphasize uniqueness and variety. On Exploratory tours, you go along as G.A.P (Great Adventure People) tries new destinations, trails, and adventures. Overall, G.A.P has hundreds of tours on seven continents. G.A.P offers a newsletter and a My Planner feature that keeps track of tours you are interested in and keeps you updated on news about those tours.

International Expeditions
www.ietravel.com

   International Expeditions specializes in small group natural history expeditions with an emphasis on enrichment, while at the same time providing top-rate accommodations. Destinations are extremely varied, ranging from Mongolia to the Galapagos to Tierra del Fuego.

Alpine Ascents International
www.alpineascents.com

   Alpine Ascents International is an example of a very specialized tour provider site, offering a mountaineering school and expeditions to the Seven Summits, four Himalayan peaks, and other climbs, treks, and tours. Even if you aren't planning on joining an expedition, you

Figure 7.2   G.A.P Adventures main page

might enjoy reading the cybercasts from expeditions currently in progress.

Earth River Expeditions
www.earthriver.com

Earth River Expeditions specializes in rafting on some of the world's classic and wild rivers in some of the most remote places on Earth, including Patagonia, Chile's Futaleufu, Peru's Colca, Tibet's Upper Yangtze, the Himalayan Po Tsangpo, and China's Great Bend of the Yangtze. Earth River Expeditions also offers sea kayaking trips to Fiji, the Lakes of Patagonia, the Yukon's Primrose wilderness, and a trek through British Columbia's Headwall Canyon.

Ranchweb.com
www.ranchweb.com

If you are considering a dude ranch vacation, Ranchweb.com can put you in touch with more than 200 dude and guest ranches, mainly in the U.S. but also in Canada, Argentina, Brazil, and Mexico. With the All Dude Ranches section or the Location Search menu, you can choose ranches by location, but also be sure to check out the other sections of the site. The Selecting a Ranch section provides lists of ranches that offer particular activities, such as riding (naturally), cattle drives, fishing, golf, and spas. The Dude Ranch Rates section has a useful comparison table for prices and activities offered. If you use the Space Availability Finder electronic form and specify the locations and dates of interest, you will get a reply showing what is available for that period.

Robert Young Pelton's Come Back Alive
comebackalive.com

If you really want "adventure," try this site! The creator of the Come Back Alive site is Robert Young Pelton, author of *The World's Most*

Dangerous Places. Most of the adventures are not as extreme as might be indicated by the title, and much of the site is *about* adventure travel and advice for travelers rather than suggestions on where to go, though you will indeed get some suggestions for destinations in the Dangerous Places section. It describes conditions, challenges, and dangers for 31 countries (including sections on dangers such as the body parts business in Brazil). The Black Flag Cafe is a very active forum (see the section on Discussion Groups at the end of this chapter).

Outdoor Travel

As a category, "outdoor" may seem quite redundant since adventure travel was just covered, and, indeed, none of the adventure sites are heavy on "indoor" vacations. The adventure/outdoor distinction is indeed somewhat arbitrary, but most of the following sites emphasize camping, hiking, canoeing, and related activities. On the pragmatic side, if a selected site claims it is an outdoor rather than an adventure travel site, it got put here. Sites included cover national (and other) parks, camping, and backpacking, and a mixture of other sites to provide a sampling of the variety of outdoor travel sites available. For national parks, the national sites for the U.K., the U.S., and Canada are included. For national parks of other countries, try a search such as *national parks Germany*. (Unless there is an English version, you may not easily find the official parks site this way, but the search will probably find sites that at least give you names, locations, and descriptions of the national parks for that country.) For parks, camping, biking, and many other outdoor destinations and activities, start with the following site, GORP. For sites more specifically about recreational vehicle (RV) camping, see Chapter 4.

GORP

gorp.away.com

GORP's claim that it is "your encyclopedic resource for outdoor recreation—hiking, biking, rafting, camping, fishing, and more" is an ambitious goal, but GORP does an admirable job of fulfilling that claim, though its geographic coverage is predominantly U.S. GORP is a part of the Away Network, which includes the Away.com site (with an emphasis on "active travel" and destination guides, interest guides, travel deals, etc.) and OutsideOnline (the site for *Outside* magazine). GORP's main page contains articles on the outdoors, featured destinations and photos, and an excellent menu and site map that clearly organizes the major content into categories: Destinations, Gear, Most Popular, Activities, Interests, Parks, Top 10 Lists, City Guides, and Active Vacations. The tabs at the tops of pages will lead you to the core features of the site. The following is what you will find under each of the tabs:

- Destination Guides – Use either the map or menus to choose a U.S. state or a continent, or use the Resources section at the bottom of the Destinations page to make your choices. In this latter section, you will find additional links for the following categories: National Parks, National Forests, State Parks, Seasonal Guide, Top 10's, and Activity How-To's. For most of the links under these categories, you will find one or more of GORP's articles on the topic or destination. For U.S. state destinations, GORP also provides Activity guides (including articles on each activity listed for that state) and information on parks, monuments, and other destinations and recreation areas. For each of those, a substantial description and other information of use to the traveler are typically included. For Canadian destinations, you will find outdoor articles on the country, provinces, and activities. For Europe, you will find articles on "Top 20 Adventures" (for about six countries) and other articles on countries and activities.

- Activity Guides – Find links to GORP articles, guides, lists, how-to's, where-to's, and recommendations for Hiking & Camping, Biking, Fishing, Horseback, Family Activities, Caving, Paddling, Climbing, Snow Sports, Drives/RVs, and Nature/Environment (Figure 7.3). For each of these, the material provided by GORP could easily constitute an entire site.

- National Parks – Check out the index to U.S. National Parks by region. Click on the name of a park for a detailed description and suggestions as to what to do there. Move On To and More On links on a park page take you to further detail about the park. By the time you have gone through all the links for a particular park, you will probably know everything you will ever need to know about it. Look for sub-tabs for National Parks, National Forests, National Monuments, Wilderness Areas, and World Parks. Most of these tabs will lead to a listing by U.S. state, with links to information on each park. The last tab, World Parks, takes you to a selective list of parks by continent and country, with links to articles, descriptions, and other details about parks in more than 30 countries.

- Close to Home (City Guides) – Read articles on outdoor activities for 50 U.S. cities that are within a weekend's drive.

- Outdoor Gear – Read articles, reviews, and buying guides (from *Outside* magazine) for just about any equipment you might need for just about any legal outdoor activity.

- Active Vacations – Use the travel agency section of the site (and the most international section) to find outdoor tours and trips for destinations worldwide. The Search form on this page enables you to search by continent, country, and activity.

Figure 7.3   GORP Activities page

In addition to the vast amount of content covered, there is even more on GORP. Look around each page for additional links. To get access to the full content, you will need to register, but it is free.

National Parks and Other Parks

For national, state, county, and provincial parks, there is usually a government site that provides lists of parks and a lot of other useful information about parks all in one place. GORP, which was just discussed, also includes extensive information on U.S. national parks and some major parks in other countries. You can also make very effective use of a search engine to get information on a specific park or parks in a specific region, for example, *Yellowstone National Park*, *Ontario parks*, *Kenya parks*, or *Virginia parks*. Depending on the nature of the park and the country, you might want to substitute some other words for "parks," such as *preserves* or *reserves*.

U.S. National Park Service—Experience Your America
www.nps.gov

The U.S. National Park Service (NPS) site is rich in information about the NPS, its role, responsibilities, and services, but for someone planning to visit the parks, the first stop should probably be the Find a Park section of the site. There you can find information about each individual park, national historic site, monument, cemetery, memorial, wild river, and trail. You can browse alphabetically by name, location, or topic. On the individual pages for each park, you will find a description, activities, fees, and, dependent upon the particular property, such things as activities for kids, history, accessibility, hours, etc. If you don't easily find a link for camping reservations, go directly to reservations.nps.gov.

Council for National Parks
www.cnp.org.uk

The Council for National Parks site provides general information about the U.K. national park system, but of more use to travelers are the links found on the map under the National Parks button. Click

The Traveler's Web

there to get to links to the individual sites for each park. Since each park authority produces its own site, the content of these may vary, but you generally will get a good overview of the park, its features, and what you can do there.

Parks Canada
www.pc.gc.ca

Parks Canada, which is the official site of the Parks Canada Agency, covers not only Canada's tremendously varied and scenic National Parks but also National Historic Sites and National Marine Conservation Areas. Click on one of the National Parks of Canada links on the main page for a page with an alphabetical list of parks, or browse by province. A search box allows you to search by keyword. The pages for the individual parks, sites, and conservation areas provide full details about hours of operation, fees, reservations, how to get there, and what to do there. Take advantage also of the Travel Planners, Reservation Service, and other resources under the Planning Your Visit section.

ILoveParks.com
www.iloveparks.com

ILoveParks.com provides links to the sites for national and other parks in 50 countries.

Camping, Hiking, Nature Tours, Etc.

There are more than 4 million Web pages that have "camping" in their title, with content ranging from philosophy to gear to recipes. All camping-related topics can be useful to the avid camper, but most of that content goes beyond the "travel" emphasis of this book. For a very broad look at camping, GORP, which was discussed earlier, is an excellent starting place. Most of the following sites focus a bit more on where to go.

America Out of Doors
www.americaoutofdoors.com

America Out of Doors is an extensive Web resource guide with links to hundreds of sites on Hunting, Fishing, Camping, Backpacking, On the Trail, Off-Roading, Skiing, and related topics. If you feel you need more U.S.-related outdoor links than are included in this chapter, America Out of Doors is a good next step.

OutdoorPlaces.com
www.outdoorplaces.com

If you are "into" hiking, camping, or paddling, or plan to be, you may want to spend some time with OurdoorPlaces.com. Look under the Features button for dozens of straightforward articles on these topics, ranging from frostbite to snowshoe basics to dealing with bear encounters. The Gear section will provide reviews, buying guides, care guides, and checklists. Though not as extensive as previous sites, OutdoorPlaces.com's Destinations section can help you locate parks by state.

Wildernet
www.wildernet.com

For someone looking for outdoor recreation, Wildernet provides a database of 40,000 area and activity descriptions throughout the U.S. Using the menus on the main page, you can select by state, from a list of 56 activities, or use the search box to search by keyword. If you select a state, you can narrow your search by type of location (national parks, state parks, national forests, lakes and dams, etc.) or by activity. Further links on a state page will identify campgrounds that take reservations, as well as local outfitters, guides, guidebooks, and maps. You can also begin by choosing an activity on the main page and then narrow the options by state. Whether you use one of those approaches or use the search box, you will be presented with a list of places that match. Click on one for a description, contact information, and, in many cases, links to a site, current conditions, and trip reports (from visitors). For some, you will find Trip Planner links to local hotels, B&Bs, car rentals, and other services. The site also sells books, maps, and gear.

Factivities.co.uk
www.factivities.co.uk

Factivities.co.uk features a listing of more than 150 types of activities in more than 1,800 activity centers in the U.K., which are browsable in the following categories: On Foot, On Wheels, On Water, On the Hoof, On the Edge (Figure 7.4), In the Air, Down Under, and Else. In addition to selecting activities by browsing through the categories, you can also search within each section by county, town (and how far from there you are willing to travel), category of activity, specific activity, group or individual bookings, age level, provider (company), and more. The site provides information on the activities and providers, but bookings are done by contacting the provider. The list of activities at Factivities.co.uk is extremely varied, from the more mundane, such as rock climbing, survival training, Nordic walking, and stock car racing, to the more esoteric, such as escape and invasion, model flying, parakarting, kite landboarding, blind driving, dragonboat racing, gypsy experience, ferreting, Llama trekking, sheepdog trials, abseiling, sphereing, aerobatic flying, wing walking, caving, and yurt experiences.

Backroads
www.backroads.com

Figure 7.4   On the Edge section at Factivities.co.uk

Backroads is an outstanding example of a tour company that specializes in active outdoor experiences. Backroads leads camping, walking, hiking, biking, and multisport excursions in Europe, Africa, Asia, Latin America, and North America. In case you are more inclined toward a nice comfortable mattress while at the same time enjoying outdoor activities, they can also provide both "premier" and "casual" inn trips.

Woodall's
www.woodalls.com

Woodall's has been known as a resource (perhaps *the* resource) for tenters and RVers since before the Internet was even imagined. As a matter of fact, it has been providing information on U.S. and Canadian campgrounds and related information since 1935, and its print publications have been used by millions. The Woodall's site provides not just one database, but several—for RV campgrounds, tenting campgrounds, RV sales, RV services/parts/accessories, on-site rentals at campgrounds, RV rentals, destinations, and activities. All databases are searchable by state or province and city, plus additional criteria depending on the particular database. In the RV campground database, for example, you can narrow your search by the following criteria: 50 amps availability, accommodations for big rigs, allowance of pull-throughs, fishing, swimming, Internet access, laundry, year-round availability, and extended-stay campgrounds. Reservations are made by directly contacting the provider. To use the directories on the site, registration is required (it's free). On the Woodall's site, also take advantage of the collection of articles, the RV and the camping links (under Off-Site Links), and the very active Open Roads Forum, with more than 2 million postings.

ReserveAmerica

www.reserveamerica.com

For many of the sites that provide directories of campsites, you are provided with information on how to contact the campsites, but there is no reservation service on the site itself. ReserveAmerica is specifically a campground reservation service, providing bookings at 150,000 campsites throughout the U.S. (plus Manitoba). It processes more than 3 million reservations per year. From ReserveAmerica's main page, you can search Facility Type (Campsite, Cabin, Day Use, etc.), Campground Name, and State or Province, plus check availability for specific dates (Figure 7.5). You can also locate sites by using the browsable map. ReserveAmerica provides extensive detail about each campground, including a map showing facilities, background on the campground, driving directions, rules, fees, and special events. When making a reservation, you can choose by site type, camp area, and even specific campsite. ReserveAmerica has a companion site, ReserveUSA.com (www.reserveusa.com), which provides reservations

Figure 7.5 ReserveAmerica main page

specifically for camping and recreation facilities run by the U.S.D.A. Forest Service, U.S. Army Corps of Engineers, National Park Service, Bureau of Land Management, and Bureau of Reclamation and covers more than 45,000 reservable facilities at more than 1,700 locations.

Canadian Rockies

www.canadianrockies.net

There are several directories covering campgrounds throughout Canada, such as Camping-Canada.com (www.camping-canada.com) and Campgrounds · Campings Canada (www.camp canada.com). Canadian Rockies ("The Website for the Rocky

Mountains") highlights only a portion of Canada, but it serves more as a general travel guide with extensive detail about activities and accommodations, including camping.

CampingFrance.com
www.campingfrance.com

If you are planning on camping in France, CampingFrance.com provides information on thousands of campsites, which are searchable and browsable by region, department, and theme. By using the Criteria Search section on the main page, you can search by name or criteria selection, which allows you to be more specific with regard to location, facilities, and activities. Descriptions of each site generally provide details about location, facilities, phone numbers, prices, and links to the campground's Web site and reservations services.

Wilderness Travel
www.wildernesstravel.com

Wilderness Travel is a tour provider offering more than 100 off-the-beaten-path tours in 60 countries. Categories include Adventure Sailing, Archaeology, Cultural Adventures, Expedition Cruising, Hiking/Trekking, Sea Kayaking, Snorkeling, Walking, and Wildlife & Natural History. If you prefer not to travel in a group, Wilderness Travel will also provide specially designed itineraries with accommodations and guides for as few as two people.

Country Walkers
www.countrywalkers.com

If you prefer to walk and quietly and healthily observe and immerse yourself in the details of the country around you, the Country Walkers tour company can provide you with walking (or hiking or snowshoeing or horseback) vacations in more than 30 countries.

Nature Tours and Outdoor Odds and Ends

Victor Emanuel Nature Tours

www.ventbird.com

Victor Emanuel Nature Tours (VENT) may be your best bet to get a look at a red-bearded bee-eater or the Malaysian rail-babbler in its natural habitat. This tour company provides not just birding tours but other nature tours to more than 100 destinations, with more than 140 tours and covering every continent.

Scuba Diving

scubadiving.com

The Scuba Diving site is not just an example of a scuba site but also a reminder that whatever your sport, there are likely to be related magazines, which will frequently have sites with useful resources, even beyond what is offered in the print issues. Scuba Diving, for example, has not only articles but guides to favorite scuba diving locations around the world, reviews of gear and accessories, and a scuba diving message board.

Educational Travel

Just as almost all travel could or should be inherently "adventurous," travel also tends to be inherently "educational." But some journeys are designed with learning not just as a by-product but rather as a primary goal. There are travel agencies, tour operators, and sites that serve that goal, and their courses and other educational portions of trips can range from hours to weeks. A number of sites listed earlier in the Adventure and Outdoor categories provide tours that could easily be placed in the educational category. The following sites provide a further glimpse of what is out there in the way of "study" vacations. Also included are some sites that provide an introduction to the whole study-abroad world, most typically offering semester, year, or longer programs. For study-abroad resources, the StudyAbroad.com and IIEPassport sites, which will be discussed later, provide many links for a fuller exploration of that broad topic.

ShawGuides
www.shawguides.com

Whether you want to study cooking or cuneiform, Chinese or Czech, ShawGuides will get you to a fun place to do it. The site is a compendium of learning vacation and career courses, workshops, and other programs from more than 5,800 sponsors in more than 140 countries. From the main page, you can browse for courses and workshops under the following categories: Cultural Travel, Art & Craft Workshops, Career Cooking Schools, Recreational Cooking & Wine Schools, Golf Schools & Camps, Photography, Film & New Media Schools, Photography, Film & New Media Workshops, Language Vacations, Writers Conferences & Workshops, Tennis Schools & Camps, and High Performance & Discovery Programs. Clicking on any of those categories will lead to a page where you can search for opportunities by topic or date, or you can browse by month, season, U.S. state, U.S. region, or country and by specific focus for most topics (Figure 7.6). For each course, you will find a description, link to the provider's site, number of programs per year, program length, group size, faculty, costs, locations, months, focus, contact information, and calendar of upcoming workshops, programs, and events.

Educational Tour Companies

For decades, companies have provided tours for students and others, usually led by a teacher or other person who has agreed to serve as a group leader in return for having all or part of their own expenses paid. These tours usually also have a "tour leader" who is paid by the

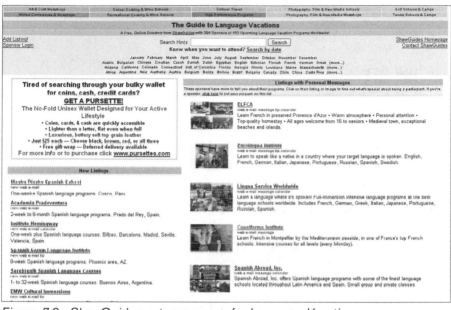

Figure 7.6   ShawGuides category page for Language Vacations

tour company and deals with the day-to-day logistics of the tour. Most of these companies provide tours to a wide range of countries and on a wide range of subjects from six to 15 days. The companies differ in price, number of participants, types of accommodations, and other factors. With the Web, the number and reach of these opportunities have expanded, making it easy to shop among them for the company and tours that best suit your needs, inclinations, and pocketbook. There are numerous reputable companies in this field, but the following are some of the better known:

ACIS

www.acis.com

eTrav Educational Travel Alliance
www.etrav.com

Explorica
www.explorica.com

CHA Educational Tours
www.cha-tours.com

Casterbridge
www.casterbridgetours.com

EF Educational Tours
www.eftours.com

NETC (National Educational Travel Council)
www.educationaltravel.com

Passports
www.passports.com

Voyageur Educational Tours
www.voyageurtours.com

Institutional Tour Providers

Numerous nonprofit and educational organizations and institutions offer special tours for their members and associates. Alumni associations of colleges and universities often promote these extensively to their members, and if you aren't getting frequent mailings about these, check out the alumni section of your alma mater's site. Museums offering educational tours include the Smithsonian and the American Museum of Natural History.

Smithsonian Journeys
smithsonianjourneys.org

The Smithsonian Institution, through its museums and magazine, brings us a taste of a tremendous variety of cultures. If you want to try some of those cultures yourself, the Smithsonian can take you there. Smithsonian Journeys, from the Smithsonian Institution, provides unique tours to 70 countries, led by study leaders who are recognized as experts in their fields. Group size is small, and the tours emphasize accommodations and top-quality cuisine that reflect the local culture. To get a feel for the range of offerings, pull down the menus on the search form on the main page to see the lists of 16 interest areas (ancient history, archaeology, performing arts, trains, etc.) and 17 types of tours (countryside, cruises, festivals, etc.).

American Museum of Natural History (AMNH) Expeditions
www.amnhexpeditions.org

From Cultural and Archeological Treasures of Bulgaria to a Hudson Bay Polar Bear Watch, AMNH Expeditions (offered by the American Museum of Natural History) are tremendously varied and unique. The site itself makes it very easy to explore the possibilities, with sections that allow you to browse by date, region, mode of travel (Jets, Planes & Trains), Family Programs, and Discovery Cruises.

Study Abroad

Most tours that have been discussed so far in this chapter have ranged from a day to a couple weeks. The phrase "study abroad" usually implies a substantially longer time period (a semester, summer, or year) and courses earning academic credits. Many colleges and universities, of course, have a semester or year abroad as part of their program. The first two sites that follow can connect you with institutions with these programs.

StudyAbroad.com

www.studyabroad.com

StudyAbroad.com provides a directory of Academic Year/Semester Programs, Summer Programs, Language Programs, Intern/Volunteer Programs, Teach Abroad Programs, and Intersession Programs. For each of these categories, you can browse by country; programs can also be browsed by subject (117 of them), country, and city. For each program, StudyAbroad.com provides a description, contacts, and links to a site whenever possible. On the main page and elsewhere, you will find links to a number of major program providers.

IIEPassport

www.iiepassport.org

IIEPassport, from the Institute of International Education, is a directory of more than 700 categories of programs around the world. From the main page, you can select by a combination of country and field of study. An Advanced Search link allows you to search by area of the world, city, organization, term (Summer and Short Term Study Year-Round or Semester and Academic Year-Length Study), and Format (Art Studio, Directed Field Study, Independent Study, etc.). For each program, the site provides location, sites, dates, duration, field of study, eligibility, costs, deadline, etc., as well as contact information, of course. IIEPassport also offers a detailed general guide to studying abroad.

Semester at Sea

www.semesteratsea.com

Whereas the previous two sites contain directories of hundreds of programs from numerous providers, Semester at Sea is an example of programs in a very unique environment run by a particular provider. Semester at Sea makes three voyages a year aboard the *MV Explorer*, a 525-foot floating campus with six passenger decks, a library, computer lab, student union, campus store, swimming pool, and fitness center. Undergraduate programs, continuing education, Summer Law at Sea, and Summer Teachers at Sea programs are also offered.

Other Educational Travel Ideas

Literary Traveler
www.literarytraveler.com

One might think of Literary Traveler as a "motivational" site for educational travel. It is neither a travel agency nor a tour provider, but if you like literature, it can provide inspiration to visit the places where famous literary figures once lived and wrote. On this site, you will find articles on the places associated with the lives and works of more than 70 novelists, poets, and playwrights. Under the Literary Tours section of the site, you will find a list of literary tour operators that can get you to Dante's Italy, the Lost Generation's Paris, Yeat's Ireland, and other places that served as inspiration for those whose works inspire us.

Elderhostel
www.elderhostel.org

Elderhostel will be discussed in some detail in the next chapter, but it also deserves a mention here because of its emphasis on learning. The name may suggest that young whippersnappers need not apply. However, the organization is generous with its definition of "elder": You only have to be 55 or older to participate in one of the 8,000 programs offered in more than 90 countries each year.

Earthwatch Institute

www.earthwatch.org

Earthwatch Institute offers an opportunity for anyone to participate in scientific field research, with projects ranging from Belarus Wetlands to Dinosaur Footprints to Early Man in Spain to Climate Change in the Rainforest. Expeditions are available in the areas of Aquatic Animals; Aquatic Environments; Archaeology and Paleontology; Birds, Insects, and Plant Studies; Climate Change, Conservation Biology; Culture and Health; Earth Sciences; Ecology and Evolutionary Biology; Ice and Snow; Land Animals; Land Environments; Marine Sciences; Plant Science; and Zoology.

Lindblad Expeditions

www.expeditions.com

Lindblad Expeditions, a pioneer in ecotourism for the last quarter-century, will take you on its ship-based, expert-led, exciting but relaxed journeys to a variety of exotic and out-of-the-way destinations. To get a feel for what Lindblad has to offer, go to the Daily Expedition Reports section of the site to read journals about what Lindblad tour members have been experiencing in the past few days.

Natural Habitat Adventures

www.nathab.com

The type of destination explored by this tour company is defined by its name, Natural Habitat Adventures. Behind that, though, is a philosophy of "responsible travel" that defines the nature of the tours. It is one of two companies endorsed by the World Wildlife Fund. You can join Natural Habitat Adventures' small groups for tours to Africa, the Americas, the Arctic and Antarctic, and the Pacific.

TraveLearn

www.travelearn.com

TraveLearn's theme is "For people who take their minds with them on vacation." TraveLearn people will provide you with tours that focus on ancient traditions and cultures as well as contemporary situations. A key part of its approach is the value of actually meeting the local people and learning from them. With more than 25 years of experience, TraveLearn emphasizes small groups, expert tour leadership, and top-quality accommodations.

Geek Cruises

www.geekcruises.com

Geek Cruises offers "High-Tech Conference-Cruises for Geeks" to Alaska, Europe, the Caribbean, and Hawaii. If you can speak Java, Linux, or Perl, or love to discuss Oracle, Photoshop, script, or networking, and have a sense of pride when friends refer to you as a "geek," Geek Cruises will probably bring you home with a smile on your face. Not only will you get to talk with those who speak your language, but you will also get to chat with industry leaders.

Other Resources for Adventure, Outdoor, and Educational Travel

Many other categories could be identified as subsets of adventure, outdoor, and educational travel or are closely related to those interests (for example, Outdoor and Adventure designations could be broken down into many specific sports). The Education designation is also virtually unlimited in terms of what interests might be included. The next chapter, "Sites for Special Groups and Special Needs," starts off with three Web resource guides that not only serve special groups and needs but also provide links to hundreds of additional sites for sports and other interests.

Discussion Groups and Forums for Adventure, Outdoor, and Educational Travel

A number of the general travel forums, such as Travel Forums.org (www.ityt.com/forums), Frommer's Travel Talk (www.frommers.com), and IgoUgo (www.igougo.com), have sections dealing specifically with adventure, outdoor, and learning travel. In addition, three of the sites discussed in this chapter have such places where you can get advice, information, and opinions on adventure, outdoor, and learning tours, providers, and destinations.

GORP—Community

gorp.away.com/gorp/interact

GORP's discussion boards, which are combined with Away.com and OutsideOnline.com forums, have sections for Hiking, Biking, Fishing, Paddling, Gear, Climbing, Wildlife, Skiing, Conservation, and Destinations. To find messages on other topics, use the discussion board's keyword search and pull-down menus for regions, activities, and topics.

Woodall's—Open Roads Forum

www.woodalls.com/cforum

Woodall's Open Roads Forum is extremely active, with more than 2 million postings and forums specifically on numerous aspects of RVing, camping, and related topics. You can expect to find multiple postings almost every day in almost every category. Using the Advanced Search form for forums, you can search by keyword, forum, dates, and author.

Come Back Alive—The Black Flag Cafe

www.comebackalive.com/phpBB2/index.php

The Black Flag Cafe is the forums section of Robert Young Pelton's Come Back Alive site. The active forum contains 15,000 topics and more than 150,000 posts.

Sites for Special Groups and Special Needs

The general goal for most leisure travelers is to see and explore a new destination or just to relax. Sometimes, though, travelers will have something more specific in mind in terms of why they want to go and what they want to do when they get there. Indeed the types of travel discussed in Chapter 5, "Cruises: Ships, Barges, and Boats," and Chapter 7, "Adventure, Outdoor, and Educational Travel," are examples of "specialty travel." Beyond those, there are many other special reasons for going somewhere or special requirements for destinations and accommodations. If playing on different golf courses, attending concerts, traveling with a group of people with whom you particularly relate, or taking tours that accommodate certain physical requirements is a controlling factor in your travel planning, then you are looking for specialty travel.

On the Web, there are a variety of starting places for planning these kinds of trips. Begin on any of the big reservation sites or, for that matter, on restaurant and hotel reservation sites, and then look for links or Web site search menu items to specifically identify providers that serve special groups and needs. On the big reservation sites, make use of the vacation packages and destinations sections, which will often highlight these types of getaways. Beyond that, there are many sites that have the distinct purpose of providing access to travel for specific groups and specific needs and even special "desires." (Just let your imagination run wild on the possibilities for the latter.) The first sites covered in this chapter are those that serve as indexes to and resource guides for specialty travel generally. No matter what your special need or interest, chances are good that these guides will lead you to providers that focus on your particular requirements. There are also, though, some specific groups of travelers who constitute a very significant portion of the traveling public. The rest of this chapter will examine sites that address some specific groups who constitute portions of travelers: families, businesspeople, seniors, gays and lesbians, and handicapped and disabled persons. You will also find it easy to locate hundreds of travel agencies that specialize in these kinds of trips. Try a search, for example, on *golf vacations* or *polo vacations* or *family vacations France*. (For student travel, take a look at the resources provided in the Educational Travel portion of Chapter 7 and also the section on Hostels in Chapter 6, "Finding a Bed and a Meal.")

Many sites in this chapter offer guides, advice, and lists of providers for trips and tours. When it comes to actually making the reservations, use these sites in conjunction with others in the book to make sure you get the best deal. For example, if you use one of the following sites and decide that your family trip will be to Disneyland Paris this summer, the best deal may indeed be right on the site. However, also take a few minutes to check out prices on some of the more general reservation sites as well.

Specialty Travel in General

The following three sites are resource guides for a broad range of specialty travel. They cover not just special groups and needs but also many specific sports and other interests. Especially for "outdoor" travel, these sites can serve as companion sites to those discussed in

Chapter 7, and two of the sites mentioned in that chapter are also included here. Remember, when using resource guides, it is usually worthwhile to examine more than one. Each covers some sites the others do not, and each has different categories. For example, only TouristClick.com has a category for Supernatural travel, only Specialty Travel Index has a category for Truffle Hunting, and only InfoHub provides a Naturist category.

InfoHub Specialty Travel Guide
www.infohub.com

InfoHub contains paid listings with descriptions and links to more than 12,000 vacations from more than 1,300 providers. To find vacations of interest, you can browse by category under 13 Popular Activities categories (which are further divided geographically), browse by 10 main Guided and Self-Guided Tours categories, or browse by Lodgings (Resorts, Outdoors, Unique Stays). Particularly with the Guided and Self-Guided categories, you can easily get a feel for the variety of specific offerings since the 10 main categories are each broken down into numerous subcategories (more than 100 in all). Under Hobby, for example, if you click on the More link, you will find subcategories for Antiques, Astronomy, Brewery/Beer Festivals, Collectors Tours, Cooking School, Crafts Tours, Gambling, Photography, Pottery, Videography Tours, and Whisky/Distillery Tours. On the main page, you will also find pull-down menus that allow you to search by a combination of Region (destination) and Category (45 of them). Try being even more precise by using keywords in the small search box on the main page, which searches not just the titles but also the descriptions for thousands of vacations.

Whether you get there by browsing or searching, InfoHub first provides an overview of each vacation with a brief description, season, destination, activity, duration, and price. Click on the name of the tour (e.g., In Touch with Ghana) for full details and contact information to book the tour, which is done through the provider, not through InfoHub. On the main page and elsewhere, Personal Tour Guides links can connect you to personal guides throughout the world. InfoHub's Review section has reviews written by travelers, and there are 10 Forum sections with numerous subsections, many of which are quite active.

Specialty Travel Index
www.specialtytravel.com

Specialty Travel Index is a directory of more than 400 tour operators providing specialty travel. Using the search menus on the main page, you can select a combination of destination and interest/activity. A strength of the site stems from its interest/activity list, where you can choose from among 360 categories, including Aerobics, Air Shows, Astrology, Bull Fighting, Chocolate Tours, Coffee Tours, Dialysis Cruises, Fashion Tours, Gorilla Viewing, Grandparent/Grandchild Tours, Jewish Tours, Legends, Metaphysical, Military History, Mushroom Hunting, Reindeer Safaris, Shamanism, Shark Diving, and Wildflower Viewing. Rather than a list of tours, a search produces a list of tour operators that offer such tours. For each operator, you'll find a description of what they do and contact information with links to each site. The Specialty Travel site, which is produced by *Specialty Travel* magazine, also includes more than 150 articles from the magazine.

TouristClick.com—Specialty Travel
www.touristclick.com/SpecialtaTravel.html

Specialty Travel, one of 10 sections in the larger TouristClick.com site, contains paid listings for more than 400 specialty tour operators. The listings are arranged in 33 categories, some with subcategories (Figure 8.1). For each operator, a very brief description is given, along

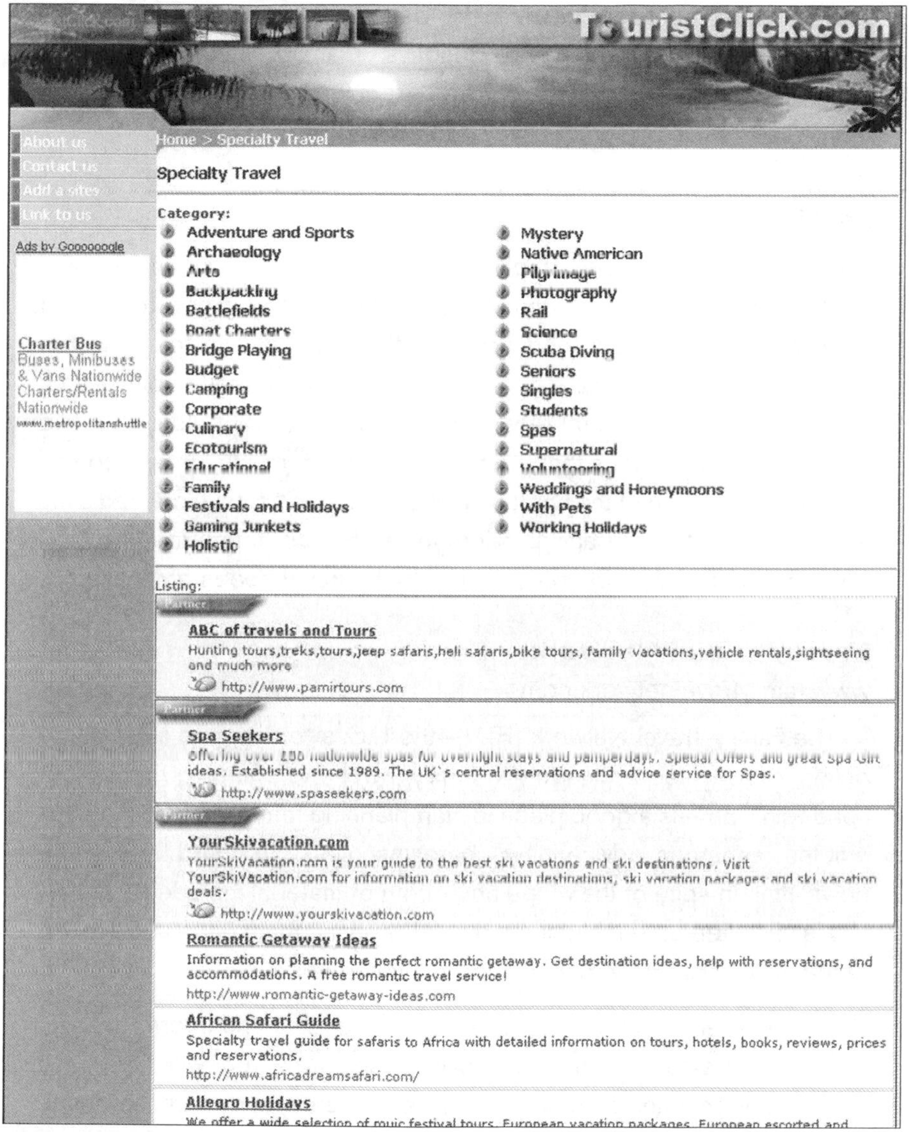

Figure 8.1   Specialty Travel categories at TouristClick.com

with a link to the operator's site for categories such as Battlefields, Bridge Playing, Festivals and Holidays, Gaming Junkets, Mystery, Native American, Pilgrimages, Photography, Science, Supernatural, and With Pets.

Families

The term "family travel" implies a number of factors that affect how one plans for travel, including traveling as a small group, choosing appropriate destinations and activities that are not just tolerable but preferably enjoyable for a range of ages, and, often, careful budgeting. You can go to the general reservation sites and travel guide sites and sort through the options that are best suited for families, or instead you can take advantage of the work of a lot of people who have created sites that sort it out for you and provide you with trips, tours, lodging, and travel advice specifically compatible with the travel needs of families.

Family Travel Network
www.familytravelnetwork.com

The Family Travel Network (FTN)—the U.S.'s "oldest and largest free online site devoted exclusively to family travel and planning great vacations with kids"—is a good place to start planning family travel. It includes articles, resources, advice, news, bargains, message board links, and a newsletter. In spite of the range and depth of material included, the FTN site is uncluttered, with highlighted articles on the main page and the rest of the main content found in the following categories:

- Current Features – A collection of readable and informative articles written from the family perspective. You will find good advice, tales of specific family adventures, and more. Most articles and other information on FTN are about U.S. and Caribbean vacations, but some of the general advice articles are universal.

- Hot Deals – This list of specific travel bargains identified by FTN provides details, contact information, and, when relevant, the expiration dates. Bookings are made through the agency or provider, not FTN.

- Destinations – Articles about family travel to specific locations.

- Travel Interests – Activity-oriented articles on topics such as river rafting, dinosaur treks, family cruising, etc.

- Kids and Teens – Articles focusing on destinations and types of trips, written from and for a teen (and younger) perspective.

- Travel News – News articles regarding events, resorts, cruise lines, tour providers, and destinations with a family focus.

- Tips & Reviews – Travel tips on such things as traveling with toddlers, budgeting, packing, and snacks.

- Travel Links – Annotated links to more than 100 sites related to family travel.

- Newsletter – Link to subscribe to FTN's free newsletter.

FamilyTravelFiles.com
www.familytravelfiles.com

FamilyTravelFiles is an online magazine with hundreds of articles about family vacations around the world. Whether you're just browsing through the titles for ideas or reading the full articles, this magazine is a great guide to family travel options. The Vacation Ideas Directory, USA, Files by State, and World links near the top of the page all provide ways to find articles about destinations. The Tours link and the Family Vacations Folders link lead to articles on tours, and the Folders option allows you to browse by Snow Places, Mountains,

Adventure Vacations, Theme Parks, Reunion Places, Beaches, Cheap Sleeps, and Cruises. The Events link (with USA, Canada, and World sub-links) leads to listings for festivals, fairs, carnivals, exhibits, and other events. For topical articles (advice, news, etc.), you can use either the E-Zine link near the top or the more detailed categories on the left of the page (Family Travel News, Family Vacations Ideas and Options, Family Events, Field Trips, Vacation Reviews, Vacation Advice, Ten Takes, and Vacation Deals). You will also find links to the signup page for FamilyTravelFiles' free newsletter. When you click on any of the categories, recent articles will appear. Don't miss the "More ... Articles" links, which lead to the archive of articles for that category. At various places on the site, you will see links to Vacation Ideas, which will take you to the sites for tour providers.

Family Travel Guides
www.familytravelguides.com

For family travel in the U.S. (and a bit of Canada and the Caribbean), Pamela Lanier's Family Travel Guides offers a database of family accommodations, road food recipes, and suggestions, articles, and links to outdoor vacation ideas, suggested vacation packages, articles on (U.S.) regional attractions and accommodations, and tips on travel safety, health, age groups, and trip planning. With the Search link, you can search for lodging by city, name, or keyword, and with the Articles link, you can search for articles by keyword. The free newsletter will keep you updated on the latest family vacation deals.

About.com—Travel With Kids
travelwithkids.about.com

As it does for so many other travel topics, About.com provides us with a collection of good advice, ideas, articles, deals, and more in its

Travel With Kids section. The site is full of articles on topics such as "Top Things to Do in New York with Teens," "Beach Vacations 101: Save Money, Have Fun," and basic practical advice such as "How to Unblock Ears in Airplanes." Many links lead to special travel offers, but under both the Essentials and Topics portions of the site, you will find lots of articles on specific family destinations, cruises, tips, games, and other activities. There are dozens of articles specifically about traveling with babies and teens and as single parents. Most articles relate to U.S., Mexican, and Caribbean destinations, but if you look under the Topics section and click on the link for "more" destinations, you will find more than 100 articles on other destinations. The About.com—Travel With Kids Forums are not very active, but it's worth taking a look. After using the Travel with Kids section of About.com, you may also want to check out About.com's Budget Travel section for family travel (budgettravel.about.com).

T+L Family
www.travelandleisure.com/family

On the T+L Family site, brought to you by *Travel & Leisure* magazine, you will find the quality articles you would expect from one of the world's leading travel publications. Look for articles on family destinations worldwide as well as tips, tales, and advice articles.

BabyCenter—Travel with a Baby
www.babycenter.com/baby/babytravel/index

Want to know what to pack when traveling with a baby, how soon you can travel after delivery, whether your baby needs a passport, whether to use cloth or paper diapers when traveling, and whether airplane water is safe for your baby? The Travel with Baby portion of the BabyCenter site can answer these and many more "baby travel" questions.

TravelWithYourKids.com

www.travelwithyourkids.com

For destinations, travel preparations, flying, moving abroad, and other topics, on TravelWithYourKids.com you will find articles as well as advice for parents, from parents. You will find plenty of good first-hand advice on dozens of topics and destinations.

GoCityKids

www.gocitykids.com

Though at present, GoCityKids covers only 20 U.S. cities, if you do happen to be traveling to one of those cities with kids, this site is worth the stop. On it you will find lists (plus descriptions, locations, opening times, etc.) for events, parks and playgrounds, activities, entertainment, services, family restaurants, and lots more. From the main page, click on a city and then choose from a list of subjects or a calendar, or use the Activity Finder search to find activities by Type of Day (Indoor or Outdoor), Kind of Fun (Get Up & Go, Thinking & Learning, etc.), and your child's age.

Travel Channel—Great Family Vacation Ideas

travel.discovery.com/convergence/familyvacations/familyvacations.html

On the Great Family Vacations Ideas section of the Travel Channel site (Figure 8.2), you will find guides to some major family destinations in the U.S. (Universal Orlando, Disney World, Busch Gardens Tampa, etc.) and a bit for Europe (Disneyland Paris, Euro Coaster Kings). The site also offers some "best" lists, including those for roller coasters, factory tours, ice cream parlors, thrill parks, and theme parks for children. Also look under the News & Events section of the main page for lists of family-oriented fairs, festivals, theme parks, zoos, and aquariums. Some lists are U.S.-only; some are international.

Figure 8.2   Travel Channel–Great Family Vacation Ideas main page

FamilyTravel.com

www.familytravel.com

FamilyTravel.com has gathered information on an assortment of family-oriented fun trips, adventure travel, cruises, ranch vacations, family camps, and more. In addition to travel deals you find here, check out the family destination guides for continents, countries, and regions.

Business Travelers

Most travel sites on the Web are aimed at leisure travel, which should not be surprising, since the vast majority of what has ever been written about travel has probably been, to at least some degree, on the "leisure" side. On the other hand, a lot of travel is, of course, done for business. That does not mean that the sites covered in this book are of no use to the businessperson, especially for self-employed business travelers who make their own reservations and other travel plans. In addition, especially for longer business trips, my own experience has convinced me that working in at least a little leisure (an hour at a museum or a long quiet meal at a local restaurant) can make a big difference in making a business trip enjoyable rather than a burden. Hence, even much of the leisure material found on the Web might be of use to road warriors, and beyond the leisure material, there are a number of sites designed specifically for the business traveler. The following sites will provide a good return on your time investment, with articles, tips, and advice on a broad range of business travel topics.

About.com—Business Travel

businesstravel.about.com

On the main page of About.com—Business Travel, you will be presented with about 10 featured articles typically containing current news and advice for the business traveler. For more, visit the Essentials and Topics links on the left side of the page. The Essentials section includes articles on booking business travel, packing, safety, and keeping records. Under Topics, you will find articles (and links to providers of business travel services and products) under the categories of Hotels, Airlines, Car Rental Services, City Guides, Travel

Loyalty Programs, Travel Safety & Health, Women's Travel, Incentive Travel, Travel Gear & Accessories, Records & Reimbursement, and Packing Tips. If you prefer to have updates and new content sent to you, sign up for the free newsletter.

Executive Planet
www.executiveplanet.com

If business takes you abroad and you don't know the best time to request a business appointment in Austria or whether it's acceptable to discuss politics in Russia, go to Executive Planet (Figure 8.3). The site provides an overview of business etiquette and protocol for 46 countries, including guidelines for making appointments, business dress, conversation, addressing and greeting people, gift-giving, deal-making, and entertaining. If you have other questions, you can take advantage of the discussion groups provided by Executive Planet.

Getting Through Customs
www.getcustoms.com

Getting Through Customs, from the authors of *Kiss, Bow, or Shake Hands: How to Do Business in Sixty Countries*, offers more than 100 articles excerpted from the authors' books, covering a variety of etiquette and how-to-do-business topics, including food, dress, greetings, gift-giving, negotiation, gestures, punctuality, and specific cultural tips for more than 20 countries.

bradmans
www.bradmans.com

If you are presented with a gift while in Beijing on business, do you know that you should first refuse it and then reluctantly accept it? Do you know whether you should then open it? If you are going to be in

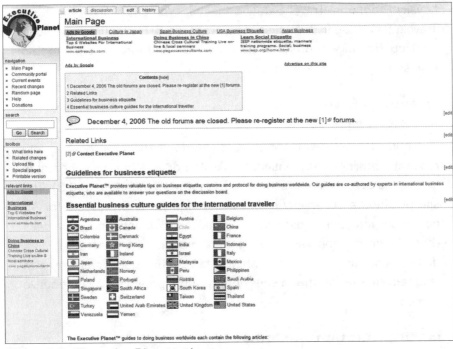

Figure 8.3   Executive Planet main page

Osaka, do you know where you can get a reputable translation service
there? If you don't know, the bradmans site is there to help. bradmans
is the publisher of guides specifically for the business traveler to Asia,
Europe, the Middle East, and Africa. The site has business guides to
more than 50 cities on those continents (Figure 8.4). For each city, typically you will find information for the following categories:
Accommodations (a substantial list suitable for business travelers),
Restaurants (also a substantial list, with a description, price range, links,
and phone numbers), Nightlife, Entertainment, In the City (useful business contacts for secretarial services, office rentals, etc.), Cultural Dos
and Don'ts, Also Know (current issues), Insider Info (advice from locals),

Figure 8.4   City guide at bradmans

Background (history, politics, religion, economy, population), Essentials (business contacts, Internet access, tipping, etc.), and Useful Phrases.

CNN Business Traveler

edition.cnn.com/CNNI/Programs/business.traveller

On the CNN Business Traveler site, you will find business travel stories that have been covered on the CNN Business Travel television program, including the Story Archive link (CNN Travel stories going back to March 2004). The Travel Kit portion of the CNN Business Travel page includes a variety of tips and background information for travelers. In case you don't want to miss the story live on TV, show times for the program are also posted on the site.

Times Online—Business Travel

travel.timesonline.co.uk

The Business Travel part of the Times Online Travel site brings you articles on current business travel news and issues, from both a U.K. and an international perspective, plus a number of relevant links to the more general business and travel articles and features on the broader Times Online site.

USA TODAY Online—Business Traveler

www.usatoday.com/travel/columnist/index.htm

Along with its other travel features, *USA TODAY* Online has two business travel columnists whom you can look to for insightful and informative travel news: David Grossman and Joe Brancatelli. For airline and other transportation news or any news that affects frequent business travelers, these two writers keep readers aware of what is happening and also what to expect in the near future.

Frequent Flyer—Making the Best of Business Travel

www.frequentflyer.oag.com

Frequent Flyer, subtitled "Making the Best of Business Travel," is presented by OAG and contains lots of news about airlines, airports, and related information. If you want to keep up-to-date on details of what is happening on the air travel side of business travel, this site will do the job. Also consider taking advantage of the bi-weekly OAG Frequent Flyer Update e-mail newsletter.

Seniors

The following sites are examples of what the Web offers for traveling seniors (aka "mature travelers"). Also take a look at the educational sites in Chapter 7 since many will feature trips specifically designed for seniors. For links to about 100 more sites related to senior travel, check out the Transitions Abroad—Senior Travel site. From the budgeting side of things, be sure to look for senior discounts on various sites such as Amtrak.

Elderhostel
www.elderhostel.org

For educational trips on culture, music, history, art, crafts, outdoor adventures, and more, from Albuquerque to Zagreb, seniors can look to Elderhostel. For travelers 55 and older, Elderhostel, a nonprofit organization founded in 1975, is the best-known organization for providing educational and cultural experiences specifically addressing their interests (Figure 8.5). Each year, Elderhostel sponsors 8,000 programs in 90 countries, ranging from one day to two weeks. On the site, you can browse for programs geographically or use the searchbox to search by keyword (subject, city, country, etc.). With the Advanced Search link on the home page, you can search for programs by country, U.S. state, dates, category, activity level, keyword, price range, and special accommodations (vegetarian, kosher, low-fat, low-salt meals, single rooms, and RV sites). For each course,

Figure 8.5   Elderhostel main page

extensive descriptions are provided and registrations can be completed online.

ElderTreks

www.eldertreks.com

ElderTreks is an adventure travel company featuring more than 60 "active, off-the-beaten-path, small-group adventures" in 60 countries, designed for people 50 and older. The tours, some by land and some by expedition ship (with one to 110 passengers), focus on adventure, culture, and nature. Tours run from six to 32 days on subjects ranging from "Valley of the Grizzlies: Sailing in The Khutzeymateen Sanctuary" to "Transylvania: Castles and Counts in the Carpathians." Destinations include all continents (as well as polar regions) and can be searched for on the site by region and by "land or sea." In addition to the detailed descriptions provided, take advantage of the colorful and detailed downloadable brochures for each tour.

Transitions Abroad—Senior Travel Resources

www.transitionsabroad.com/listings/travel/senior/resources.shtml

The overall Transitions Abroad site contains a wide range of articles and hundreds of links related to working, studying, traveling, and living abroad. The Senior Travel Resources section features articles and dozens of links for seniors, including links to Educational Programs, Home & Hospitality Stays Abroad, International Tours with Substance, Senior-Friendly Volunteer Vacations, general senior travel sites, and information on print resources.

AARP—Travel

www.aarp.org/travel/destinations/?sitrackingid=171190

For travelers, AARP (formerly known as the American Association of Retired Persons) may be best known for member discounts at thousands of hotels. The travel portion of AARP's site provides information about those discounts, plus information on discounts on hotels, airlines, car rentals, cruises, vacations, and tours. The site also includes more than 100 articles on worldwide destinations of particular interest to seniors, articles on travel themes (jazz, botanical gardens, spas, aircraft carrier museums, etc.), and articles on lodging and transportation tips. The message board is active, so if you are a senior and have travel questions, you will probably be able to get some responses there.

Walking the World
www.walkingtheworld.com

Walking the World is a tour company that provides "outdoor adventures for people 50 and better," especially walking tours (hence the title). Destinations include North America, Europe, and elsewhere. The company promises high-quality accommodations and cuisine as well as a healthy, close-up look at the localities.

50plus Expeditions
www.50plusexpeditions.com

50plus Expeditions specializes in adventures for active travelers 50 and older. Trips fall into three categories (Small Group Adventures, Expedition and Adventure Cruises, and Independent Adventures) with destinations in 20 countries on six continents. The site also contains an interesting collection of links for 50-plus travelers.

Seniors Home Exchange
www.seniorshomeexchange.com

Seniors Home Exchange, which was also mentioned in Chapter 6, provides home exchange and hospitality exchange opportunities exclusively for seniors.

Seniors Go Travel

www.seniorsgotravel.com

Seniors Go Travel is an online magazine that contains several dozen articles, written from a senior perspective, on destinations in Canada, the U.S., and elsewhere, plus a number of articles on travel tips.

About.com—Senior Travel

seniortravel.about.com

The Senior Travel section of About.com contains a broad collection of "mature travel" articles on discounts, adventure activities, cruising, dream trips, RV travel and road trips, adventure travel, volunteering, learning vacations, cultural travel, health, safety, and more.

Gay and Lesbian Travelers

Gay and lesbian travel has become a major market in the last decade or two, and there are a large number of companies and Web sites that provide guides and tours especially designed for this community, with an emphasis on gay and lesbian-friendly providers, destinations, accommodations, and services.

GayGuide.Net

gayguide.net

GayGuide.Net is a site that brings together individual Gay Guides that have been written for hundreds of countries and cities. Since each guide is written by a different person, the content differs greatly: Some concentrate on gay news and events, and some focus on clubs, bars, restaurants, resources, etc.

International Gay and Lesbian Travel Association (IGLTA)

www.iglta.com

The International Gay and Lesbian Travel Association is a trade association for businesses involved in the gay and lesbian travel industry. Its site serves as a directory of its members as well as a directory of travel services, including hotels, tours, galleries, transportation services, and entertainment. Using the search options on the main page, you can search by category (more than 30 of them), business name, city, state or province, or country. For a list of gay and lesbian travel agents, choose Travel Agents in the category search for a list of more than 200 gay and lesbian, or gay-friendly travel agents, arranged by country. For each business, you are typically given the name, address, phone number, e-mail, description, and link to its site.

Gay.com—Travel

www.gay.com/travel

Gay.com is owned by the PlanetOut media company, which includes Gay.com, PlanetOut.com, Kleptomaniac.com, and other properties. In the Travel section of the Gay.com site, you will find articles on cruises, budget travel, luxury escapes, outdoor adventure, and ski vacations (Figure 8.6). Travel guides for destinations from OUT&ABOUT are also included, but access requires a subscription. You will also find yellow-page listings for lodgings, tours, travel agents, and bars and clubs, and an extensive directory of events throughout the world.

QT Magazine

www.qtmagazine.com

QT magazine is an online gay and lesbian travel magazine containing more than 100 destination guides (about two-thirds of which are for the U.S.), hundreds of features and news articles, tour packages, and a business directory for hotels, resorts, restaurants, entertainment, and other businesses.

Figure 8.6   Travel section at Gay.com

Orbitz—Gay & Lesbian Travel
www.orbitz.com

Orbitz.com has a Gay & Lesbian section with deals you can browse by destination or by the following categories: Deals of the Week, Gay & Lesbian Cruises, Resorts & Gay/Lesbian Tours, and Deals to Popular Destinations. Look for the link to the Gay Travel section under Explore Destinations and Interests and under various Deals sections.

Travelocity.com—Gay Travel
www.travelocity.com

The link for gay travel deals on Travelocity moves around, but try looking under Vacation Packages or Travel Tools. You will find a variety of gay and lesbian travel deals for cruises, vacations, tours, last-minute deals, hotels, and flight–hotel combinations. You will also find links to gay and lesbian travel offers in the Cruises section and elsewhere on the Travelocity site.

Handicapped and Disabled Travelers

The Web provides a variety of sites that are useful to travelers with disabilities. Some sites offer advice and tips, some provide tours, and some address travel issues for those with specific disabilities. The following sites are resource guides that will lead to hundreds of these sites. For lists of travel agents and tour providers that offer accessible travel, the resource guides will lead to an assortment of companies.

Access-Able Travel Source
www.access-able.com

Access-Able Travel Source was created by a couple with firsthand experience dealing with accessible travel issues and is enhanced by the contributions of other travelers. It is an impressive directory of thousands of resources and links for accessible travel, arranged in the following categories: World Destinations (accommodations, attractions, etc.), Travel Professionals (travel agents and tour operators), Cruise Ships (with details on accessibility for various cruise lines), Travel Tales (travelers' stories about their trips), Links & Resources (more than 400 links to sites relating to accessible travel), Feature Destination (featured articles), and Summer Fun (links for summer travel). The Travel Agents list is searchable by those providing services for particular categories of disabilities or needs (Developmentally Disabled, Blind and Low Vision, Hearing Impaired, Mobility Restricted, Dialysis, Oxygen, and Diabetes). The site also provides travel tips, lists of organizations and magazines, and more. Though the amount of information on each resource (such as hotels) will vary, site users will probably be impressed by both the number of resources and the level of detail provided.

Disability Travel and Recreation Resources
www.makoa.org/travel.htm

Disability Travel and Recreation Resources is a no-frills resource guide with links to more than 150 sites relevant to travelers with disabilities. Sites are arranged under categories including Travel Planning, Destinations, Transportation, Air Travel, and Especially for Children.

MossRehab ResourceNet—Accessible Travel
www.mossresourcenet.org/travel.htm

Accessible Travel is a resource guide with advice for accessible travel and an extensive collection of links on the topic. It contains general travel tips, a cruise checklist, a Driving with a Disability Factsheet, and Featured Trips articles. For links, it provides lists of Web resources for Travel Agencies, State Tourism Offices, Tourism Offices by Country, Airlines—Trains—Buses, Hotels—Motels, Automobile

Rental Agencies, Van Rental Companies, Driving with a Disability, Travel Alerts—Warnings, Travel Resources, Travel Publications, Government Resources, Weather, and Newsgroups—Mailing Lists. Accessible Travel is created by MossRehab, a rehabilitation hospital and research and diagnostic center, and is a part of the MossRehab ResourceNet Web site.

Discussion Groups and Forums for Special Groups and Special Needs

If you want to read travelers' own opinions, tips, complaints, questions, and answers regarding types and aspects of specialty travel, take a look at the following sites. Most of them are sections of sites covered earlier in this chapter. For almost all of these, anyone can read the messages, but you need to register (it's free) to post messages.

InfoHub Specialty Travel Guide—Forums
www.infohub.com/forums

InfoHub has a general forum and specific forums for most of the major categories of specialty travel on the InfoHub site. Altogether the forums contain more than 20,000 postings. You can read and even contribute without joining, but membership is recommended (it's free). Since the forums have moderators, the quality of content of messages is quite good.

Family Travel Boards
www.familytravelboards.com

Family Travel Boards has forums that cover various destinations (continents, etc.) and the following topics: Reunions and Multi-Generational, Safety and Security, Single Parents, With Pets, Deals from the Travel Trade, and Vacation with Teens. Each forum has an administrator and one or more moderators, and most administrators require that you resister (it's free) to post messages. There are a total of more than 5,000 postings.

About.com—Travel With Kids—Forums
travelwithkids.about.com/mpboards.htm

The Travel with Kids Forum at About.com includes individual forums for General Interest, Destinations (U.S., Europe, etc.), Offers, Tours, Lodgings, Vacation Ideas, and Disney Vacations. Anyone can read messages, but to post, you must register (it's free). The forums, which are only moderately active, feature between 1,000 and 2,000 postings going back to 1998.

Frommer's
www.frommers.com

Click on the Travel Talk tab to get to the Frommer's Forums, and then choose the category of interest. Among the choices are Disabled Travelers, Family Travel, Gay & Lesbian Travel, Honeymoons, Senior Travel, Single Travel, Student Travel, and Women Travelers. The level of activity varies (from a few dozen to several hundred postings). The Family Board is the most active. Anyone can read messages, but you must register to post (it's free).

AARP Message Boards—Travel
community.aarp.org/rp-travel

The Travel section of the AARP Message Boards is quite active, with several hundred postings each month in categories that include destinations by continent, Travel Talk, and Cruises. Anyone can read messages but to post, you must join (the forums, not necessarily AARP).

Lonely Planet—The Thorn Tree
thorntree.lonelyplanet.com

Lonely Planet's Thorn Tree message boards address a number of categories of specialty travel, including boards for various activities (sports, etc.), Gay & Lesbian Travelers, Women Travelers, Travelers with Disabilities, and others. The boards are very active, each typically with hundreds or thousands of topics and thousands or tens of thousands of postings.

Executive Planet—Forums
www.executiveplanet.com

If you have questions about business culture and etiquette anywhere in the world, try the Executive Planet Discussion Boards. Executive Planet has a General Discussion forum and forums for each region of the world. Anyone can read messages, but registration is required to post messages (it's free).

Exploring Countries and Cultures Online

Though you obviously don't need to be an expert or even generally conversant in the history, economics, geography, and other facets of the places you visit, knowing a bit about those topics can enhance your trip. Especially if you are planning on meeting the locals, knowing more than the "average tourist" about their land can gain you some respect and credibility. For business travelers, this is obviously important. The travel destination guides covered in Chapter 2, "Travel Guides Online," which provide some very basic information on history and other facets of countries, regions, and cities, are a good place to start. If, though, you want a more in-depth understanding, the Web provides a wealth of much more detailed background information. You can find not just fascinating but very useful information about cultures, traditions, etiquette, religions, politics, economics, the arts, history, cuisine, and more. By using the language resources on the Internet, you can even learn some polite language basics to help you be polite and be understood when you have questions and needs. The Web also provides a way for you to easily find and read newspapers from thousands of cities around the world and even be alerted by e-mail to events, topics, and locations of specific interest to you.

The following sections begin with encyclopedias and country guides that provide overviews and a variety of details about countries. Other sections cover maps (beyond the road maps featured in Chapter 4, "Train, Car, and Ferry Travel"), a variety of language tools, and other sources for cultures, traditions, and more.

Encyclopedias

For general overviews and specific information relating to countries, cultures, history, and more, encyclopedias can be a great resource. Explore the content of the following free online encyclopedias for background on a country and to get a feel for what they provide. Also use them for information on cities, historical figures, foods, and, for that matter, any interesting aspect of a place on which an encyclopedia article may have been written. Try topics such as Russian culture, Latvian cuisine, and Chinese opera.

Wikipedia
wikipedia.org

This Internet-only encyclopedia is an example of a WikiWiki site, a collaborative project that allows easy input and online editing by any Internet user. Though encyclopedia "purists" have criticized the reliability of Wikipedia information (because anyone can change or add to an article), a good argument can be made that Wikipedia articles may be actually *more* reliable for exactly the same reason. If an error is introduced or an article is "vandalized," it is often corrected within minutes. (Remember, whether its Wikipedia or another resource, do not, of course, make life-changing or critical financial decisions based on a single source.) That issue aside, Wikipedia is more extensive by far than any other free online encyclopedias, offering more than 180,000 articles, which are often more extensive and up-to-date than those you will find in other encyclopedias. Try it for just about any topic

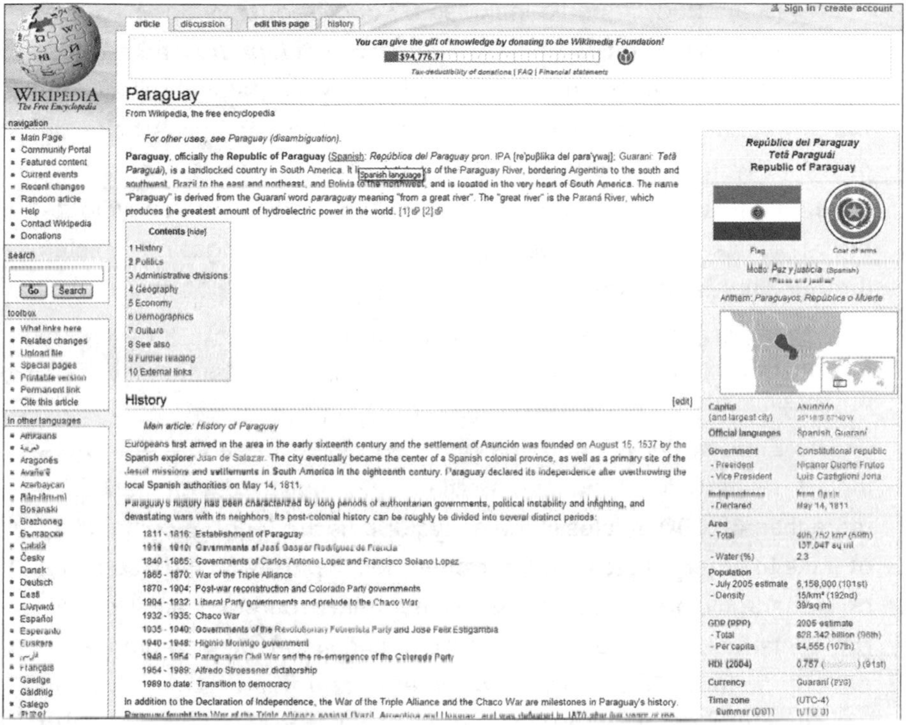

Figure 9.1   Wikipedia country article

that interests you. Wikipedia is both browsable and searchable, with versions in numerous languages. For countries, you will usually find sections on history, politics, geography, economy, demographics, culture, plus flags, maps, and statistics, as well as lots of links to related articles and often numerous photos (Figure 9.1). Check out the articles on cities, national and regional music, cuisine, arts and crafts, mythology, and pastimes.

HighBeam Encyclopedia

encyclopedia.com

HighBeam Encyclopedia includes 57,000 frequently updated articles from the sixth edition of the *Columbia Encyclopedia*. The articles, which are free, can be located either by browsing alphabetically (as with a "regular" encyclopedia) or by using the search box. Articles on countries typically include information on the land, people, economy, government, and history, with links to related topics in the encyclopedia. The site also provides links to news and magazine articles through HighBeam Research for a fee.

Encarta

encarta.msn.com

The Encarta encyclopedia is one part of the Encarta site (others include a dictionary, thesaurus, atlas, and multimedia center). The more than 42,000 articles in the encyclopedia are lengthy, contain lots of links to other articles, and, for countries, typically include sections on geography, plant and animal life, natural resources, climate, environmental issues, people, ethnic groups and languages, religion, education, culture, economy, government, and history. Articles on countries and other major topics are usually free, but links for more specific articles usually require a subscription.

Country Guides

Just as the guides discussed in Chapter 2 are intended primarily for tourists, there are also a number of places on the Web for getting guides that provide both more general and more detailed background information on countries. Some of these country guides are from a general perspective, and some provide profiles from a business perspective. In each case, they provide an easy way for moving to another level of understanding about the nature and flavor of any specific country.

The World Factbook
www.odci.gov/cia/publications/factbook

The World Factbook, compiled by the U.S. CIA and often referred to as the *CIA World Factbook*, is one of the best-known reference tools on the Internet. Revised annually and updated throughout the year, it provides clearly presented and highly detailed data and narratives on 272 countries, territories, and other entities. To get to the page for a country, use the pull-down menu on the main page. For each country, the data is arranged in the following sections: Geography, Communications, People, Transportation, Government, Military, Economy, and Transnational issues. The icons next to data items lead to ranked and alphabetic comparisons with other countries and to notes regarding the definitions and gathering of the data items.

BBC Country Profiles
news.bbc.co.uk/2/hi/country_profiles/default.stm (International version)

news.bbc.co.uk/1/hi/country_profiles/default.stm (U.K. version)

BBC Country Profiles for 201 countries and 51 territories can be found by clicking the Country Profiles link on BBC's main news page. Each profile includes an Overview and Facts, Leaders, and Media sections. The profiles are brief (compared with the World Factbook), but they provide a good quick look at the country. The Media links take you to the major news services for the country (press, TV, radio), and, just in case you happen to bump into him or her, a photo of the leader of the country is included.

U.S. Department of State—Background Notes
www.state.gov/r/pa/ei/bgn/

The U.S. Department of State has prepared a page of Background Notes for about 200 independent states, dependencies, and areas of special sovereignty. For each entry, you will find information on the land, its people, history, government, political conditions, economy, foreign relations, and U.S. Embassy officials, plus contact information and links to travel and business information.

Foreign & Commonwealth Office
www.fco.gov.uk

The U.K. Foreign & Commonwealth Office (FCO) site contains a Countries & Regions section (click on the Countries & Regions link on the main page). Click on the link in that section for Country Profiles. For each of the more than 200 countries (or other political entities) listed, you will find a report with information on the country's history, geography, economy, international relations, human rights, and health, and a link to travel advice.

Library of Congress—Portals to the World
www.loc.gov/rr/international/portals.html

For a very rich collection of links for 214 countries (and territories), go to the Portals to the World site from the Library of Congress. For each country, you will typically find links on the following topics: General Resources, Business, Commerce, Economy, Culture, Education, Embassies, Genealogy, Geography and Environment, Government, Politics, and Law, History, Language and Literature, Libraries, Archives, Media and Communications, National Security, Organizations, Recreation and Travel, Religion and Philosophy, Science and Technology, Search Engines, and Society (Figure 9.2). For larger countries, you will usually find at least a dozen links for each category. Take advantage of this site to get a really good feel for the wealth of Web information available on individual countries.

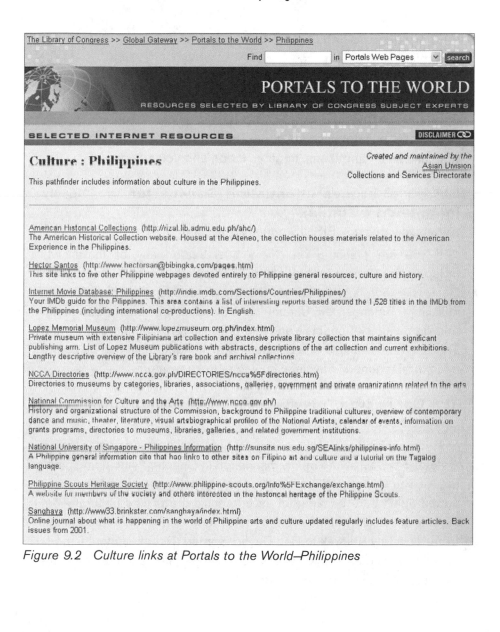

The Library of Congress >> Global Gateway >> Portals to the World >> Philippines

Find [   ] in Portals Web Pages [v] [search]

PORTALS TO THE WORLD
RESOURCES SELECTED BY LIBRARY OF CONGRESS SUBJECT EXPERTS

SELECTED INTERNET RESOURCES   DISCLAIMER ∞

Culture : Philippines

*Created and maintained by the
Asian Division
Collections and Services Directorate*

This pathfinder includes information about culture in the Philippines.

American Historical Collections (http://rizal.lib.admu.edu.ph/ahc/)
The American Historical Collection website. Housed at the Ateneo, the collection houses materials related to the American Experience in the Philippines.

Hector Santos (http://www.hectorsan@bibingka.com/pages.htm)
This site links to five other Philippine webpages devoted entirely to Philippine general resources, culture and history.

Internet Movie Database: Philippines (http://indie.imdb.com/Sections/Countries/Philippines/)
Your IMDb guide for the Philippines. This area contains a list of interesting reports based around the 1,528 titles in the IMDb from the Philippines (including international co-productions). In English.

Lopez Memorial Museum (http://www.lopezmuseum.org.ph/index.html)
Private museum with extensive Filipiniana art collection and extensive private library collection that maintains significant publishing arm. List of Lopez Museum publications with abstracts, descriptions of the art collection and current exhibitions. Lengthy descriptive overview of the Library's rare book and archival collections

NCCA Directories (http://www.ncca.gov.ph/DIRECTORIES/ncca%5Fdirectories.htm)
Directories to museums by categories, libraries, associations, galleries, government and private organizations related to the arts

National Commission for Culture and the Arts (http://www.ncca.gov.ph/)
History and organizational structure of the Commission, background to Philippine traditional cultures, overview of contemporary dance and music, theater, literature, visual artsbiographical profiles of the National Artists, calendar of events, information on grants programs, directories to museums, libraries, galleries, and related government institutions.

National University of Singapore - Philippines Information (http://sunsite.nus.edu.sg/SEAlinks/philippines-info.html)
A Philippine general information site that has links to other sites on Filipino art and culture and a tutorial on the Tagalog language.

Philippine Scouts Heritage Society (http://www.philippine-scouts.org/Info%5FExchange/exchange.html)
A website for members of the society and others interested in the historical heritage of the Philippine Scouts.

Sanghaya (http://www33.brinkster.com/sanghaya/index.html)
Online journal about what is happening in the world of Philippine arts and culture updated regularly includes feature articles. Back issues from 2001.

Figure 9.2   Culture links at Portals to the World–Philippines

HLB International: Doing Business In ...

www.hlbi.com/DBI_list.asp

If you do business abroad, make use of the country business guides provided by HLB International, an organization of accounting firms and business advisors. The site has guides for 48 countries, with each including information on topics such as investment factors, types of business organizations, taxation, labor, and accounting.

BISNIS (Business Information Service for the Newly Independent States)

www.bisnis.doc.gov/BISNIS/countryindex.cfm

If you are planning on doing business in any of the Newly Independent (former Soviet) states (particularly Armenia, Azerbaijan, Belarus, Georgia, Kazakhstan, Kyrgyz Republic, Moldova, Russia, Tajikistan, Turkmenistan, Ukraine, and Uzbekistan), use this site to get a large number of specialized reports relating to commercial affairs. This site is an example of a business-specific guide but can be useful even for the general traveler who wants to know more.

The Connected Traveler

www.connectedtraveler.com

If you get tired of reading about destinations, consider just listening instead. Podcasts were briefly discussed in Chapter 2, including mention of The Connected Traveler by Russell Johnson. His site is mentioned again here because of its emphasis on travel's cultural side, including a healthy helping on foods around the world. Topics range from Nine Tiny Reinyak to Bad Day in Borneo. Not all content is podcasts, however: All articles are available in text, and some articles are available in audio and even in video.

Maps

If a picture is worth a thousand words, then a map can be worth much more. The Web provides thousands of maps that not only help you get around a country but can also help you understand a country. Road map sites, including Maporama, ViaMichelin, MapQuest, MapBlast, Rand McNally, Google Maps, and Yahoo! Maps, were discussed in Chapter 4. The following map sites provide other map perspectives, including political, relief, historical, thematic, and more.

Perry-Castañeda Library Map Collection
www.lib.utexas.edu/maps

The Perry-Castañeda Library Map Collection, brought to you by the Libraries of the University of Texas, is a tremendous collection of current and historical maps and includes links to other map sites, gazetteers, etc. Most of the more than 5,000 maps available are in the public domain, and a large portion of the maps are produced by the CIA. For any country, you will usually find relief and political maps, plus for many countries, maps of major cities and various thematic maps on topics as varied as economic activity, land use, vegetation, gas and oil, minerals, climate, and ethnolinguistic groups. The Perry-Castañeda site also contains an outstanding and fascinating collection of historical maps. So if you want a map of Britain in 410, Dublin in 1610, or France in 1789, or formerly top-secret maps for the Normandy landings, this is the place to come.

Global Gazetteer
www.fallingrain.com/world

Global Gazetteer is a "directory of 2880532 of the world's cities and towns sorted by country and linked to a map for each town." You can browse the alphabetical list to find latitude and longitude, altitude, time zone, satellite images, nearby cities and towns, current weather (graphs), and nearby airports.

World Gazetteer

www.world-gazetteer.com

The World Gazetteer offers population figures for countries, administrative divisions, larger cities, towns, and other places, plus geographic coordinates, area size, maps, flags, links to online data sources for the statistics, lists of largest cities, and other data. Browse through the alphabetical list to find places of interest or use the Contents link to browse by topic. A pronunciation table is provided for dozens of languages and will be useful not just here but for other applications.

Google Earth

earth.google.com

The hottest cartographic item since Mercator, Google Earth is a downloadable program that provides online access to satellite and aircraft imagery of every place on Earth. Download the free program that allows you to display the images, and then while online, Google Earth delivers the images to you. You can zoom in and out and tilt the image and move forward as if you are "flying over," and then you can overlay roads and many other objects.

Google Earth's main page presents a control console and an image of the entire Earth. Click on an area of your choice, and then zoom to exactly where you want to see—your own backyard, Tonga, or Timbuktu (Figure 9.3). You can also zoom directly to your destination by typing in an address. At an "altitude" of your choice, you can have Google Earth superimpose roads, railways, schools, parks, hotels, restaurants, etc., as well as political boundaries, statistics, driving directions, and much more. For 38 major U.S. metropolitan areas, you can see 3-D images of buildings and terrain. You can add your own placemarks and annotations, and even share these with others.

Images (all taken within the last three years) are available for the entire world, with higher-resolution images available for most major

Figure 9.3 Google Earth view of Geneva, Switzerland

cities in the U.S., Canada, the U.K., and Europe. Road maps are available for the U.S., Canada, the U.K., and Western Europe. Google's Local Search features are provided for the U.S., Canada, and the U.K. For the lower resolution sites (more remote parts of the world), the resolution will allow you to see at least major geographic features and towns. The higher resolution sites let you identify an object that is the size of a car or larger.

Unless your computer is a few years old, it can probably handle Google Earth. But check the Google Earth site for detailed requirements. More powerful versions, Google Earth Plus and Google Earth Pro (with enhanced features, including GPS device support), are also available for a fee.

News

Being aware of the local news in places you travel to has many advantages and is surprisingly easy. Not only will you be familiar with and prepared for various situations, but assuming that you are prepared to add an appropriate level of tact and diplomacy, knowing what's in the news can make you a much better conversationalist while you are there. As you examine news sites, look for links for free e-mail alerts (the news is sent, usually daily, to your e-mail) and/or the orange symbol for RSS (which stands for either "really simple syndication" or "rich site summary"). RSS provides an easy way to have news headlines (or, additionally, summaries or full stories) fed to you, rather than you having to go to multiple sites to get the news. With an RSS "reader," you can have the reader automatically gather news headlines (or more) from whichever RSS-equipped sites you have specified. For more information, the Fagan Finder site (www.faganfinder.com/search/rss.shtml) has a good explanation of RSS. Another easy way to get acquainted with and use RSS (with minimal explanation required) is to sign up for My Yahoo! (my.yahoo.com) and use that as your reader. My Yahoo! will walk you through the process.

Newspapers and Radio Stations

If you are planning on spending several days in Singapore, you can bring yourself up-to-date on what is happening there by reading a local newspaper or listening to a local radio station. Where can you find a Singaporean newspaper if you are in Peoria or Peterborough and don't even know the names of papers in Singapore? The Web, of course. There are literally thousands of newspapers online, and they are very easy to locate by using any of several Web resource guides for newspapers, radio and TV stations, and other media channels. Two of the best of these resource guides are Kidon Media-Link and ABYZ

News Links, which are described in detail in the following section. They provide links to thousands of news sites around the world. You can also find a fair amount of national news by making use of the major news network sites, such as BBC and CNN, where you can browse or search for articles about your destination. Six of these network sites, each with somewhat different content, perspectives, and organization, are also included in this section.

Kidon Media-Link

www.kidon.com/media-link

Kidon Media-Link provides links to more than 18,000 new sources, including sites for newspapers, news agencies, magazines, radio, television, teletext, and Internet-only news sources. With Kidon Media-Link, you can easily browse by continent and by country. The Search link on the main page enables you to search by title words, city name, and specific kind of media (newspapers, etc.). In case you don't speak the country's native language, you will find that for most countries there will be at least one newspaper that is published in English. A link on Kidon Media-Link's home page offers a list of sources by country that are in English (or in your choice of nine other languages). For each source, you will see the language and city in which it is published (Figure 9.4). Symbols next to the source listing indicate the presence of audio and video on the site. Click on the name of a specific source to go directly to its site.

ABYZ News Links

www.abyznewslinks.com

ABYZ News Links is very similar to Kidon Media-Link but contains some sources that the latter does not (and vice-versa). It has links mainly to newspapers but also includes links to many broadcast stations, Internet services, magazines, and press agencies. You can find

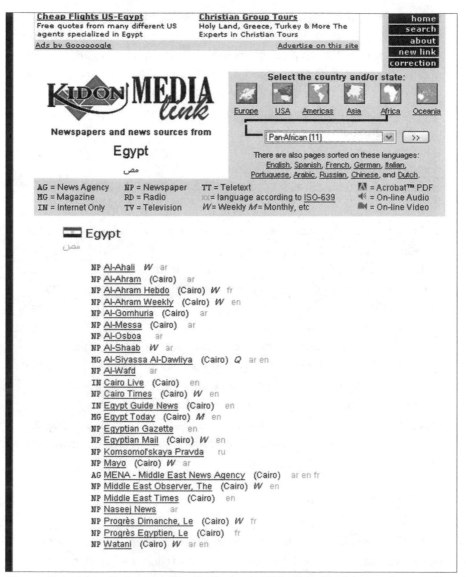

Figure 9.4   List of news sources in Egypt at Kidon Media-Link

news sources by either browsing by continent and country or using the search box. For each country, you may find news sources about the country that are published elsewhere, as well as publications from the country itself. When browsing, the lists will show the type of media, whether it is a national or foreign publication, the media focus (business, general, or sports), and the language.

News Networks

All the major news networks have "international" coverage. However, international may mean that only news about big events and issues of global interest will get covered. It does not mean that events that are mainly of interest to a specific country will get the same detailed coverage. For example, the election of a prime minister in a small country may get coverage, but a local flood may not. The following networks have a generous definition of international and offer quite a few stories about somewhat more local events for many countries.

BBC News

news.bbc.co.uk

For international coverage, many people will argue that the leader among news network sites is BBC News. The site contains almost all news published by BBC News since the site opened in November 1997. Sources of stories include BBC News itself, BBC World Service, The Press Association, Associated Press, Reuters, and Agence France-Presse. You can easily hone in on news from a particular region of the world by using the links on the left of the main page for Africa, Americas, Asia-Pacific, Middle East, or South Asia. You can also search for news about a particular place or topic by using the search box in the upper right corner of the main page. Also take advantage of the audio and video available on the site. When you have clicked on one of the continent links, the audio and video on that page will be specific to BBC World service stories for that area.

Reuters
reuters.com

For reporting on news throughout the world, Reuters is definitely a leader, widely respected for its international coverage. Particularly make use of the International and World Crises link on its news categories menu. Content goes back about one month.

CNN.com International
edition.cnn.com

The menu on the main page of CNN.com International leads to sections for Asia, Europe, the U.S., and the World. Click on the World link for sections on Africa, Americas, and the Middle East. Mobile phone access is available through CNNtoGo (www.cnn.com/togo).

World News
wn.com

World News is a news aggregation site that partners with more than 300 news organizations to provide news that it categorizes into more than 5,000 country, regional, and thematic categories. On the main page, look at the menu on the left for a sense of the breadth of coverage. Click on one of the menu items to get a feel for the further level of specificity of categories. For example, if you click on WN Asia, you will see Breaking News for Asia, but you will also find links to dozens of specific categories by country and topic. From there, if you click on the Indonesia Life section, you will get Indonesian headline stories and links to additional specific categories. You can also sign up for a free e-mail newsletter with daily headlines for more than 50 WN categories.

EINnews

www.einnews.com

EINews is a business information and online news service that draws from 25,000 sources and has extensive news for more than 300 countries, regions, U.S. states, and topical areas. The catch is that the most you will see is the headlines unless you subscribe. However, if you are very serious about tracking news for a particular country, it may be worth the subscription. (EINews does offer a free seven-day trial.)

Worldpress.org

worldpress.org

Worldpress.org is a press "review" site that uses a number of correspondents around the world who draw from the world press to "illuminate" issues and provide "a succinct view of the political and economic climate globally" by "translating, reprinting, analyzing, and contextualizing the best of the international press from more than 20 languages."

Language Tools

If you speak the native language of the country you are visiting, your trip can be significantly different than if you don't. Even if you have never spoken a word of the language, your trip can be different (and better) if you at least learn a half dozen basic phrases. When you meet someone who doesn't speak English, just being able to say "Excuse me," "Where is ...," "Please," and "Thank you" will literally get you a long way. You may not understand a word of the reply, but hand gestures will get you going in the right direction, and the "Thank you" part will probably also get you a smile. Add to that some basic local etiquette (and frequent smiling), and you will leave behind a much better impression of your own country than, unfortunately, is left by many tourists. For many languages, the Web provides you with the basic phrases to use and, unlike the printed phrase book you will want to bring along, may have a feature that allows you to actually *hear* the pronunciation

For those who speak the language but significantly less than perfect, the Web can also be helpful in "brushing up" language skills. The previously listed news sites will provide audio from radio stations and many other news sources that you can tune in to. The Web also provides dozens of dictionaries for most languages. To practice your reading, the Web can provide you with literally millions of pages in any of dozens of languages. (Use the advanced search page on Google or Yahoo! or another search engine to search on any topic, and use the language section of the search page to specify that you only retrieve items in the languages of your choice.) As you are practicing your reading, you can make use of not just online dictionaries, but the several translation tools on the Web.

The following sections feature sites that will take you to language lessons, collections of dictionaries (yourDictionary.com), examples of dictionaries for a few of the more common languages, and sites that translate words, phrases, and larger text selections. For the latter function, remember that these are machine translations. If you use them to translate a paragraph, the translation will almost certainly not be perfect. A perfect translation is not the purpose here, but rather a rough idea of what the author is talking about—so if you are concerned more with precision than with general concepts, you may want to not use translation sites. For the dictionaries, the online versions may be quite old, but most should be useful for some basic language needs.

Learning Some Language Basics

Don't expect the Web to make you conversationally adept in any language, but for many languages, sites exist that can provide you with at least a few useful words and phrases. The following site is a Web resource guide with links to a broad range of language sites, and the remaining sites in this section are examples of specific sites that will help you get acquainted or reacquainted with language basics.

iLoveLanguages
www.ilovelanguages.com

iLoveLanguages is a directory of more than 2,400 language-related sites, including online courses, language schools, software, dictionaries, translation sites, and other resources. This site is a good starting place to explore the possibilities.

Travlang—Foreign Languages for Travelers
www.travlang.com/languages

Travlang provides an introduction to more than 80 languages. For each language, you will find basic vocabulary and phrases arranged in the following categories: Basic Words, Numbers, Shopping/Dining, Travel, Directions, Places, and Time and Dates. Under each category you will find from 10 to 50 words or phrases of use to travelers, and each has an audio file so you can hear the language spoken, as well as a quiz you can take. To increase your vocabulary, Travlang also offers a free e-mail Word-of-the-Day service.

BBC Languages
www.bbc.co.uk/languages

BBC Languages has one of the most extensive collections of free introductions to languages on the Web. The site provides lessons and quizzes for introductory French, Spanish, German, Italian, Mandarin, Chinese, Portuguese, and Greek, or for those who just need to brush up. The site also provides Quick Fixes with audio for a dozen "holiday phrases" in 37 languages, including Albanian,

Basque, Belarusian, Bosnian, Bulgarian, Catalan, Croatian, Czech, Danish, Dutch, Estonian, Finnish, Flemish, French, German, Greek, Hungarian, Icelandic, Italian, Latvian, Lithuanian, Luxembourgish, Macedonian, Maltese, Norwegian, Polish, Portuguese, Romanian, Russian, Serbian, Slovak, Slovene, Spanish, Swedish, Turkish, and Ukrainian. These lessons are also downloadable as MP3 files. You will also find a variety of other language resources in BBC's impressive collection.

Fodor's—Living Language
www.fodors.com/language

At first glimpse, you may think this section of the Fodor's site is just an ad for Living Language courses. If you look farther down on the page, you will find that the site actually contains an introduction to French, German, Italian, and Spanish. For each language, you will see choices for the following categories: Useful Expressions, Dining Out, Sightseeing, At the Airport, Personal Services, Shopping, Finding Your Way, Health Care, Leisure and Entertainment, Accommodations, On the Road, General Information, Socializing, and Communications. Each category features a fairly extensive list of useful words, phrases, and sentences, any of which you can click on to hear the pronunciation.

About.com
about.com

About.com, which has been mentioned a number of times in this book under a variety of travel topics, has several sections for specific languages. The following sites contain a variety of subsections about different aspects of the language. Each one includes an introduction to speaking the language. The other content will vary considerably, but much of it will be of use to travelers. The Italian section offers guidance about using hand gestures, and the French section provides instruction on how to greet acquaintances with *La bise*, the kiss.

About.com—French Language
french.about.com

About.com—Italian Language
italian.about.com

About.com—Japanese Language
japanese.about.com

About.com—Spanish Language
spanish.about.com

About.com—Judaism—Learn Hebrew Online
judaism.about.com/od/learnhebrewonline

GermanForTravellers
www.germanfortravellers.com

The GermanForTravellers (GFT) site provides free language lessons for topics including Basics, Travel, Food, Shopping, and Situations, plus Grammar, Vocabulary, and Sounds. Access to the full collection of lessons on the site, however, requires a paid membership. Beyond the language lessons, the site also offers very useful sections on culture and travel and a collection of more than 200 links to history, news, literature, radio, TV, music, movies, learning German, and more. The Culture section has lists and articles on topics such as holidays, travel, food and drink, and etiquette.

Bonjour!
www.bonjour.com

Bonjour.com has an easy-to-use set of audio lessons with several hundred words, questions, and expressions under the categories of

Greetings and Courtesies, Alphabet, Numbers, Days, Months, Seasons, Questions, Quantities, Weather, Time, Asking For Help, Emergencies, Banks, Taxis, Restaurants, Transportation, Finding Your Way, Touring, Socializing, and Famous Expressions.

Voice of America—Pronunciation Guide

names.voa.gov

Should you need to mention the name of the leader of the country you are visiting, you will make a better impression if you pronounce the leader's name correctly. The Voice of America Pronunciation Guide provides the correct pronunciation of more than 6,000 people and places.

Dictionaries and Translation Tools

yourDictionary.com

www.yourdictionary.com

yourDictionary.com is a tremendously rich and valuable site—valuable not just because of the variety of useful things that you can do on the site but because it displays a good example of the overall richness of the Web. The main page has a variety of language tools, and if you go to the pull-down menu under Dictionaries, you'll find links for several languages. Instead of clicking on any one of those, click on the menu item for "280 more," which is a collection of links, not to 280 more dictionaries, but to sites that have dictionaries for 280 more *languages*. For each language, you will typically find several dictionaries. The extensiveness and general quality of the dictionaries will vary, but for most languages, you should find a dictionary that will be adequate for general use. The lists of dictionaries yourDictionary.com shows for a language will usually include dictionaries specifically of that language, plus dictionaries for translations. You will also often find specialized and technical dictionaries, such as for acronyms, medicine, biology, and chemistry. The dictionaries you find here and elsewhere on the Web may be quite old, but most of them work well for basic language needs.

At the center of the main page of yourDictionary.com, you will find a search box to translate single words between English and 24 other languages. Near the top of the page is a link for Multilingual that leads to a search box that will translate any of 50,000 phrases simultaneously into English, French, German, Italian, and Spanish. Warning: If you have a passion for languages, you may find yourself spending a very long time exploring the amazing things that yourDictionary.com has to offer

WordReference.com

www.wordreference.com

WordReference.com is a combination of dictionaries that translates English into Spanish, French, and Italian, and from those languages to English. On the main page, type your term in the Enter a Word box, and choose the translation you want (e.g., English to Spanish). The results page will show one or more Principal Translations, as well as relevant additional translations, compound forms, and common phrases using the term (Figure 9.5). Though it is not obvious, many of the words on search results pages are clickable for more in-depth definitions and better understanding of the terms and their usage.

The ARTFL Project

machaut.uchicago.edu

The ARTFL Project site contains several French and English language reference tools, including a French-to-English dictionary, an English-to-French dictionary, and a French verb conjugator. On the main page, enter a word in the Quick Lookup box and then click the button for the operation you wish (e.g., French > English). For translations,

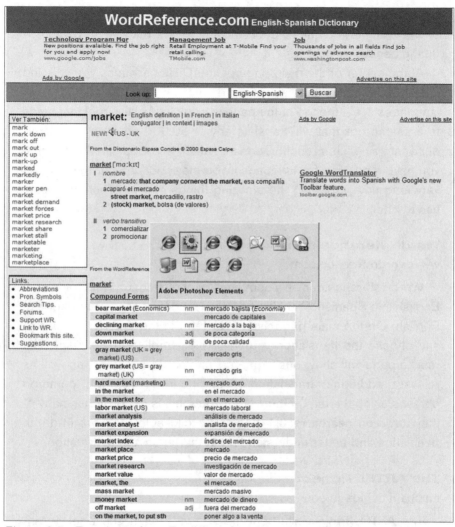

Figure 9.5   Translation from English to Spanish at WordReference.com

the resulting page not only provides a simple translation but links to full definitions and examples. The definitions come from a variety of dictionaries dating from 1606 to 1935, so don't expect to find definitions for television, podcasts, or other modern terms. (The word "computer" *is* there. Try it and find out why.)

LEO (Link Everything Online)
dict.leo.org

For powerful German-English and English-German translation dictionaries, LEO provides more than 400,000 entries. The results can be very extensive. For example, if you search for the English word "shoe", LEO will return 13 corresponding German nouns, three German verbs, one phrase/collocation, and more than 80 composed entries (pairs such as "shoe polish" and "*die Schuhcreme*"). The search results pages provide links to a detailed definition in German, conjugation and inflection tables, and an audio file that lets you hear the actual pronunciation. You will also find here a nice display of usage and idiomatic expressions, with links to such things as declension tables.

Chinese-English Dictionary
www.mandarintools.com/worddict.html

The Chinese-English Dictionary site, which is an implementation of the CEDICT Chinese-English Dictionary Project database and contains about 100,000 definitions, enables you to enter an English word and have it translated into traditional, simplified, and pinyin Chinese. Click on the pinyin translation to hear the pronunciation.

Foreignword.com
foreignword.com

Foreignword.com combines the power of 265 dictionaries to enable you to translate terms from 69 source languages into 73 target languages, for a total of 400 combinations. Click on the Tools link for a feature that allows you to translate entire portions of text using 28 different machine translation tools for 38 languages. With Foreignword.com's Eureka Search, you can search a database of more than 4,000 sites that contain dictionaries, glossaries, and lexicons.

PROMT-Online
translation2.paralink.com

PROMT-Online offers translation capabilities between most pairs of English, French, German, and Russian words. Click on the More Languages menu for additional options. The site also provides an on-screen "keyboard" for German, French, Italian, Russian, and Spanish. Choose one of the language keyboards to type words in that language.

Free2Professional Translation
www.freetranslation.com

FreeTranslation can translate text into English from French, German, Russian, Italian, Dutch, Portuguese, and Russian. Likewise, English can be translated into Spanish, French, Italian, German, Dutch, Portuguese, Russian, Norwegian, Chinese, or Japanese. Paste a block of text into the text translator box and choose the language. As emphasized before, keep in mind the limitations of machine translations.

Government, Politics, and Religion

Depending on where you are traveling and to whom you are speaking, government, politics, and religion are topics of conversation that, at one extreme, you may want to avoid, and at the other extreme, topics that people you meet will be anxious to discuss. (Actually, this is true at home as well.) Whether or not you will be discussing these topics, knowing something about all three in regards to any country you visit may make your trip more meaningful, more educational, and even safer. The country guides discussed earlier in this chapter provide some basic information on each of these topics; the following sites will provide a deeper reach into each subject area.

In addition, consider visiting an embassy site for your destination country. What and how much information is available will vary greatly, but the sites can provide extensive and useful information about a country, including news, history, culture, customs, cuisine, and travel tips. Several sites provide good collections of links to embassies throughout the world, but if you are looking for an embassy for a specific country, try a simple search engine search. If you just search for *embassy Japan* or *embassy Latvia*, you will most likely find what you are looking for quickly. On the first page of search results, there will usually be links for the embassies in several locations, but look particularly for the country's embassy site in a major city, such as Washington, D.C., or London. Information from those embassies may be more extensive. One example of such an embassy site is Russia's, which is included in the following list.

Governments on the WWW

www.gksoft.com/govt

For those who want to get acquainted at a fairly detailed level with the makeup of a country's government, Governments on the WWW is a resource guide with links to official government sites for more than 220 countries, including sites for parliaments, ministries, offices, municipal institutions, and embassies. Links are also available to the Web sites of political parties, public broadcasting corporations, central banks, and more.

Political Resources on the Net

www.politicalresources.net

If you want to know "straight from the horse's mouth" about a country's major political parties and what they say they stand for, the Political Resources on the Net site will provide links to the parties' sites.

Politics & International Relations
socio.ch/journals/politics.htm

If you are up for reading some scholarly articles on politics and international relations, the Politics and International Relations site identifies and links to individual online journals.

Religion Resources on the Web
www.lib.iastate.edu/collections/eresourc/religion.html

Religion Resources on the Web is a Web resource guide that provides an extensive collection of links to sites that will help you understand the background, history, and tenets of major religions around the world. The encyclopedias covered earlier in this chapter are also good resources for this topic.

Embassy of the Russian Federation
www.russianembassy.org

The Web site for the Embassy of the Russian Federation (in Washington, D.C.) is a good example of the kinds of information that embassy sites can provide. On this site, you will find information on Russia's government, economy, culture, geography, science, cuisine, religion, holidays, foreign policy, and more (Figure 9.6).

Cuisines

Just as "an army travels on its stomach," you might say the same for some ordinary travelers. If this describes you, then getting to know the gastronomical terrain before you embark will help you accomplish

Figure 9.6   Embassy of the Russian Federation main page

your mission. As in many cases, for finding Web sites that discuss the cuisine of a particular country, employing a search engine may be one an effective tactic. Try a search for something like *cuisine Argentina* or *cuisine Portugal.* Another good approach is to use Wikipedia, which has good overview articles for the cuisine of many countries.

Wikipedia—Cuisine

en.wikipedia.org/wiki/cuisine

Wikipedia has articles on many national cuisines (as noted in Chapter 6), in addition to articles on specific countries and articles on various specific aspects of life in those countries. The links provided at this URL lead to articles for more than 70 countries.

Museums

If you are reading this chapter, then you are interested enough in the "cultural" side of travel that it is likely you will be visiting at least one museum on your trip. Knowing ahead of time what museums there are at a destination and what those museums offer can save you time, make you more prepared, and whet your appetite. The guidebooks covered in Chapter 2 provide lists (and usually brief descriptions) of museums for the cities they cover. Other Web sites have information on a lot of museums, and, of course, many or perhaps most museums have sites of their own.

MuseumStuff.com
www.museumstuff.com

As indicated on its main page, MuseumStuff.com concentrates its attention on U.S. museums. But it also contains information on a large number of museums throughout the rest of the world. Altogether, the site has 22,000 items on museums or related to museums. For each museum listed, there is a brief overview of the museum and a link to the museum's site. Some links are to pages that are directories of museums in a particular city (e.g., Museums of Morocco). Use the search box to search by location or topic (or other keywords), browse by main subject (Art, History, Science), or use the Museums Online link to browse by state, country, type, genre, etc.

MUSÉE
www.musee-online.org

MUSÉE is a directory of 37,000 museums worldwide, though, as you will see from the main page, the emphasis is on museums in the U.S. You can use the box on the main page to search or click on Advanced Search to search by keywords, museum name, location, and time frame for events and exhibitions. You can also browse using the categories listed on the main page (Art & Design, Food, Fashion, Film and Music, History, Kids, Science and Nature, Sports, and Special Interest). Each major category has an extensive list of subcategories (more than 130, including topics such as Comedy, Mining, Whaling, Theatre, Pop Culture, Wax, and Costume). The amount of information provided for each museum varies considerably, ranging from basic location, phone number, and a brief description of the collection, to more detailed listings with fuller descriptions, lists of activities, links to the Web site, list of facilities, museum hours, and admission fee.

Virtual Library Museums Pages
vlmp.museophile.com

The Virtual Library Museums Pages is a resource guide with links to thousands of museum sites around the world. You can browse by continent and country, or you can use the search box to search by keywords for subject, location, name, or other terms.

24 Hour Museum
www.24hourmuseum.org.uk

The 24 Hour Museum is an extensive guide to more than 3,800 publicly funded and nonprofit museums, galleries, and heritage sites throughout the U.K. The site also contains articles; news; sections for kids, teachers, and volunteers; and museums and heritage guides for 10 cities. For information on specific museums, use the search box on the main page or the Advanced Search page to search by keyword, museum or gallery name, time frame (for events, exhibitions, etc.), collection type, event type, age range, and museum facilities. A description, location, hours, contacts, admission charges, links to articles, and more are provided for each institution.

Festivals and Conferences

If you want to plan your vacation around specific festivals or conferences or just find out what events of this type are happening in the places you are headed, check out these Web sites or try a Web search to find special events (for example, *festivals brazil*).

Festivals.com

www.festivals.com

Festivals.com enables you to browse or search a database of more than 40,000 festivals, fairs, and special events. Though the site has some worldwide coverage, it predominantly covers the U.S. (compare 10 entries for England to 20 for Alabama, including the Down Home Psaltery and Hammered Dulcimer Festival and the Alabama Chicken and Egg Festival). Look for festivals by searching by keyword or browsing by topic (Arts, Culture, Kids, Motorsports, Music, and Sports). For each festival, you will usually find a description, date, location, directions, admission and parking fees, phone number, e-mail, and a link to the festival's site. The site includes primarily "commercial" festivals and not the thousands of religious and similar festivals around the world.

Bugbog—Festivals and Events

www.bugbog.com/festivals/festivals.html

Bugbog's Festivals and Events page features dates and brief descriptions for about 200 festivals worldwide, which are arranged and browsable by the following categories: Best Arts Festivals, Best Colorful Festivals, European Festivals, Exotic Festivals, and English-Speaking Festivals and Events. The Exotic category leads to festivals such as the Bikaner Camel Festival in India, Khmer New Year in Cambodia, the Water Splashing Festival in China, the Dragon Boat Festival in Hong Kong, Redneck Games in Georgia (U.S.), and Buffalo

Races in Thailand. While you are on the Bugbog site, also check out the excellent Travel Pictures for countries and cities.

FilmFestivals.com
www.filmfestivals.com

If film festivals are on your list of preferred activities, visit FilmFestivals.com. The site contains news about festivals, films, and film people, and a searchable database of festivals and films worldwide. From the main page, you can browse by country, events taking place this week or this month, and other criteria. The Advanced Search page lets you search for festivals and films by country, film name, director, production company, and production year. Information about each festival includes festival name, a brief description, dates, organizer, and, depending on the particular festival, venue, opening hours, admission, links to the festival's sites, and festivalgoer comments.

Wcities
wcities.com

Wcities, which was discussed in some detail in Chapter 2, also deserves mention here because of its extensive coverage of museums, concerts, festivals, and other events. From the site's main page, browse to find the city you wish, then use the Events section to search by date range and themes (Arts & Museums, Concerts, Cultural, Family, Festivals, Holidays, Sport Event, Theatre, Tours, and Other). For each event, you will find a description, dates, phone numbers, and, in some cases, reviews and links to the event's Web site.

AllConferences.com
www.allconferences.com

AllConferences.com is a directory of conferences, conventions, trade shows, exhibits, workshops, and business meetings. It contains information on thousands of conferences worldwide—however, do not consider it to be exhaustive. (For example, the Library category only listed one upcoming event and only four for Literature.) You can browse for events by the following categories, each of which has a number of browsable subcategories: Arts & Humanities, Business, Computers & Internet, Health, Society, Reference, Science and Technology, Education, Social Science, Recreation, News, and Government. You can search using the simple search box on the main page or the Advanced Search to search by title, city, country, date, category, or keyword. The amount of information for each event will differ, but the descriptions usually include the name, dates, location, and a link to the event's site.

Discussion Groups and Forums for Exploring Countries and Cultures

The discussion groups covered in previous chapters contain lots of discussion about particular countries and cities, but their primary focus is on the "travel" aspect rather than on background, culture, and politics. If you would like to read more about and perhaps get involved in discussions on those topics, try Yahoo! Groups and Google Groups. Be warned that both have a large proportion of messages that are spam, advertisements, and "tales told by idiots." However, if you poke around a bit, you can find some interesting information, comments, and perspectives.

Yahoo! Groups
groups.yahoo.com

Yahoo! Groups contains hundreds of thousands of discussion groups, most created by individuals or small organizations. The main Yahoo! Groups page has an entire category devoted to Cultures and Community. Under that category, look at the Countries and Cultures subcategory for more than 28,000 groups. In addition, try the search box and search for the name of a country. For some groups, anyone can read the messages, but for others you have to join the group (it's easy to do and even easier to undo). To join a group, you need a Yahoo! ID, which is also easy to get and for which you can, shall we say, use a different persona.

Google Groups
groups.google.com

The main content at Google Groups is the collection of Usenet discussion groups that contains messages going back more than 25 years. It also contains the more recently created groups that Google established, which are patterned after Yahoo! Groups. You can browse by category or use the search box. Google's Advanced Groups Search page allows you to narrow your search by specific groups, message author, date, and subject. Most messages can be read by anyone, but for some groups, you will need to join the group, which requires a Google account.

Bits and Pieces and Practicalities

Choosing your destination, planning your itinerary, and making your reservations are (hopefully by now) obvious tasks and activities for which the Web provides extensive resources. There are, though, numerous other travel-related tasks and activities for which the Internet provides information, assistance, and tools. A selection of Web sites providing a lot of "nitty-gritty," everyday odds-and-ends information is included here for passport and visa information, time, weather, currencies, ATMs, weights and measures, flight tracking and airports, subways, health and safety alerts, wired travel, electrical connections, packing lists, travel supplies, finding your way to religious services, and a few miscellaneous items.

Passport and Visa Information

Official governmental Web sites are good starting places and serve as the "definitive" place to get information on passports and visas. However, they also generally provide a wealth of other information of interest to those traveling abroad.

U.S. Department of State—Travel
travel.state.gov

The main page of the U.S. State Department's Travel.State.Gov Web site serves as a Web portal for both American citizens traveling abroad and for non-U.S. citizens traveling to the U.S. The site contains information on passports, visas for entering the U.S., services for U.S. citizens abroad, news regarding traveling to the U.S., and links to resources regarding laws and policies that relate to Americans living or traveling abroad. You will also find Consular Information Sheets with information about traveling to other countries, including Entry Requirements, Safety and Security, Crime, Medical Facilities and Health, Medical Insurance, Traffic Safety and Road Conditions, and more.

U.S. Department of State—Passports

travel.state.gov/passport

U.S. citizens will find just about everything they need to get or renew a passport from the Passports page of the U.S. State Department's Travel.State.Gov site. Application forms can be filled out online, or they can be printed out.

Foreign & Commonwealth Office

www.fco.gov.uk

British citizens can use the Foreign & Commonwealth Office (FCO) Web site for a wide range of information and advice about traveling abroad. Click on the Travel Advice link on the main page to get to the FCO's Travel page, which will provide information on passports and visas as well as health, safety, money, drugs, travel checklists, and more. The Travel Advice by Country link will take you to a list of countries you should avoid or only travel to if necessary, and also a menu that will provide a travel summary sheet for any country.

Time Differences

When planning your trip or planning a time to phone family and friends back home, it is good to know the time differences between home and your destinations or between destinations. Several places online provide the current time in any country or the difference between two time zones. The first site that follows (time and date.com) brings together a number of useful tools. The other two familiar sites— Google and Yahoo!—offer shortcuts for finding times in other cities.

timeanddate.com
www.timeanddate.com

Among the tools offered by timeanddate.com are its World Clock, which displays the current time in more than 150 cities around the world, and a Full World Clock, which does the same for more than 450 cities. If you click on the name of a city for either clock, you will be shown the current date and time, time zone, Daylight Savings Time information, difference between its time and Greenwich Mean Time, sunrise and sunset times, dialing codes, and latitude and longitude. With the World Time Search option, you can search for times by continent or city. The Time Zone Converter will calculate the differences in times between cities.

Yahoo! Time Shortcut
yahoo.com

From Yahoo!'s main page, just type in a phrase such as *time in Ankara*, then click Search. At the top of the search results page, you will see the current time and the difference between that city's time and UTC (Coordinated Universal Time). For Ankara, you will see something like:

```
Local time in Ankara, Turkey is 9:09 PM,
Tuesday, Jul 17, 2007
    Coordinated Universal Time (UTC) + 2:0
hours
```

Google Time Shortcut
google.com

From the main Google page, type the word *time*, followed by the city, just as with Yahoo!. Google will respond with the local time for that city.

Weather

Wondering what to pack for your trip and whether you should take an umbrella? You may already have a favorite weather site with the current weather conditions and forecasts for cities around the world. If not, try one of the following.

The Weather Channel
www.weather.com

For weather in just about any city in the world, enter the city name or a ZIP code in the Local Weather search box on the Weather Channel site and click Go. If there is more than one city with that name, you can choose from a list of options. Choose the city, and you will be shown the latest weather conditions (in great detail) and a 36-hour forecast. Links on the page will lead to a 10-day forecast, a month forecast, a video forecast (U.S.), traffic conditions, and more.

Weather Underground
www.wunderground.com

The Weather Underground site provides a tremendous number of weather details worldwide (Figure 10.1). In the search box, enter the city and state, or ZIP code, airport code, or country. If you receive a list, choose the place of interest. You will be shown the current conditions (including temperature, wind-chill, humidity, dewpoint, visibility, flight rule, wind speed, and more), a five-day forecast, a seven-day forecast, historical maximum and minimum temperatures, astronomical times (sun and moon rise and set, length of day, etc.), plus links to satellite and radar images, ski conditions, weather maps, and marine weather. You can easily spend an hour exploring this site.

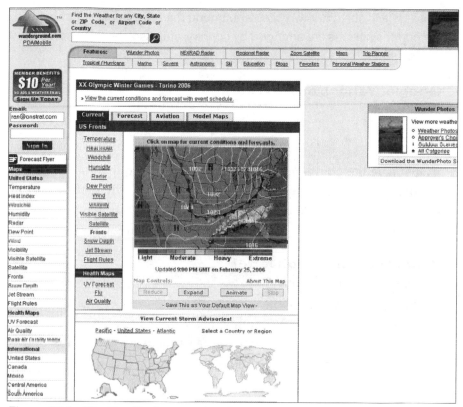

Figure 10.1 Weather Underground main page

Currencies

Many Web sites offer currency converters, which show not just the exchange rates, but do the calculations for specific amounts. Sites will differ in terms of which currencies they cover, how up-to-date the rate is (worst case: today's rate, but often rates are only minutes old), and how much additional information they provide, including historical figures. If you want a straightforward figure without additional data, you can use the search boxes at Google, Yahoo!, or Ask.com. For getting more details, the other two sites are among the most popular. For each, the currency menus are arranged by country, and also show the name of the currency.

Google, Yahoo!, and Ask.com
google.com
yahoo.com
ask.com

Just type the conversion you are looking for into the search box. For example, search for *convert 400 dollars to yen*. The results page will supply your answer. All three of these search engines cover most currencies.

Yahoo! Currency Converter
finance.yahoo.com/currency

The Currency Converter in Yahoo!'s Finance section provides conversions for more than 160 currencies, with charts showing recent changes, a table comparing exchange rates for major currencies, and links to news stories related to currencies.

FXConverter
www.oanda.com/convert/classic

FXConverter converts 164 currencies and shows the day's medium, minimum, and maximum rates. You can request that the conversion show the interbank rate, the typical credit card rate (+2 percent), the typical cash rate (+4 percent), or interbank rates with from 1 percent to 10 percent additional percentages applied.

ATMs

Gone are the days when before you left home you had to go to the bank (or a currency exchange) to get a supply of local currency for the countries to which you were headed. Now wherever you land and stay, you are probably near an ATM where you can not only get the currency you need, but get it at a good rate. If you want to check ahead of time (or while you are there) for ATM locations, try the following sites. One is for Visa and the other is for MasterCard. In each case, the institution that owns the ATM is probably—but not necessarily—a member of one or more of several networks such as Cirrus or Plus, one of which will accept your bank card or credit card.

Visa ATM Locator

visa.via.infonow.net/locator/global

On the Visa ATM Locator site, you can search by region, country (150 of them), city, and postal code. Depending upon the city, the Advanced Search link can limit your search to those ATMs that are open 24 hours, have wheelchair access, are Braille compatible, etc. You can also ask for airport ATMs, a list of ATMs, or a list and a map.

MasterCard ATM Locations

www.mastercard.com/atmlocator/index.jsp

At the MasterCard ATM Locations page, you can search by address or airport for ATMs in more than 230 countries and limit your search to those with 24-hour access, handicapped access, or drive-through. You can also identify those for your own financial institution.

Weights and Measures

Trivia question of the day: "What do only Myanmar, Liberia, and the U.S. have in common?" Give up? They are the only three countries in the world that have not officially switched to the metric system (however, Myanmar and Liberia use the metric system in practice). So, for probably at least another generation, travelers will be making conversions to and from the metric system. If you read that Paris is 832 kilometers from

Munich and want to know the distance in miles, you can turn to the Internet (among many other places) for help if you don't remember the conversion factor. But those sources may not help if you want to take a pair of slippers home for your daughter, because clothing sizes are a different problem. For conversions, see the following Web sites.

Google and Yahoo!
google.com
yahoo.com

In both of these search engines, you can calculate a metric/Imperial conversion simply by entering phrases like the following in the search box:

> *convert 832 km to mi*
> *convert 250 miles to kilometers*
> *convert 30 gallons to liters*

In Google, you can also do the following:

> *1.32 euros/liter to dollars/gallon*

You can use either the abbreviation or the words, and, in Google, you don't actually have to use the word "convert."

Tyzo.com
www.tyzo.com

Tyzo's clothing size comparison chart is one of several handy tools found in the Travel Tools section of Tyzo's main page. Not only is there a Clothing link there, but you will also find links to databases to look up an airfare comparison (recent historical fares within the U.S. from the U.S. Department of Transportation), airport codes, dialing codes, electricity requirements, and time zones. Tyzo also provides a metric converter.

Johnny Jet—Clothing & Shoe Sizes
www.johnnyjet.com/clothingsizes.html

You may recall we mentioned Johnny Jet site in Chapter 1, "What's Out There? The Real World and the Cyber World," where it was discussed as an extensive travel resource guide. This particular part of Johnny's site provides a printable list of clothing size equivalents for Japanese, American, British, and Continental sizes.

Flight Tracking and Airports

Before you rush to the airport, you probably will want to know if your flight has been delayed by 30 minutes, and likewise, so would the person who is planning to meet you at the other end of your flight. If you will be hurrying to catch a connecting flight when you land or want to know the layout of an airport, having an airport map and information about airport facilities and services can be useful. All this information is readily available on the Web, although the sites vary in how much information they provide, how it is displayed, and how easy it is to use. For flight status information, consider going directly to the airline's own site, particularly for non-U.S. flights, since most sites included here provide information from the U.S. Federal Aviation Administration. (Be aware that the arrival and departure times on the airline sites may differ from the other sites because the airline may report the time an aircraft left and arrived at the gate, whereas the non-airline sites may provide "wheels up" and "wheels down" times. All of us who have spent long times on the tarmac appreciate the difference.) For an impressive amount and variety of flight and airport information, try the following sites and see which suits you the best. (Tip: When searching for flights, you may notice a flight is booked through one airline, but "operated" by another. This "code-sharing" assigns two flight numbers to the flight. If your search for one flight number does not work, try the other.)

Yahoo!

yahoo.com

Both Yahoo! and Google provide shortcuts to flight information. Just enter a flight number into the search box, click the search button, and links to your answers will be shown near the top of your results pages. On both search engines, the shortcuts are often more productive for U.S. flights. The data provided for these shortcuts is usually collected from other Web sites mentioned in this section. On Yahoo!, if you search for a flight number (e.g., *ual 1197*), an answer such as the following will be returned:

> Check the status of United Airlines
> flight 1197

Click on that link, and a page with information about the flight's status will appear.

Yahoo! also provides a shortcut for airport information. (Expect Google to follow Yahoo!'s lead on this.) If you enter a three-letter airport code in Yahoo!'s search box, you will get a link to information about the airport, including any current arrival or departure delays.

Google
google.com

With Google, if you search for *ual 1197*, you will find an answer like this one at the top of your results:

> Track status of United Airlines flight
> 1197
>   on Travelocity - Expedia - fboweb.com

Click on any of the three links for details about the flight status.

FlightAware—Live Flight Tracker
flightaware.com/live

The information from FlightAware may be overkill for someone who just wants to know when a flight left, where it is, and when it is expected to arrive. But Flight Tracker is so easy to use that you may find yourself digging deeper into what this site offers. On the main page of the Live Flight Tracker, you can use the search boxes to find the flight you want by entering the flight identification number (e.g., UAL884) for private or commercial flights or the airline name and flight number for commercial flights. (For the airline name, just start typing. The site will help you get to the correct name.) You can also use the airport code box to "View Airport Activity" to see information on current arrivals, departures, and en route flights for that location. For any flight you select, FlightAware displays a map with the flight route and a table with the type of aircraft, origin, destination, route, duration, status, the "Proposed/Assigned" departure time and "Actual/Estimated" arrival time, altitude, and ground speed (Figure 10.2). Typically, there is a six minute delay in the flight data you see on the site. FlightAware tracks commercial and private flights in the U.S. that are being tracked by the FAA. Free registration provides the option to get e-mail status alerts, post to discussion groups, as well as get personalized and more detailed displays. If you use the airport codes, be aware that they are not the ones you usually see on your airline ticket. These are ICAO codes with four letters for U.S. airports in the "lower 48" and typically have the letter "K" in front of the code on many sites (e.g., KDFW instead of the usual DFW). To check any code, click on the "Don't know the code?" link, and the site will help you find the right one.

FlightArrivals.com
www.flightarrivals.com

For U.S. and Canadian flights, FlightArrivals.com gives you reports on arrivals, departures, delays, schedule changes, and airport status. Arrival and departure requests can be specified by airline and flight number, but if you don't know the number, you can check by city and airport within a two-hour period, by airline and airport within a six-hour period, or by airline, origin, and destination within a 16-hour period. The status for each flight is provided (scheduled, in flight, and

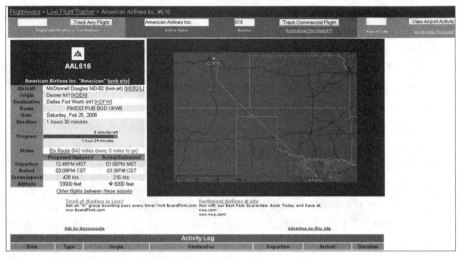

Figure 10.2   FlightAware flight display

completed) as well as departure and arrival times, airport weather, notes about airport delays, and more. If the flight has any stopovers, that information is also shown for each segment.

FlightView
flightview.com

FlightView has both a flight tracker and an airport tracker. With the flight tracker, you can select flights by flight number and either airline or airline code or by city, where you can specify either the departure or arrival city and time of day and date. Results show scheduled and actual/estimated times for arrival and departure. Flight details include aircraft type, ground speed, altitude, and operator (airline). For flights en route, a map is displayed with the plane's location. If you click the Launch Live button, a pop-up screen will display an animated, zoomable, continually updated view of the plane's track and location. Click the Weather option for current conditions.

The airport tracker portion of FlightView is a clickable map of the U.S., indicating current U.S. airport conditions (normal, delays, and major delays). Click on an airport location for a chart with arrivals and departures and the percentages of flights that are on time, late, or very late.

fboweb.com
www.fboweb.com

This site offers a range of information for the aviation professional or enthusiast, or for ordinary users who wants to track flights. On the main page, the Quick Track section will probably interest most regular travelers. You can choose the airline, enter the flight number, and then click the Track button. You will be shown flight information, including the kinds of information (times, status, etc.) shown by other flight tracking sites and a zoomable (left-right-up-down pan-able) map that shows the flight's progress, which is updated automatically every minute. Links on the flight information pages lead to additional options, but some require a subscription. On the main page, another search box can be used for flight tracking by entering an airport code to get detailed aviation-related airport information. Much of the site consists of information more of interest to aviation professionals. But for the casual user, the Aero Info section includes a Find Airports option for locating airports near a specific destination. This can be useful for any traveler who needs to fly to a smaller city or town and does not know what airports are closest.

Just for fun, click on the Toolbox link near the top or bottom of the page and watch the videos monitoring U.S. and U.K. airspace for a 24-hour period. The main page also features a "3D Flight Tracking" link for a "real-time," 3-D "Google Earth" view of current inbound flights for selected airports.

FlyteComm
www.flytecomm.com/cgi-bin/trackflight

For flight tracking, FlyteComm provides a straightforward form where you can select an airline and enter a flight number, or you can view a list of all current flight activity by choosing either a departure or destination airport. Results for a flight search offer the same basic information (times, status, etc.) as all other flight tracking sites. For flight activity by airport, you are shown a list with the departure/destination city, airline, flight number, arrival/departure time, status (planned, scheduled, in-flight, arrived), and the weather at the airport.

FAA—Flight Delay Information

www.fly.faa.gov/flyfaa/usmap.jsp

For flight-delay information at U.S. airports "straight from the horse's mouth," try the Federal Aviation Administration's Flight Delay Information page. Information covers airports, not individual flights.

Transportation Security Administration (TSA)—Security Checkpoint Wait Times

waittime.tsa.dhs.gov

In any airport, there are times when you can zip through security, and other times when you wait in line so long you notice that the hair of the person in front of you is substantially longer than when you started. The Transportation Security Administration's Security Checkpoint Wait Times site can give you at least a rough idea of what you are likely to encounter. On the site, you can choose a state, then an airport, the day of the week, and the hour of the day. The site will then provide a reasonably good estimate of wait times, based on recent historical data. For each hour, it will show you the average and maximum wait times.

Another section of the TSA site (www.tsa.gov/public) contains links to other information of interest to flyers, including lists of prohibited items, information on transporting special items, and other tips.

The Airline Codes Web Site

www.airlinecodes.co.uk

If you need the code for airlines or airports or have become obsessed with knowing every code you find on tickets and itineraries, go to the Airline Codes Website to find the codes for aircraft, airlines, airports, and countries. You will also find links to the sites for 1,651 airlines.

World Airport Guide

www.worldairportguide.com

World Airport Guide is produced by World Travel Guides, which also provides a collection of city guides mentioned in Chapter 2. For each of more than 200 airports, the site provides an address, phone number, Web site, airport map, and information in the following categories: Country Code, Airport News, Transfer Between Terminals, Driving Directions, Car Parking, Car Hire, Public Transport, Information and Help Desks, Airport Facilities, Conference and Business Facilities, Disabled Facilities, and Airport Hotels. Many of those sections have sponsored links for local services such as car rentals, airport shuttles, limousines, and hotels. Other links on the page can take you to Columbus' guides for the country, the city, and its attractions.

LongTermParking.com

www.longtermparking.com

On LongTermParking.com, you can identify, get information about, and book long-term parking at airports in the U.S. and 16 U.K. airports. Not all parking facilities participate, and even for some very large airports, you may find no listings here. For airports not listed here, try the Web site of the airport itself. You can find it by means of World Airport Guide, previously discussed, or usually very easily by just searching on the name of the airport in a search engine.

Subways

You can find information online for most of the world's subways and bus systems. A search engine will often work well for finding a subway or bus route map (e.g., *subway washington dc*), but the following sites compile this information in one place for many of the world's cities.

Subway Navigator
www.subwaynavigator.com

Subway Navigator pulls together information for nearly 140 subway systems around the world. Information from subway Web sites is used to provide users with a "route finder" so you can specify a departure and arrival station and then see the exact route you need to take, including which train to take (e.g., Line E) and its direction (e.g., Haussmann-St. Lazare), transfer points, and your estimated travel time (Figure 10.3). For cities for which the route finder is available, you can enter the names of your departure and arrival stations or search from a list of stations. For most of those cities, you can also select the stations by clicking on a map of the system. Even if the route finder is not available, you can find a link to the subway's official site and, in some cases, links to specific pages for fares, help, itinerary finders, timetables, and traffic loads. For some cities, Subway Navigator provides a "thematic search" that identifies points of interest near selected subway stops.

The Subway Page
www.reed.edu/~reyn/transport.html#maps

The Subway Page is a combination map collection and resource guide for subways and related local and regional transit services. The City Subway Maps section contains maps or links to maps taken from various sources for more than 150 subway systems (some cities have more than a dozen different maps). There are several other sections

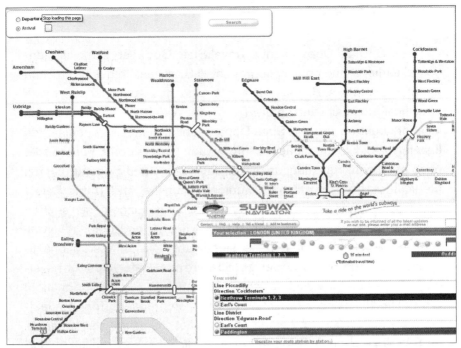

Figure 10.3   Results of route finder at Subway Navigator (with inset showing
            requested route)

to the page, but of particular interest to travelers is the collection of
tram, bus, light rail, and rail system maps for about 60 cities.

Health and Safety Alerts

Governmental agencies and international organizations provide
extensive, up-to-date information on health and safety conditions
throughout the world. The first four of the following sites are particularly noteworthy for keeping informed on these aspects of travel. The
fifth site is an example of a site describing the kinds of health and
medical services available from private companies for international
travelers.

U.S. Department of State—International Travel

travel.state.gov/travel

The U.S. State Department's Travel.State.Gov Web site was mentioned earlier as the primary source for U.S. citizens to get information about passports and visas. The site also has sections that relate specifically to health and safety. The Travel Warnings section includes a list of countries that the State Department specifically recommends travelers avoid. In the Consular Information Sheets portion of the site, each country has sections that deal with Safety and Security, Crime, Medical Facilities and Health, Medical Insurance, and Traffic Safety and Road Conditions. The Current Public Announcements section contains notices about current "terrorist threats and other relatively short-term conditions that pose significant risks or disruptions to Americans." The Safety Issues section provides safety tips for travelers, information for victims of crime abroad, and related information. Under Health Issues, information focuses on preparing for and dealing with medical care and emergencies. Fact sheets are also available on SARS, avian flu, and foot-and-mouth disease, and you'll also find a collection of links to private companies that provide air ambulance service and insurance for travelers. The other sections of the site are also worth a glimpse.

Centers for Disease Control and Prevention—
Travelers' Health

www.cdc.gov/travel

The Travelers' Health portion of the Centers for Disease Control and Prevention site offers details beyond the information on the Department of State site, including sections on Destinations, Vaccinations, Travel Medicine Clinics, Yellow Fever Vaccination Clinics, Mosquito and Tick Protection, References and Resources, Diseases, Illness and Injury Abroad, and Safe Food and Water (Figure

10.4). Additional sections cover specific groups and settings, such as Traveling with Children, Special Needs Travelers, Disaster Relief Workers, Traveling with Pets, and Travel by Airplanes and Cruise Ships. The Destinations section features specific information for each region of the world on vaccines, diseases found in that region, other local health risks, what you need to bring with you, staying healthy during your trip, and things to do after you return home. Most of the individual sections provide extensive detail.

Foreign & Commonwealth Office
www.fco.gov.uk

The Foreign & Commonwealth Office, mentioned earlier, provides a significant amount of health and safety information on its Web site. On its main page, click on Travel Advice, and on the resulting page you will find links to travel warnings (under Travel Advice by Country) and to information on Avian and Pandemic Flu, Risk of Terrorism, Travel Insurance, Travel Health, River and Sea Safety, and Hurricanes.

World Health Organization—International Travel and Health
www.who.int/ith/en

This part of the World Health Organization (WHO) site has a publication, *International Travel and Health*, that is downloadable (by chapter). The publication covers health risks you might encounter in specific destinations and those associated with certain types of travel (business, humanitarian, leisure, backpacking, adventure tours, etc.). It also has chapters on travel by air, environmental health risks, and other topics.

International SOS
www.internationalsos.com

Figure 10.4   The Travelers' Health section of the Centers for Disease Control and Prevention Web site

The International SOS site is included here as an example of a company site that offers health and safety-related services to international travelers, including medical assistance, international healthcare, and security services.

For the Wired Traveler: Cybercafes and Other Options

If you want to keep in touch by e-mail while traveling, take advantage of everything the Internet has to offer in most cities and even smaller towns by finding a nearby cybercafe. Though cybercafes are usually easy to find once you've arrived at your destination, the following sites will help you find them before you even leave home. If you are taking your laptop with you, one of the following sites will help you find WiFi hotspots, and for those who want to access their own mini-office from anywhere in the world, take a look at the last site listed in this section, My Yahoo!.

If you have a laptop with you, here's another possibility for Internet access when you're traveling internationally: If your hotel allows free or inexpensive local calls, and if your Internet Service Provider (ISP) at home provides a list of free numbers to dial in, purchase a phone card abroad that offers reduced international call rates and then call one of your ISP numbers back home. For example, in Frankfurt, I purchased a phone card that I could use to call the U.S. for just a few cents per minute. Since my hotel provided free local calls, I hooked up my laptop to the data port on the phone. Then I configured the dial-up program on my computer to first dial the toll-free number on the phone card, then the PIN for that phone card, and then one of my ISP numbers in the U.S. Be sure to build in the appropriate pauses (indicated on most dial-up programs with commas). The overall cost was just the price of the phone card. Configuring the appropriate numbers may involve some trial and error, but it means you can use the Internet without going to a cybercafe or paying for sometimes very expensive Internet access through your hotel.

Cybercafes

Among the several cybercafe directories available, the following are among the most extensive and informative. All the establishments listed here provide the cyber part, though they may or may not provide the cafe part.

Cybercafe.com
www.cybercafe.com

Cybercafe.com offers a database of more than 4,200 Internet cafes in 140 countries. You can browse by continent and country (and sometimes by city, state, or province), or you can search by city or country. For each cafe, you will typically find the name of the cafe, the city, address, phone number, fax, e-mail, home-page link, hours, prices, facilities, and in some cases, a description of what the cafe has to offer.

Cybercafe Search Engine
cybercaptive.com

The Cybercafe Search Engine provides a search for more than 5,000 "verified cybercafes, public [I]nternet access points and kiosks in 161 countries." You can search by city, state/province, or country. Each establishment includes the name, address, city, phone number, home page, and e-mail.

Netcafeguide.com
www.world66.com/netcafeguide

Netcafeguide.com, which is now a part of World66, provides an extensive collection of destination guide articles written by site users.

For many destinations, there is a list of Internet cafes, each with the name, a description, a rating, phone number, home page, address, price, e-mail, and hours.

Finding WiFi Hotspots

There are numerous WiFi hotspot directories online, but among them, JiWire seems to be as large or larger than others (larger than at least one that claims to be definitive) and with more search options than most. Some other WiFi locators use the JiWire database.

JiWire
jiwire.com

JiWire provides information about various aspects of WiFi, and on its main page you can search for WiFi Hotspots. To search, click on the Locate and Map WiFi Hotspots link. You will find a search page with options that will let you search by address or airport code, city, country, state/region, ZIP/postal code, proximity, business or location name, location type (airport, bar, golf course, hotel, and 40 other types), and provider, and for either free or pay connections (or both). It lists a total of more than 130,000 hotspots in 131 countries. Each listing includes the name, address, location type, provider, and links to a map, directions, and connection options. JiWire also provides a hotspot directory that you can download to your mobile device.

Your Mini-Office on the Web

My Yahoo!
my.yahoo.com

If you would like to access some of your own resources (files, bookmarks, calendar, phone numbers, addresses, etc.) from any-where in the world with an Internet connection, consider setting up and using a My Yahoo! account. If you already have a Yahoo! account for e-mail, that account will also work for My Yahoo!. My Yahoo! is a general portal that will let you personalize a variety of modules (Figure 10.5). All the information is stored on the Yahoo! Servers, which you can access wherever you go. In addition to providing easy and immediate access to your choice of thousands of news sources, you can use the Briefcase feature to store files that you might need; store names, addresses, and phone numbers using the My Yahoo! Address book; create and store notes using the Notepad; keep a list of your favorite sites under Bookmarks; use the full-featured online Calendar; check your investments with the Yahoo! Portfolio module; and access

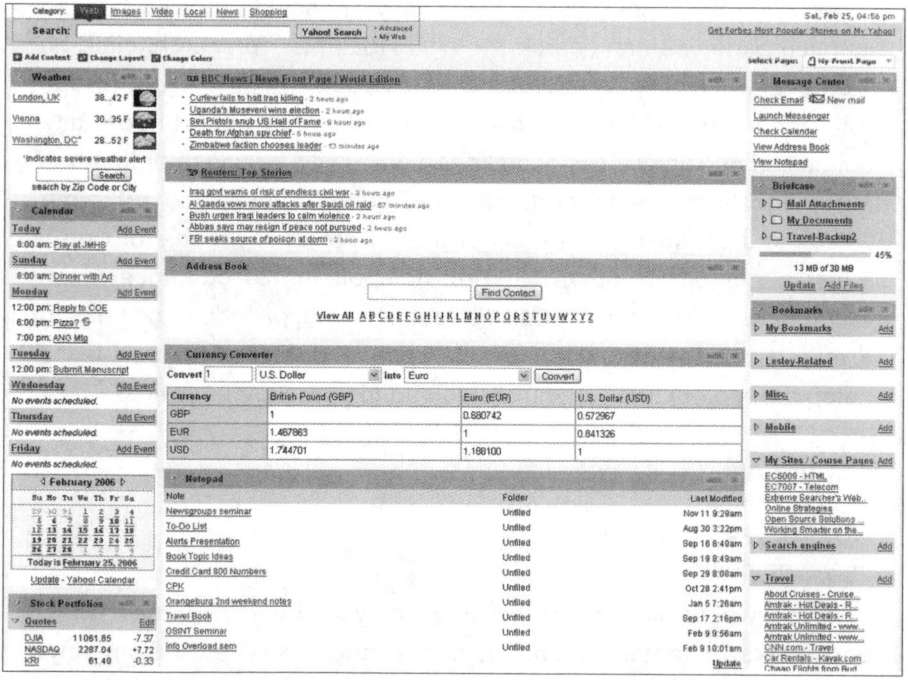

Figure 10.5 My Yahoo!

your Yahoo! e-mail and, through it, your other POP e-mail accounts. (If you want to go beyond what you can do with My Yahoo! and access your computer at home or your office, you can use a paid subscription to a service such as GoToMyPC at www.gotomypc.com.)

Electrical Connections

Tyzo, which was mentioned earlier, provides information on voltage and frequency for more than 200 countries and territories. The following site also provides that information, plus a photo of the plugs needed.

World Electric Guide—Electric Power Around the World
kropla.com/electric2.htm

Electric Power Around the World gives you the standard voltage, frequency, and type of plug (with a photo) for more than 200 countries.

Packing Lists

If you travel a lot, you probably have created a packing list of your own. If you haven't, check out the following sites.

Universal Packing List
upl.codeq.info

The Universal Packing List site will create a personalized packing list for you, depending on where and when you are going and other variables. You specify the dates of your trips, your gender, the minimum and maximum expected temperatures (a link to a climate site is provided), the type of accommodations, ages of kids on the trip, types of activities and transportation, and some other choices, and the Universal Packing List site will create a list just for you (Figure 10.6).

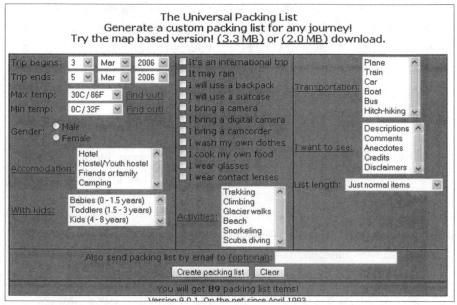

Figure 10.6 Universal Packing List form

You can also specify that you want a list with just critical items, most items, etc.

One Bag—The Art and Science of Traveling Light
www.onebag.com

In addition to providing advice on packing and traveling light, the One Bag site provides an annotated list of what to take as well as a shorter checklist that can be downloaded. Be sure to check out the pages on What to Take It In and How to Pack It.

Johnny Jet—Packing Lists
www.johnnyjet.com/popup/packing.html

Johnny Jet, who provides the excellent collection of travel sites discussed in Chapter 1, includes on his site three packing checklists: for men, women, and children. The lists are inclusive yet at the same time short enough to print conveniently.

Travel Supplies

The following three sites are examples of the variety of online stores specializing in gear and supplies for travelers.

Magellan's
www.magellans.com

Magellan's can outfit you with clothing, appliances, maps, books, optics, picnic gear, rain gear, and things from a dozen other categories. The site also provides a useful collection of travel tips and articles.

Travelwares.com
www.travelwares.com

Travelwares.com's catalog contains hundreds of items in categories such as Comfort and Convenience, Currency and Voltage Converters, Money Belts, Packing Organizers, Safety and Security, Lights, Camera, Action!, Kid's Stuff, luggage, globes, clocks, and more.

Family on Board
www.familyonboard.com

Family on Board, "The Family Travel Gear Specialists," features a range of products designed for travel with kids, from car seats and drink bottles to puzzles and games.

Finding Religious Services

When you are traveling and want to find the nearest place of worship, the following sites may be helpful. If readers want to recommend similar sites that list all or most locations for other religions or denominations at a national level, I will add those to this book's companion site (www.extremesearcher.com/travel).

Masstimes.org
masstimes.org

Masstimes.org lists Mass times and locations for more than 90,000 Roman Catholic churches around the world. You can browse geographically or search by place name, postal code, or even phone number.

Kosher Delight
www.kosherdelight.com

Kosher Delight, Your Online Jewish Magazine, contains a wide variety of information on Jewish life and Jewish communities around the world. The site's Kosher section has lists of restaurants and hotels, and the Jewish Stuff section has directories of Synagogues, Mikvaot, Chabad Houses, etc.

Masjid Addresses in the United States
www.msa-natl.org/resources/IS_USA.html

Masjid Addresses in the United States is a directory of Masjids and Islamic Centers throughout the U.S. and is browsable by state and also searchable by keyword or phrase. The site is being expanded to include Canadian locations and a Prayer Times Scheduler.

Miscellaneous

The following are sites that did not conveniently fit into any specific category. The variety of these sites is also a reminder of the variety of content on the Web for travelers.

MyTripJournal.com

mytripjournal.com

MyTripJournal.com is a site that enables any traveler to create a site to share travel experiences, stories, and photos with friends and family. It's also a place where travelers can plot their journey on maps, share stories and photos, exchange messages, and control who can see the site. The first 45 days of use are free, but there is a fee to keep the site longer.

Kodak—Taking Great Pictures

www.kodak.com/eknec/PageQuerier.jhtml?pq-path=38&pq-locale=en_US

If you want better photos but don't want to have to go through an entire do-it-yourself book or class on photography, try the Taking Great Pictures site from Kodak. You will find easy-to-understand tips that will make a significant difference in the quality of the photos you bring home from your vacation.

Infobel

www.infobel.com

If you need to find a phone number anywhere in the world, chances are Infobel can lead you to the appropriate phone directory. Infobel is a resource guide that contains links to phone directories (white pages, business directories, and other options) for more than 200 countries. While not all countries have either white or yellow pages, some actually have an e-mail directory. You may also want to take advantage of a link on the main Infobel page for a list of international dialing codes.

Yahoo! Mobile—Travel and Transportation WAP Web Sites

mobile.yahoo.com/resource_center/wapdir/travel_and_transportation

Throughout this book, you have occasionally seen mention of versions of sites that are compatible with cell phones and other devices. Expect the number of these sites for travel to increase rather rapidly. Depending on your wireless service provider, you will probably find some travel sites already listed if you have Internet capability on your cell phone. The Travel and Transportation WAP Web Sites section of Yahoo! Mobile's directory has a list of selected travel-related sites organized in the following categories: Automotive, Flight Information, Destination Guides, Events, Lodging, Regional, and Train Travel.

Conclusion

As I said in the Introduction, the major thrust of this book is "aware-ness"—awareness of what is on the Internet for travelers, awareness of the variety and breadth of content, and awareness of what individ-ual sites can accomplish for you.

A lot of material has been covered, including quite a bit of detail as to what the sites provide, how you can search them, etc. I recommend that you not worry about the details. Of much more importance is the "awareness" of what is there, knowing that there are sites that provide very specific kinds of cruises, sites that help you choose your airline seat, sites that help you to be "polite" in foreign countries, sites that ... well, you get the point. If you remember all the things you *can* do, you can always come back to the book for the where and how.

Be sure to take advantage of the Web site at www.extremesearcher. oom/travel. It is organized in chapters and sections, just like the book, to help refresh your memory about the resources available and to help you use them with ease, and it includes any updates uncovered after *The Traveler's Web* was published.

Have a great trip!

About the Author

Randolph Hock, PhD

Ran divides his work time between writing and teaching. On the teaching side, he specializes in customized courses to help people use the Web effectively (through his one-person company, Online Strategies). His courses have been delivered in more than a dozen countries, to companies, government agencies, nongovernmental organizations, schools, universities, and associations. On the writing side, *The Traveler's Web* is his fourth book.

Ran has been a chemistry teacher and a librarian, and for many years he held training and management positions with Dialog Information Services and Knight-Ridder Information. He loves to travel, plan travel, think about travel, talk about travel, and write about travel. He has traveled extensively in the U.S. and abroad for both pleasure and work (but even counts most of the "work" travel also as "pleasure"). He has traveled by plane, train, ship, ferry, boat, canoe, car, bus, bicycle, horse, and rickshaw. He lives in Vienna, Virginia, with his wife, Pamela, and his two younger children, Stephen and Elizabeth. His older son, Matthew, like the rest of the family, is a traveler and spends considerable time traveling the U.S. and Europe with his band The Explosion.

Index